ALSO BY DAVID LOTH

A Long Way Forward — *The People's General: The Story of Lafayette* — *Woodrow Wilson, the Fifteenth Point* *Lorenzo the Magnificent* — *Book of the Seven Seas* (WITH PETER FREUCHEN) — *Report on American Communism* (WITH MORRIS L. ERNST) — *American Sexual Behavior and the Kinsey Report* (WITH MORRIS L. ERNST)

SWOPE OF G.E.

The Story of Gerard Swope and General Electric in American Business — by DAVID LOTH

SIMON AND SCHUSTER NEW YORK 1958

PUBLISHED BY SIMON AND SCHUSTER, INC.
ROCKEFELLER CENTER, 630 FIFTH AVENUE
NEW YORK 20, N. Y.

FIRST PRINTING

LIBRARY OF CONGRESS CATALOG CARD NUMBER: 58-6276

MANUFACTURED IN THE UNITED STATES OF AMERICA
BY AMERICAN BOOK-STRATFORD PRESS, INC., NEW YORK

To HELEN *for her help*

Contents

AUTHOR'S NOTE

Gerard Swope died of pneumonia after an illness of only three days on November 20, 1957, while this book was on the press.

I felt that to change the present tense, in those passages where I had employed it, would be a mere exercise in grammar, and so I have left them as they were written.

I think it should be added that Gerard Swope's last months were of a pattern with the rest of his very active "retirement." They included a trip to Europe and Israel, where he received an honorary degree from the Technion-Israel Institute of Technology; elaboration of a plan for extending his favorite social-insurance programs; a good deal of reading and theatergoing. He went to his office three days a week for the work he did in connection with his own affairs and those of organizations in which he took an interest until the Friday before his death. It was characteristic of him that he requested absolutely no funeral services of any kind be held—and that his request was observed.

David Loth

I *The View from the Top*

Corporations have no souls, but they are well equipped with nerves, and on May 16, 1922, those of the General Electric Company were quivering like the strings of Paderewski's piano. In forty-two American cities and assorted offices around the world the corporate jitters were acute enough to be remembered by the survivors thirty-five years later as the outstanding feature of the day.

The attack was confined to a small minority of the sixty-one thousand employees. Only vice-presidents, department heads and their assistants, office managers, plant superintendents, officials of subsidiaries, research directors, were affected. But they make up a corporation's nervous system. This one was twitching because General Electric was getting a new Chief Executive for the first time in its thirty-year history, and a stranger to most of its men at that. They fretted impotently, worrying about what he might do to them and their jobs.

Sitting around their handsome table on the twentieth floor of No. 120 Broadway, in the heart of New York's financial district, a dozen of the fifteen distinguished bankers and businessmen who composed the Board of Directors were concerned less with nerves than figures. These showed that their business had shrunk almost half in less than two years. It was no consolation to them to know that this was a national trend. They wanted it reversed for General Electric and made that fact quite clear to the man they elected president, Gerard Swope. He was virtually unknown to the public, but he had a reputation in the electrical industry itself for knowing more about it than any man on earth.

He succeeded in more than changing the curve of his company's earnings. He also gave a twist to the American industrial system which has affected its course ever since. The big, complex, diversified corporations of today operate on some of the principles and practices which he established.

First of all, he instituted a different use of mechanization than the masters of mass production had yet employed, doing for managerial techniques what Henry Ford accomplished for the assembly line a few years earlier. Gloomy prophets were saying in 1922 that scientists and mechanics had invented machines which made more goods than the businessmen knew how to distribute. Swope showed business how to catch up with the machines.

Secondly, he put into practice principles by which the heads of corporations which number their products by scores and their employees by hundreds of thousands can manage problems of personnel.

Thirdly, he molded the relations between corporation and community into new patterns by directing business management into fields where previously it had avoided responsibility.

These accomplishments were mercifully hidden from the directors—some of them did not like his methods later on even when the results were good—and opinions differ as to whether Swope was an originator or an adapter. Whichever way one looks at him, however, he was a man who got them adopted, for better or worse.

On that bright, warm spring Tuesday he was crowned with as much real sovereignty as an American can win: virtually autocratic rule over one of the chief productive enterprises on the industrial scene. Some members of the Board who were voting him that power regarded him with a good deal of curiosity because they didn't know him very well.

They saw a short, slender man of forty-nine, very quick in his movements, disconcertingly decisive in his speech, sharp-eyed even when he raised his glasses on their black cord to scan a set of figures. His thick, dark hair was parted in the middle; a big, strong beak of a nose and a sharp angle of chin jutted over his high stiff collar. Co-workers found him coldly impersonal, impatient and dead set on getting his own way. They said he always was in a hurry, but they were only partly right. He so hated to waste time that his remorseless regimenting of the day's fourteen hundred and forty minutes gave bystanders an impression of almost supersonic velocity, when to himself he seemed merely to be moving with deliberate speed.

The Board meeting ended, he accepted the good wishes of the directors with an old-fashioned courtesy which surprised people who had experienced his impatience, but he did not linger over the amenities. Walking fast, he returned to his office on the nineteenth floor, from which, for the past three years, he had managed the foreign business of the company. He did not pause even for a word with the new chairman of the Board who had been elected with him, Owen D. Young, a tall, good-looking lawyer with deep-set eyes and a leisurely manner who had been the company's general counsel for nearly a decade.

"We already had agreed so completely on what we would do that there was no need for us to say anything to each other that first day," Young explains.

He was more intimately acquainted with Swope than most General Electric officials, and months earlier they had mapped their respective roles with mutual respect and admiration. The words they used to describe the chart to each other were characteristic.

"I will do all the work—I like it," Swope had assured his future teammate.

"One of us will be the captain and the other navigator," was the way Young put it.

No doubt existed in the mind of either that the bridge of the good ship General Electric had moved temporarily to the nineteenth floor. There its windows commanded a wide view of the nation's finance as expressed in steel and stone, with the oil-slick East River looking deceptively clean in the bright sun. A man could have been forgiven for looking out complacently over the offices and banks while congratulating himself on reaching the top of the industrial ladder. But Gerard Swope was not the man to gaze idly out of windows no matter how delightful the view or his own thoughts. Besides, not all his prospects were rosy.

The United States was going through one of its periodic business depressions, the third since Swope came of age. In the spring of 1922 the whole economy was in a slump, although mass production had revolutionized American factories and taken industrial leadership of the world away from England. The result of that, and of war, seemed to be that farm values were crashing and unemployment lists mounting; General Electric had laid off twenty thousand men, nearly one fourth of its 1920 force. The depression already had removed such industrial notables as William C. Durant from control of General Motors, which he had promoted into a billion-dollar corporation, and the Seiberling brothers from Goodyear Rubber, which they had founded. Although the American slogan of "a car for every family" was repeated with touching faith, the automobile industry was in the doldrums with men idle and unsold cars accumulating by the thousands. Building, despite urgent needs for more urban homes and better rural ones, had slowed almost to a standstill.

However, the public displayed little general interest in news of the business world other than the scandalous. The two most important corporation stories on May 16, 1922, were the changes at

General Electric and a merger between Bethlehem Steel and Lackawanna Steel. The merger got by far the more space, but both events were relegated to the financial section, even in the business-minded *New York Times*. The page one place of honor went to Secretary of State Hughes, who was announcing terms on which the United States Government would consent to meet Soviet Russia's delegates in a conference to settle all international issues. The Supreme Court had upset unanimously a Federal law clapping a 10 per cent tax on the products of child labor. A New York State commission was interrogating schoolteachers in closed hearings about their loyalty to American institutions, and there was the usual argument as to whether liberty or security was in greater danger. A Chicago labor dispute had erupted into bombings. Prohibition was drenching New York with illicit liquor; the day's news stories told of smuggling by sea, land and air. Colorful Sam Untermyer was in the midst of an investigation of the construction industry.

In the world of which these newspaper columns were a reflection, the General Electric Company loomed larger than one might suppose from the headlines. For it was an electrical age, and in spite of the slump, Swope thought that both the company and the industry were only on the threshold of their expansion. He himself was older than the industry although he was only forty-nine, and he had seen it grow from a toy to the key to limitless power. Every year electricity did a little more of the work of men—and of women. Every year it opened up new possibilities for progress. Why, tucked away in this very morning's newspaper was some small print which hinted at a great potential branch for the industry. The programs of no fewer than six radio stations which broadcast every day were presented, although, to be sure, the editors had to go as far west as Chicago to find that many. Five of them were hopefully commercial, too; the sixth, only one in New York City, was an Army Signal Corps job. General Electric's own WGY in Schenectady was listed as going on the air twice a day, once with commodity prices and again with stock market quotations, baseball scores and news.

Although many people thought that General Electric was as large as it was possible for a corporation to get, and perhaps too large for the safety of the country, Swope expected it to expand not only in the lines along which it had operated for thirty years but into many new fields as well. Already, and in spite of recent bad times, it was the fourth largest industrial firm in the country and did twice the business of its nearest electrical competitor. A sprawling aggregation of complex machines, inventive brains and busy sales offices, it had been formed by amalgamation and purchase as well as growth. Now, in 1922, it had plants or offices in forty-two American cities, and branches in dozens of foreign countries. It was primarily a great engineering company making the increasingly heavy power equipment of the electrical age, and a hodgepodge of incandescent lamp factories ostensibly competing with each other under the intermittently suspicious eye of the Department of Justice. In the vast field of household and office appliances, it was represented only by an electric fan.

General Electric also was a little world of people, sixty-one thousand of them at this time. Swope was very conscious of being regarded as an outsider by those with whom his contacts would be closest—vice-presidents and department heads, superintendents and office managers, who had grown up in the company. They were sure he could never understand, much less manage, the biggest corporation in the industry. The manufacturing, engineering and research brains of the organization were especially scornful of him as a mere merchandiser, for so they called him. Dr. William D. Coolidge, who had made it possible to use tungsten in lamps, did mention to his colleagues in Schenectady that he and Swope had started together at the Massachusetts Institute of Technology in 1891, but couldn't remember what his fellow freshman had looked like. Coolidge's boss, Dr. Willis R. Whitney, creator of the first modern industrial research laboratories, recalled that as a young instructor he had taught Swope chemistry and found him a more than satisfactory student. These two were among the small minority who knew or cared that he was by profession an electrical engineer.

That he had come through engineering to business, and in just this period of American industrial development, was one of the reasons he had such an impact upon the company, the industry and indeed the country. Other reasons, of course, were his own personality, abilities and luck, the men and women who influenced him, and perhaps above all the spirit of the times in which he lived.

II *A Long Shadow at Dawn*

"St. Louis," it has been said by men born in the city who prospered elsewhere, "is a great place to come from."

As evidence some of them mention, along with their own, the name of Swope. But the people who remain do not accept this rather slighting verdict, and on December 1, 1872, when Gerard Swope was born, the one-time French trading post on the Mississippi was booming. Rosy dreams of greatness floated through the air, almost as tangible as the flakes of soot which already were a notable feature of St. Louis atmosphere.

Boom fever, however, was not one of the ailments current in the home of Isaac and Ida Swope way out on Olive Street near Grand Avenue, a thoroughfare recently opened along the western edge of the city to become, its planners fondly predicted, "the boulevard of the Western Continent." This sort of talk was alien to

Isaac Swope. A man of adequate initiative but little driving ambition, he had come to America from his ancestral Saxon village in the wake of his younger brother fifteen years before, looking for peace and enjoyment of life rather than greatness.

The wave of German immigration after 1848, which caught up the Swope boys along with thousands of others, created large German populations in some Midwestern cities. Isaac went first to Cincinnati, where his brother was established, but soon moved to the even larger German settlement in St. Louis. A tall, good-looking young fellow more remarkable for the unfailing amiability of his expression than anything else, he prospered sufficiently in a series of merchandising enterprises through the Civil War to go back to Germany for his bride, Ida Cohn, in 1865.

She was a dozen years younger than her husband, a sharp, eager, round-faced girl whose small figure contained a boundless energy. Her family had higher educational advantages than most German immigrants, including the Swopes, and her father, Chief Rabbi of Thuringia, was the first Jew to win a Ph.D. degree at the University of Breslau. Ida herself, although barred by her sex from anything more than the simple German schooling for girls, acquired through her own efforts and family environment considerable taste in literature and learning in the humanities.

Isaac Swope was forty when their second child and first son was born—a girl, Golda, was five years old—and named Gerard after Ida's father. The immigrant of 1857 had started a modest manufacturing business in watch cases, the works being imported from Switzerland, and had bought a comfortable brick and stone house in a neighborhood where trees and lawns somewhat mitigated the dust. It was a typical middle-class home except that there were more books in it than most—Goethe and Schiller in the original along with Dickens and Thackeray. Unlike a very large proportion of St. Louis families, however, Isaac and Ida Swope saved German for reading; English was spoken exclusively.

German was the tongue of a considerable part of the population. One out of five of the city's more than 300,000 people had been born in Germany; an equal number had seen the light in other European countries, principally the British Isles, France, Switzerland and Bohemia. Only a few hundred had as yet come from Italy, Poland or Russia, and parts of the city were more German than melting pot. Of the eight daily newspapers, three were in German, and on one of them a young Hungarian immigrant, Joseph Pulitzer, was making quite a journalistic reputation.

Fourth largest city in the country, St. Louis was inordinately proud of its flour mills and breweries, its iron works and foundries, its fifty-seven banks, its packing plants and planing mills, the bridge which Captain James Eads was building across the Mississippi, the mile and a half of wharves where sometimes as many as one hundred steamboats could be counted, the increasing number of gaslit homes, even the smoky air which Pittsburgh itself could hardly surpass. Boosters gravely assured protesting housewives that the seasoning of sulphur and iodine, so objectionable to smell and taste, "is highly favorable to lung and cutaneous diseases."

While the small Gerard was growing into an awareness of his surroundings, the fashionable and some of the just plain clean were rejecting this doubtful health advice and moving out beyond Grand Avenue in hopes of escaping the soot and smoke. In his early years, however, the boy would have heard more about the commonly admired features of his city than of its drawbacks. People never tired of telling each other or strangers about the great Eads bridge and tunnel bringing sixteen railway lines into the splendid Union Station; of the Grand Exchange Hall at Third and Pine with its magnificent ceiling rising sixty feet above the floor and its seventy great French plate-glass windows; of William Lemp's Western Brewery, largest individually owned manufactory under one roof west of New York; of the E. Annheuser Association's seven acres of buildings and the wondrous office of its young general manager, Adolphus Busch, elegant in imported furnishings and paintings, marble fireplace, Axminster carpets and fine draperies. There was talk of glamorous parties at Tony Faust's Oyster House and Saloon, of ornate mansions rising on Lindell Avenue toward Forest Park, of the fleet of three hundred streetcars which horses hauled every day along eighty-six miles of track.

In his own home he heard, too, about books and current events which his mother's clubs met to discuss, about the plays appearing in the leading theaters, where Edwin Booth and Joseph Jefferson, young John Drew and Ada Rehan were familiar performers, about "Mr. Shaw's jewel of a garden," a rich man's gift to those of his fellow citizens who wanted to study or enjoy the wonders of botany, even about such civic problems as the growing juvenile delinquency in Kerry Patch, the North Side slum where street Arabs in gangs fought and feuded, stole and gambled while serious people like the Swopes wondered how to restore the younger generation to a decent appreciation of the morals and manners of an earlier time.

For a little boy this talk was to some extent unreal, hardly in the same world with the everyday routine of home. Thanks to Ida Swope, Number 3530 Olive Street was an orderly dwelling, for she made and enforced the rules. Of an outgoing nature, her discipline was tempered by her genuine love of people, but it was in contrast to the easygoing Isaac, who could hardly bring himself to be severe enough for discipline.

Gerard's horizons widened as he grew old enough for school, in his case the Stoddard Public School, although Golda was sent to a private institution as more fitting for girls. They attended jointly the Sunday School of the congregation to which their parents belonged, a synagogue on Seventeenth and Pine which was rapidly becoming notable for its progressive or "Reform" tendencies. The children, therefore, were not exposed to ritualistic forms and observances. The dietary and behavioristic peculiarities which set the Orthodox obviously and sharply apart from their Gentile neighbors had vanished from the Swope home before the boy learned about them.

When he was three years old, a sister, Dolly, was born, and eight years later another boy, Herbert Bayard, so that in her preoccupation with them Ida Swope had something less than her full attention to give to the older children. They, however, were what was known as exceptionally "good" youngsters. In Gerard's case this meant that when he played hookey or raided a neighbor's pigeon loft, he was careful not to be caught, or not often enough to disturb the serenity of his parents.

He was an undersized, wiry boy, quick and active like his mother, with thick, straight, dark brown hair, a thin face, large nose and strong jaw. Although small, he refused to be handicapped by lack of height or bulk, and his agility enabled him to keep up in sports or tramps through the woods with larger boys. There were six or eight in his "bunch," but his particular friend was Sidney Schwab, son of a prosperous clothing manufacturer whose home was near by.

Gerard maintained an undistinguished average in his studies, his sisters displaying more brilliant scholastic gifts than he. His outstanding achievements in school were a high proficiency in competitive spelling and a talent for reading assigned literature clearly in the loudest voice in the classroom. He also had an excellent record for promptness; at school and at home he was never tardy, and this was a virtue which Ida Swope regarded highly and cultivated tenderly.

"On time?" her younger son once commented. "She thought that meant twenty minutes early."

Outside the classroom, Gerard developed an interest in mechanics and chemistry and especially that strange toy, electricity, whose portents of change were rising throughout the country although still generally unappreciated. The electrical manufacturing industry was being born in the late 1870s, and then its first products were arc lighting equipment. Gerard was not quite seven years old when Edison turned on the world's first incandescent lamp, in 1879, the same year that the first electric light company to sell service to the public provided San Francisco with Charles Brush's flaring arc lights. A few months later, Wabash, Indiana, opened the first municipal electric light plant, designed to illuminate the whole town with a battery of Brush lamps shining from the top of the courthouse. Wild-eyed visionaries were braving the ridicule of sensible folk to predict that one day the world would be not only lighted but powered by electricity.

To a boy, such daring prophecies were perfectly reasonable, and as the miracles of invention followed close upon each other in the 1880s, he began to delve into some of the mysteries for himself. He was not as precocious as one of the new geniuses, Elihu Thomson, who at eleven had produced in a battery of Leyden jars an electric charge so powerful that it nearly knocked his father down. Thanks to Thomson, Edison, Brush and a dozen others, the toy was proving to be practicable. Gerard was not yet ten when an Edison plant opened in New York City to light the premises of fifty-nine customers. He was eleven when the first electric car ran on a Cleveland street, scaring horses almost as much as pedestrians. By the time he was fourteen, in 1886, satisfied customers were buying Edison's "little light in a bottle" at the rate of 200,000 bulbs a year, and the inventor needed so much room for his various manufacturing enterprises that he moved his factory from New York to two uncompleted buildings of a locomotive works in Schenectady. That year, too, electric motors replaced steam in more than a hundred industries and were running sewing machines and looms, emery wheels and lathes, printing presses and ventilators, even an elevator in Boston. In Lynn a young fellow named Edwin Wilbur Rice, Jr., son of a famous scholar, had been for a year superintendent of the Thomson-Houston Company, Edison's chief rival, although as recently as 1880 Rice was only the prize student of those Philadelphia high-school teachers, Thomson and Edwin J. Houston. Gerard Swope, getting ready for high school himself, was attracted by the strange power which could be generated and harnessed with bits of metal and coils of wire. In the basement at 3530 Olive Street, Isaac Swope good-naturedly consented to the setting up of a workshop where the boy could tinker to his heart's content.

Here, with the help of a diagram in *Scientific American*, he put together a motor which worked and would run a little wagon up and down the street. Encouraged, for this was a triumph of ingenuity in the eyes of his parents and admiring small brother, he went on to invent an electric machine which would cut cloth, and actually won the praise of Sid Schwab's father, made more convincing by an offer to buy an interest in it. Gerard was by no means indifferent to money, but he knew that his invention would not work very well, and he modestly declined.

After that there could hardly be any doubt as to his choice of a career. He would be an electrical engineer, and in preparing for that profession nothing less than the best would do. It was no small sacrifice for a modestly circumstanced family to put a son through the Massachusetts Institute of Technology, but pedagogues agreed that this was the best training ground for any engineer, so the Swopes studied ways and means of setting aside the $750 a year which their boy's education would cost.

Meanwhile he proved his worth by earning somewhat better marks at Central High School than he had in the elementary grades. He was especially keen on the sciences, and years later he and some of his classmates chuckled together over memories of their French physics teacher, Professor Peltier—in those days high-school teachers rated the title—"with his little goatee artistically dyed black." They sniffed in retrospect the air of the "wonderful laboratory strategically located in the basement so that the fumes could find their way throughout the building, especially when some wag spilled the stink stuff." At least one of them thought that here began the career of Gerard Swope.

The boy was settling into permanent habits and mannerisms. He did his assignments for school or his chores at home on time, concentrating on each until it was finished. He said what he had to say in his loud, positive tones, and did not wander off into speculative discursiveness. Sidney Schwab was preparing for Harvard and a medical degree; when the two boys talked about their plans, Gerard spoke of facts and Sidney of dreams.

Central High School, which both boys attended in the late 1880s, was two and a half miles down Olive Street, but it never occurred to Gerard or his family that he might travel on the horsecars. Father's place of business was still farther downtown, but he walked the distance. Not only was the carfare five cents each way, but Isaac Swope's long legs easily covered the ground as fast as the plodding horses. At fifteen, Gerard's head hardly topped his father's shoulder, but as they strode down Olive Street together, the boy stretched his legs to match the man's long, rapid step. It was a matter of pride with him to keep up, and before long he had the habit of a pace which gave him the appearance of being always in a hurry.

The summer before he entered high school he saw something of the larger world. His sister, Golda, reversing usual procedure, was going to Germany to be married and live in Berlin. The whole family went along, a delightful experience which gave Gerard a lifelong taste for travel. They went through Washington and New York, and met delightful European relatives—Gerard was especially impressed by his sprightly Grandmother Cohn, far livelier and younger looking than the elder ladies of his acquaintance in St. Louis.

It had taken extra studying in the hot summer vacations to get him through elementary school, shortly after his fifteenth birthday, but he made up for it by working hard enough in high school to finish the four-year course in three and a half, and did well enough to be one of the speakers at graduation exercises in June 1891. Nearly all boys who entered high school dropped out to go to work so that in Gerard's class of one hundred four graduates, all but eighteen were girls.

In his teens, Gerard developed a more than average bossiness, displayed most vigorously when, at fourteen, he imposed upon himself the task of rearing his much younger brother in the virtues of obedience and promptness. It was not an unalloyed success. Herbert had a will of his own, a lofty disregard for the clock and a vast capacity for mischief. He had neither their mother's passion for the orderly use of hours nor their father's gentle amenability. (Seventy years later Gerard still was trying to get Herbert to keep appointments on time—and failing.) Gerard established penalties for tardiness, impertinence and misbehavior, gave stern warnings and did not hesitate to deprive his brother of afternoon play hours when he thought the offense justified such punishment.

"He was severe but just," Herbert recalls, "and he really brought me up."

If Gerard's precepts failed to impress, his example in certain respects did, and there was the flattery of imitation in the younger boy's manner of speech. When both were at the peaks of their careers—the elder as president of General Electric, the younger as executive editor of the New York *World*—Gerard's secretary noted:

"The only man I've ever seen who can talk louder and faster than Mr. Swope is his brother, Herbert."

If Herbert supposed that fraternal supervision was to be relaxed by Gerard's removal to M.I.T., he was speedily disillusioned. Even at nineteen, the young man was not one to abandon a task half-finished. He was excited at the prospect of setting off alone to embark upon a career, but he took time to devise a way to maintain a wholesome discipline over Herbert. He commanded the child to send him every week a written report on his behavior. Not the least of Gerard Swope's successes in establishing his authority over men was that the unruly Herbert, whom most people were to find quite ungovernable, obeyed.

III *The Education of an Engineer*

There was no better school in America for training an engineer than M.I.T., nor, if one may judge by the records of its graduates, for training an industrialist. But in 1891, when Tech was only thirty years old, a great deal of that reputation was still to be won. Fortunately for Gerard Swope and most of his contemporaries, the entrance requirements were relatively easy, although once admitted, boys found the curriculum of mathematics and science arduous enough.

Lectures and laboratory work were scheduled from nine to five on weekdays and all Saturday morning. Studying occupied most evenings. "A place for men to work, not for boys to play," the faculty boasted. The setting was unimpressive. M.I.T.'s thousand students lived and studied in the heart of Boston. Its only building which could be considered imposing was Rogers Hall with its columned portico and wide steps up from Boylston Street, where a mild traffic rush of hansom cabs, delivery vans and carriages prevented any semblance of academic hush.

Later generations would consider the social life pitiful. Most of the budding engineers lived in private boarding houses; there was no dormitory or fraternity life to distract them from their studies; the roistering of Harvard undergraduates, although indulged in by only a minority even there, was unknown at Tech. The boy from St. Louis found the somewhat Spartan regime to his taste. One of his earliest adventures was his first poker game, and with true beginner's luck, he raked in pot after pot.

"The winnings burned in my pocket," he recalls, "and I wasn't happy until I had spent it all on hot chocolate and sandwiches for all of us."

He avoided poker after that, playing only penny ante when it would have been churlish to refuse, but the abstention was no sacrifice. Games of chance bored him; his gambling instincts were not so easily satisfied, and when he did indulge it would be to take bigger risks than a few dollars on the turn of a card.

He was acutely aware of the expense to which he was putting his parents. The average cost of a year at M.I.T. was $750, including $200 tuition, but Gerard was determined not to live as lavishly as that implied. When Isaac Swope died eight years later, they found folded carefully into his wallet one of the first letters Gerard had written from Boston. It read:

> DEAR FATHER AND MOTHER:
>
> Here is what I think a very close estimate of my year's expenses, excluding all clothes, etc. As you will see, it is $100 below what is usually allowed as an average.

Tuition		$200.00
Board, Lodging, Light and Fuel		270.00
Stationery, Books, Societies for School		45.00
Chemistry	$10.00	
Uniform	15.00	25.00
Laundry	$25.00	
Room	10.00	35.00
Sundries		75.00
Total		$650.00

This was a modest but not a hardship budget. Fifty dollars a month was a living wage for a fairly skilled workman in those days, considerably more than common labor could command. It did not, of course, lend itself to riotous living, but the traditional temptations of wine and women, fast horses and fast company had small appeal for this slender, sharp-featured, dark-haired youth who developed at M.I.T. the capacity for concentrated work which he had begun in high school.

He did well in his classes without achieving a record for outstanding brilliance, on a par with such members of his class as Alfred P. Sloan, Jr. There was rather a strong element of non-engineering studies. M.I.T. in those days stressed economics, and this, as much as the precision of an engineering education, produced some future industrial managers of great eminence—Sloan at General Motors; Paul Litchfield, who was in the class of '96, at Goodyear; Frank Park at Singer Sewing Machine; and Irénée Du Pont, who was a freshman when Swope was a senior.

A popular member of the faculty was a young instructor of chemistry, Willis R. Whitney, who, like most brilliant pedagogues, had some arbitrary devices by which he measured the quality of his students. One was a simple experiment in which the student lit a bit of pine, blew it out and plunged it into a jar of oxygen. The usual report was that "the stick burned up," but the real point, according to Whitney, was the bright glow that leaped up as soon as a spark hit the oxygen. More than sixty years later, Whitney pays tribute to Swope's powers of observation by saying:

"He was one of the few on whose reports of experiments I did not have to write, 'Repeat and note the glow.' All his life, he was alert enough to note a glow. He was an excellent student. He worked as hard as the grinds but he had more initiative and was more popular. Still, he was a mighty serious young fellow."

The serious young man learned more than chemistry from Whitney. The instructor, already one of the better scientific minds, was as much concerned with the philosophy of science as with its achievements. He used to say:

"My only religion is nature and the truths we can learn from nature."

From teachers such as this, even the most practical youths, if they have imagination, broaden the range of their interests through an awareness of the fact that there is more to the world than their particular specialty.

Outside of the regular engineering course, too, Gerard studied philosophy with Davis R. Dewey and enjoyed the privilege of hearing a brilliant young lawyer, Louis D. Brandeis, lecture on business law. This seemed perilously like the law of the jungle if one looked at the exploits of Goulds and Vanderbilts, although these were much admired in the nineties. But Brandeis offered a different ethic, one of public service. Not yet forty years old, the lawyer attracted the serious student by profundity of learning rather than wit. He considerably broadened young Swope's understanding of the nature of business and of society itself, without converting the youngster to his own passionate belief in the dangers of corporate size.

In the process of mastering the electrical knowledge of the day, the student thrilled to talk of preparations for the Chicago World's Fair of 1893. Here were to be assembled all the wonders of the age, at least all of those which mattered to an electrical engineer. Most of them had been developed since the toylike show which had dazzled beholders at the Centennial Exposition in Philadelphia only seventeen years earlier.

The year 1893, however, was notable for a less entrancing phenomenon than the Fair. A business "panic"—the pseudonym of "depression" had not yet been coined for these periodic disasters—swept the country, and one victim was Isaac Swope. While not ruined, his circumstances were so much reduced by the panic that the financing of a stay in Chicago was out of the question. Not that Gerard probably would have asked anyway, he was too conscious of the burden of his schooling upon his parents for that. But he was determined to see the Fair. Travel to Chicago was no more expensive than to St. Louis, so at the end of his sophomore year, he stopped off there looking for any sort of work which would keep him. Something in the electrical line would be preferable, and fortunately the lavish electrical display of the Fair had created extra jobs.

One of them was in the repair shops of the General Electric Company, which had set up the most elaborate electrical exhibits ever seen. The company, formed only a year earlier, was out to make a big impression, but it had regular customers to serve. The man in charge of the Chicago branch, a benevolent but demanding pioneer of the industry with the appropriate surname of Sunny, was willing to give a college student a temporary job if the boy would take a dirty one. So that summer Gerard spent his days in the grime and grease of the repair shop, and future generations of candidates for a start in General Electric were invited to reflect upon the possible significance of an 1893 entry in the Chicago branch's books: "G. Swope, helper, $1 a day."

G. Swope himself did not consider it an omen. His dollar gave him food, a bed and the opportunity to spend evenings and all day Sunday enjoying the wonders of the Fair. He could gaze with budding professional appreciation upon the biggest generator yet built, a monster of no less than 2,000 horsepower. He could ride on the moving sidewalk which carried 6,000 people for nearly a mile in less than ten minutes, or on the electrified elevated railway which surrounded the entire exposition grounds. He could inspect all kinds of motors. Above all, in the warm summer nights he could gaze with awe and fascination upon the blaze of light which distinguished this fair above all others in history. Searchlights played with highly spectacular effect upon the soaring sprays of fountains. A luminous column rising from the ground was said to have no fewer than 4,000 incandescent lamps. The great Electric Hall, shining with a splendor such as gas never had achieved, had only the sun as a competitor.

G. Swope, helper, returning to M.I.T. in the fall, was more convinced than ever that his choice of a career was wise. Electric light and power companies were springing up all over the land, and although they often had a great deal of trouble with their financing—it was hard for conservative investors to believe that queer mechanics and inventors were making a whole new world—the public liked the ease and effectiveness of "the little light in a bottle." Manufacturers were converting to electricity to run their machines in increasing numbers.

In the midst of his studies, young Swope had his minor extra-curricular triumphs. He was chosen as a speaker at the Junior Class Dinner, which still operated in the old oratorical tradition of "responses to toasts," and the class had drunk to nine of them by the time Swope's turn came. He had written almost all his speech in verse, of which a fair sample was:

> *I see that the gentlemen to follow are getting impatient*
> *Afraid I observe they'll forget their oration*
> *And the toastmaster too frowns upon me, I notice.*

This lyric effort so impressed his mathematically minded comrades that they invited him to be class poet at commencement. "But I had enough sense of my limitations to decline it," he said.

Perhaps the most revealing incident of his college career was his entry into student politics. He devised and persuaded his fellows to accept an extremely complicated system of voting for class officers, resembling proportional representation, so intricate that no one knew how to count the ballots except Swope. There was some good-natured, ribald comment on his discovery that he himself was among the victors. The success did not turn him toward politics; he never ran for elective office again.

All this time he was under the influence of a remarkable man, General Francis A. Walker, as the president of M.I.T. often was called because the stern, maturing process of the Civil War had raised him from a private at twenty to brevet brigadier general at twenty-four. For twenty years he had been one of the leading academic economists in the country and would be acclaimed by some successors in his specialty as the most important and original American economic thinker of his time. He expounded some unusual and even, cautious scholars said, radical economic ideas. He had developed a novel theory that wages were not necessarily dependent entirely upon the amount of capital which was put behind the individual worker. Rather, he argued, the most important factor governing pay should be the productivity of labor, in which capital in the form of machinery and power was only one element along with the worker's skill, efficiency and ingenuity. Walker was among the few who believed that the efficiency of labor could be improved by cutting the day's working hours from fourteen to eleven, or even ten. (He was not so visionary, he said, as to suppose that an eight-hour day ever could be achieved, but in the seventies and early eighties the reduction of the prevailing eighty-four-hour week to forty-eight was as much ridiculed as the proponents of a thiry-hour week would be a couple of generations later.) In later life Swope could remember few details of Walker's teaching, but it bore a striking similarity to his own philosophy.

Meantime, the four years of college passed so pleasantly that an affection and regard for the place and its staff remained one of the strong emotions of his later life. There was a genuinely exalting moment when in June 1895 Gerard Swope became possessed of a sheepskin testifying to the fact that he was now a Bachelor of Science in Electrical Engineering.

It was a document in which he and all his family took pride. But it was not a passport to professional employment. In the 1950s a graduate of Swope's standing at M.I.T. would have his choice of dozens of highly attractive offers. But in the 1890s the men who mattered in the mushrooming electrical companies were for the most part self-taught in their wonderful new trade; there had been no other way to learn. They were grand mechanics, imaginative craftsmen, geniuses whether tutored or not in the humanities. Almost all of them were profoundly suspicious of college boys.

IV *The View from the Bottom*

Influence sometimes opens doors which remain obstinately closed to merit. In 1895, a letter from one of his father's old friends in St. Louis to the manager of the Western Electric Company in Chicago was more helpful in getting Gerard work than his degree from M.I.T. He did not win immediate admittance to the practice of his profession. The manager would do no more than refer him to the general foreman, and obviously was reluctant to do that. The foreman in turn looked with sour distaste upon the neat dark suit, high stiff white collar and carefully knotted necktie which indicated to him that the wearer was too proud to soil his fingers.

"You know, you'll have to get your hands dirty," he said sharply.

"I am perfectly willing," Gerard replied.

"Well, when do you want to start?" the man conceded.

"I am ready now."

"All right, come back at seven tomorrow morning."

The foreman condescended to add that the pay would be twelve and a half cents an hour, the work week fifty-six hours. It did not need an engineer's training to calculate that Gerard would have seven dollars a week to live on. Fortunately this was a subsistence wage in 1895, and the hours were fewer than had been customary before the panic.

"I was assigned to the dirtiest work in the shop," the president of the General Electric Company would recall with retrospective relish, "tearing down old machines that had been returned for repairs."

The Western Electric shops, then located on the near West Side of Chicago, in a grim and grimy waste of factories and slums, never saw the dark suit and white collar again. The newest hand, though small, was wiry and capable of holding his own in the hardest manual work. He felt that he had proved himself with his companions when, not long after he started, a group of well-dressed youths from a local school of engineering came through on a conducted tour.

"You know," an older workman with whom Gerard was grubbily dismantling a motor told him, "when you first came in here, we thought you were one of those damned college men."

"Well, what do you think now?"

"Oh, hell," was the cheerful reply, "I don't know if you ever seen the inside of a school."

Gerard did not let the flattery go to his head. He kept his hands in the grease and dirt of the old machines, and before long was transferred to the slightly cleaner task of building new ones. But if his fellows accepted him as one of themselves, his foreman knew him for an engineer, and when inventory time came around, assigned the newcomer to prepare the sheets. These—"done as any young engineer would, clearly and neatly," he recalls—so impressed the general foreman that he ordered Swope to draw up the inventory for the whole department.

"But if we need you for the rough work, you'll go back," he warned gruffly.

Actually he was so glad to have his paper work well done that he proposed to make the youth a permanent clerk.

"But he was fair about it," Swope says, "and when I told him I preferred to go through other departments and learn as much as I could, he gave me the opportunity."

Living on seven dollars a week presented no serious problems to a young fellow whose tastes were simple and whose dissipations were nil. He found quarters in a small South Side apartment with a budding lawyer. Late nights were ruled out by his inclinations and the necessity of getting up in time to go halfway across Chicago by seven o'clock. His only extravagance was the nickel carfare morning and evening.

Into this Spartan life he invited his younger brother. He found the boy a factory job, not quite so grimy as his own first one, but even in his teens Herbert was conspicuously unsuited to regular hours or routine work. He was called "wild," and at home his reputation was such that almost any peccadillo in his circle was likely to be attributed to him, even when he was innocent. He was far from satisfied with the lack of diversion in Gerard's life and returned speedily to St. Louis to become a newspaper reporter, a calling in which his taste for odd hours and excitement was an asset.

Gerard continued at one job after another in the shops. He supplemented his seven dollars a week with a few dollars paid for articles published in one or another of the electrical journals which were seeking to keep abreast of the rapidly moving industry. Hardly a month passed in these days without some significant advance in electrical engineering or its application. Niagara was harnessed to its first dynamos in 1895, and across the continent, Sacramento drew light and power from the falls of the American River over a transmission line running the unbelievable distance of twenty-five miles.

This was the electric industrial revolution, and Swope was just in time to see it from the beginning. Since 1885 wires from central power stations had been providing current to run machinery in shops, but for a radius of only a few thousand yards. Now long-distance transmission set the factory free to locate wherever labor or raw materials or markets were most favorable. Power had given its long reach to industry, which no longer would be confined to the neighborhood of streams or coal.

Swope noted other signs of progress in addition to this exhilarating prospect. In New York City, Edison's station on Pearl Street furnished light to five thousand customers, some of them as far uptown as Sixty-first Street. An electric locomotive, powerful as any ever propelled by steam, this year began hauling railroad trains through long tunnels without any of the smoke, cinders and coal gas which had made the run hazardous for train crews, agony for passengers. Civilians in the Navy persuaded doubting admirals to experiment with an electric motor to turn gun turrets. Sales of incandescent lamps were counted in millions in 1895, instead of thousands, and the best makes lasted for seven hundred hours. Almost every city of any size was expanding an electric street railway or planning to install one. In hundreds of shops, mechanics and scientists were tinkering with novel ideas for better ways to produce electric power, better methods of transmitting it, better apparatus to use it.

To a young man at a bench who was trying to write about some of these phenomena, the industry ought to have seemed a chaotic mass of contradictions. But Swope was able to make some sense of it. In 1895 there were more companies manufacturing electrical equipment than there would be thirty years later; for a decade they had spawned, grown or died, merged or reincorporated in a bewildering kaleidoscope.

The pace was something to which Americans of his and succeeding generations would have to accustom themselves. Gerard now worked for the oldest company in the field, and in the mere twenty-six years since it started as a maker of telegraph instruments it had been through two forms of partnership and two incorporations. His first employer, the General Electric Company, was the biggest on a gross business of about $12,000,000 a year.

Every new device—even a good copy of an old one—was likely to produce a new company to exploit the patent or the inventor. George Westinghouse had organized the most important of these corporations around his own inventions and the purchase of some foreign patents. Out of his shops had come William Stanley to found his own company which, in 1895, was the foremost maker of transformers. Dozens of independents, large and small, were making incandescent lamps; hundreds were turning out motors or electric elevators or dynamos. An observant youth reflecting on the confusion while riding the streetcar to and from work could see a trend emerging. It was a trend toward fewer and more solid if not always larger companies.

Western Electric, for example, had confined itself to telegraph instruments only for its first three years. In 1872 its second set of partners incorporated it as the Western Electric Manufacturing Company with an expanded line. Nine years later it was reorganized with one hundred times its original capital, 60 per cent of it supplied by the American Telephone and Telegraph Company, for whom it made instruments while continuing to compete in the market with motors, generators, transmission equipment and electrical supplies generally.

General Electric illustrated the trend even more clearly. The merger of the two biggest companies which formed it in 1892 had been preceded by a good deal of consolidation, and it was difficult to see how without it the progress of the industry could have been as swift.

The Edison General Electric Company had been an amalgam in 1889 of what at one time or another had been eight different Edison enterprises. The variety was a tribute to the ingenuity of lawyers and financiers as much as to that of the Wizard of Menlo Park. By 1892 this group had absorbed Bergmann and Company, started by a former Edison employee to make auxiliary appliances. It also had purchased the Sprague Electric Railway and Motor Company which, in 1888, opened in Richmond the first practical electric streetcar system, inspiring the exclamation by a Negro observer: "Fo' Gawd, what am de white folks a-gwine do nex'? Fust dey freed de darkey, an' now dey freed de mule."

The other half of General Electric, the Thomson-Houston Company, had grown out of an enterprise formed in 1880 to exploit the patents of Professors Thomson and Houston of the Boys' Central High School in Philadelphia. Their inventions ranked second only to those of Edison and were in part complementary to his. Reorganized in 1883 with a Lynn shoe manufacturer, Charles A. Coffin, at its head, this corporation had acquired the Van Depoele Company, whose chief assets were electric railway patents. Then it paid more than $3,000,000 to the originator of the double-carbon arc lamp for the Brush Electric Company of Cleveland.

A motive for these mergers and purchases can be found in the natural desire of men to acquire wealth and power. This accounted for many of the consolidations in steel and railroads and oil, to mention only a few. But the two biggest electrical manufacturers had a different reason and one that stands better the test of public service. Their industry was a mass of patents crisscrossing each other. Hardly anyone, even Edison, had confidence in his rights to be making and selling his products. Under these circumstances it often was more sensible to merge than fight. Purchase of the Brush Company had been inspired by just such litigation.

Shortly before the merger which created General Electric, the field had been reduced when Edison won a suit to protect his lamp filament. The court battle, lasting three years with one expert on the stand for three months, defeated the claim of infringers that the filament was merely an improvement on the old carbon rod, not something new. One of the classics of patent litigation, the case drew the two biggest manufacturers together. Edison had his lamp patent; Thomson-Houston had patents on generators of alternating current which used the lamp most effectively. Each had additional patents which were as necessary to the other. So they combined in 1892, and it was taken as a measure of the industry's stature that J. P. Morgan and Henry L. Higginson of an almost equally eminent Boston banking firm consented to go on the Board of Directors.

Consolidation, however, had not stopped here. The new company promptly bought out a relatively small but, for that time, highly efficient plant in Yonkers, Eickemeyer and Osterheld. The General Electric engineers were attracted originally by the firm's patents for armatures. Later they were heard to assert that a greater asset was a man, a little, hunched-up, carelessly dressed, cigar-smoking young German only three years in this country, Carl (later Charles) Steinmetz.

The net effect of these mergers and purchases was to create a network of factories and facilities almost twice as big as either of the two main constituents boasted in 1891. But the new company's business was only about 20 per cent more than either had done separately. Some said this was entirely due to that panic of '93 which had permanently crippled Isaac Swope's modest fortunes. Others thought that General Electric failed to hold customers because it dropped Edison's name from its title. In any case, scores of competitors remained.

The growth of the young electrical industry paralleled that of manufacturing generally. Gerard Swope's first twenty-five years saw the expansion of population and transportation which made the United States a single market for steel, textiles, machinery, consumer goods—all the products of mill and mine. As yet no public regulatory bodies interfered with the way a man ran his business; the only two attempts, an Interstate Commerce Commission of 1887 and an Anti-Trust Act of 1890, had been virtually nullified by court rulings. When Western Electric's new hand was born, manufacturing was local or regional at best. By the time he got his first job, railroads had opened up the whole West and South, while the census of 1900 would show that the population had almost doubled. He was in on the ground floor to exploit these conditions—as close to the bottom, in fact, as it was possible to get.

Gerard was content to build his career upon this foundation. He appraised himself objectively. His liking for hard work and his very orderly mind could take him as far as engineering genius, which he knew he did not possess. Although he remained a laborer with an occasional clerical assignment, he believed that opportunities would open to an alert, persistent watcher. He still expected to find his own in engineering.

One of the factors in his contentment was an absorbing interest quite unconnected with the electrical industry. More than a year after he had come to Chicago, a friend introduced him to Hull House, the settlement which Jane Addams and Ellen Gates Starr had started in the West Side slums in 1889—"two lovely women," he describes them. (Swope uses this adjective in a spiritual rather than a physical sense when he talks about people he likes.) They invited the visitor to join their teaching staff (unpaid), and he accepted with an enthusiasm rare for him. He liked to teach, and a close acquaintance with the handicaps of poverty—observed rather than experienced—gave him the uncomfortable feeling that something ought to be done about it. He lacked crusading spirit, but he approved the theory of Hull House—a group of people actually settling in a needy area to work as neighbors with neighbors, and without any airs of superiority. Especially was he attracted by the opportunity which education and skills might give to individual slum dwellers bent upon improving themselves.

Thus inspired, he taught algebra and electricity at night after his day in the shops. His students included workmen and even foremen from the Western Electric plant. They were as alert as he after their long hours of work. They kept him on his toes mentally as they dug determinedly into the lore he could impart, and he learned at least as much as he taught. When he was able to get one of his pupils into the University of Chicago—contributing a few dollars and a lot of encouragement and special tutoring—he was as pleased as if he had been promoted to an engineer's job.

This was not his only inspiration from Hull House. The place had attracted a remarkable group of women in addition to the founders. Especially impressive to the young teacher were Julia Lathrop, who left to head the Federal Government's Children's

Bureau when it was established; Florence Kelly, who contributed a great deal to the progress of factory inspection; Mrs. Alzina Stevens, an intelligent and forceful leader in the labor movement; Alice Hamilton, that unusual nineteenth-century phenomenon, a woman doctor of medicine, who was a professor at the Women's Medical College and deep in the interests which would lead to pioneer work in combating industrial diseases.

A special paragraph—some would say a special book—should be reserved for one more in this group, Mary Dayton Hill. A year older than Gerard and a couple of inches taller, she came to Hull House some months after he had begun teaching there. Originally from New Jersey, she was fresh from assisting John Dewey in his unorthodox studies of education at the University of Chicago. She herself was an enthusiast for the newest education theories and practices, was widely read and possessed a mind which Dr. Hamilton, who was her roommate at Hull House, nearly sixty years later still thought one of the finest she had ever encountered. But her learning and accomplishments were not what led her friends to proclaim so fervently their devotion to Mary Hill. Not only was she kind but she was perfectly willing to listen to other people talk about themselves.

An island of fine thoughts and splendid talk in a sea of poverty, misery and ignorance, Hull House was not without its problems. Dr. Hamilton remembers that the worst of them in the 1890s was garbage disposal and rats. (Forty years later, returning for a visit, she asked the new generation of Hull House workers what troubled them most. "Garbage disposal and rats" was their reply.) Notable visitors contributed to Hull House pleasures, which rose above sanitary deficiencies. Sidney and Beatrice Webb came from England with some of the ideas and information which went into their monumental history of the trade-union movement. Ramsay Macdonald, known as yet only to a limited circle and then as a Socialist writer, gave the settlement samples of his eloquence. Prince Kropotkin, the aristocratic Russian nihilist, spun his theories of social justice. Frank Lloyd Wright dropped in to expound what some of his contemporaries called architectural heresies, only to find them to be the creed of a new generation.

Swope gained a closer view of slum life when he moved to Hull House to live in 1897. The neighborhood was a polyglot pool of immigrants, mostly Italians, Czechs and Russian Jews, with a sprinkling of Irish who ruled the roost. Largely illiterate, bewildered and afraid, the denizens of this Nineteenth Ward were systematically victimized by sweat shops and corrupt politics. Joining in abortive efforts of reformers to oust the district boss, Gerard came to understand something of the hold such a man can have on a thoroughly exploited population through petty favors and protection in return for votes. It was a civics lesson, and from it he drew the moral that the correct answer was decent housing, adequate schooling and elemental security for workers. It also was an off-beat sort of life for a man who was to be manager of one of the world's largest corporations.

If he was one of the more thoughtful members of the Hull House family at this time, he was not one of the more vocal. Dr. Hamilton remembers him as singularly well informed on current events but more interested in drawing out the information of others than in airing his own.

"We were at once aware of a pulsing vitality in him," she says, "but he never was one to try to impress himself upon the company. He certainly deferred to Mary Hill when the subject was anything he thought she knew more about than he."

It was not all work and talk at Hull House. Sundays and holidays, especially in good weather, there was the call of the open road, answered by the well-to-do in shiny carriages behind sleek horses and by such as Gerard Swope and Mary Hill on safety bicycles. Since the introduction of these machines in 1887, they had become a national craze. A country-wide association of cyclists agitated for better roads and even got a few built. Bicycle manufacturers were taking business away from makers of carriages. Neither gave much thought to the crazy tinkerers of automotive power. The first automobile had appeared on an American road in 1893, and promptly broke down. E. P. Ingersoll's magazine, *The Horseless Age,* launched in 1895, was popularly believed to be the work of a madman. That same year Gerard read the humorous and then sensational newspaper stories of America's first road race, run from Chicago to Evanston and back, with two cars actually completing the fifty-two-mile course the same day. If he had thought about it, he would have endorsed the advice of the president of the Detroit Edison Company who, in 1896, warned his chief engineer, a stubborn fellow named Henry Ford, to quit fooling around with gasoline engines and stick to electricity, obviously the thing of the future.

Cyclists, then, were not disturbed by automobiles, and it was a pleasant run out along Lake Michigan, whose shores were scarcely built up as yet. Gerard and Mary pedaled tandem on a bicycle built for two—Hubbard Woods was a favorite destination but sometimes they went as far as Lake Forest. Alice Hamilton was usually along, as friend and chaperon. Other times the Hull House staff would make up a picnic party. One of these outings when Miss Addams was his partner lived long in Gerard's memory. They were an oddly matched couple on a tandem bicycle, the lady outweighing her escort by more than it would be gallant to estimate.

"She never knew what pedals were for," says Alice Hamilton. "She just sat and let the wheels go round and talked. It was hard work for Gerard, for after all she was a heavy woman and he was rather light."

On this particular day they had sojourned on the North Shore some thirty miles from Hull House, and coming back, the cyclists faced one of those stiff breezes which, even more than the boasts of its citizens, give Chicago its name of "Windy City." It was all Gerard could do to keep the tandem moving, but Miss Addams rested her feet and discoursed animatedly, pausing at intervals to suggest: "Don't you think we might go a little faster?"

Meanwhile the Bachelor of Science in Electrical Engineering became an electrical engineer. The promotion came early in 1898, a transfer to the Western Electric Engineering Department and a raise in pay to $10 a week. It had taken a long time, even in the face of the then common prejudice against college training. This year, for example, Herbert Hoover, a mining engineer with no more family influence than Swope and a degree of the same vintage, '95, was in Australia on a professional mission which paid more in a month than Swope earned in a year, even after his raise. Hoover, too, had been forced to take a laborer's job when he came out of college, but he had the real engineering flair. Swope was merely earnest and competent, as his first assignment indicated. This was to determine whether the shaft of an engine was strong enough to support the armature of an electric generator.

"I got out my old textbooks, and figured and figured and finally got a result," he says.

He had wasted a lot of time since, as an older engineer pointed out, such calculations are to be found in handbooks. But he justified the useless effort, saying; "My answer, which I had worked out so laboriously, was near enough to show my calculations were along the right lines and gave me more confidence."

From calculations, he progressed to designing small motors and then to work on plans for the largest machines made. Finally he branched out on new lines and developed some improvements in the "boosters" by which central power stations kept their current steady. The company took out several patents on them.

On the way up to these increasingly responsible tasks, he decided that his services were worth more than $10 a week. He expressed this view to the head of his department, who already had recommended Swope for a raise. But the company had adopted a policy of no salary increases during hard times. Gerard asked and received permission to appeal the ruling to the president.

This was Enos M. Barton, one of the original partners in the firm and the guiding spirit in its growth. A strong-featured, handsome man with a stern manner and a scornful look, he was at this time in his middle fifties. Starting as a messenger boy, he had been in the telegraph and electrical business all his life, with one brief interlude of schoolteaching.

"He had a cold exterior but a warm and responsive heart," Swope characterizes him. "I had never seen him before and didn't know him or his traits, but was fortunate in accidentally making just the proper approach. I said, 'Mr. Barton, I haven't come to you to ask for more money; I am asking for justice,' and then told him the circumstances."

One may doubt that the approach was quite so accidental, for he had heard a great deal about the character of the big boss from fellow workers. Anyway, the auspicious start won him little immediate satisfaction. Barton was not to be stampeded by even the most serious engineer, especially one who looked even younger than his few years.

"Let me suggest," he replied stiffly, "that you go back to work and when the next advance-in-pay period comes along, if your pay is not increased, then maybe we don't value your work as highly as you think we should, but, on the other hand, we will consider it and you will see by our action how you should guide yourself for the future."

The young man had a dogged patience in those days; later colleagues would have been surprised that he held his peace for six months. Then the raise came through, to $15 a week and retroactive at that, so he had more than $100 in a lump. It was a lot of money, and welcome, but even better was the notice of a man who could speed his advancement.

There were other opportunities, and Swope was not one to neglect them. He went to St. Louis for the Christmas holidays of 1898—it was the last time he saw his father, for Isaac Swope died suddenly less than two months later—and there heard of a factory which was planning to convert to electric power. Sidney Schwab's father introduced him to the owners, and he spent a good deal of his vacation working with the architects and engineers to convince them that they should use Western Electric equipment. He went back to Chicago with an order for more than $10,000, a sizable achievement for a youngster who never had tried to sell anything before.

"Bonus for getting the business?" he asks in some surprise. "I don't remember any, but the incident established me in the minds of the people in the company as possibly having some commercial ability."

It also established that fact in his own mind. Hitherto he had felt an aloofness toward commerce which many professional men adopt as a badge of superiority. Swope's discovery that Western Electric was a business did more than his most ambitious engineering project to put him into the main stream of American development. Now that the whole country was linked by rails into a single potential market, the United States was well embarked on the expansion which led European observers to deprecate it as a purely business civilization. Bankers, railroad organizers and manufacturers earned more lavish praise than ever had been given to men in trade before. Rockefeller and Carnegie were national heroes, their wealth popularly regarded as evidence of services performed rather than acquisitiveness.

At Hull House, Swope sometimes heard such men criticized for antisocial manipulations which benefited only themselves. But the newspapers and people generally were willing to take the masters of money, steel, oil, coal and railroads at their own valuation, which was high. It was hard to take seriously the eloquent protests of a Bryan when his panacea was the free coinage of silver, or even of a Sockless Jerry Simpson, the Populist, who advocated public ownership of railroads.

So Swope saw the business world essentially in the same light as most of his contemporaries who never entered Hull House. Business, in this view, was making the nation great and giving the people opportunities. Exploitation of immigrant and other labor, railroad discrimination in rates against farmers and small shippers, manipulation of credit and stocks for the benefit of insiders, were evils, of course. But these practices did not seem to be essential. Barton, for example, had built a successful business without them.

Swope's new interest in the commercial aspect of the electrical industry confirmed him in his decision to make his career in

Western Electric although friends assured him that his technical education and practical experience could command more money elsewhere. He positively liked Barton's hard-driving ways and the fierce tenacity which enemies called stubbornness. He could accept a rebuff from this man with uncharacteristic meekness. It came after Gerard had revived the electric cloth-cutting machine of his high-school days and "entirely on my own time and outside my work in the engineering department" improved and patented it. He also had an offer for it, but felt that he ought to submit it to his own company first. Barton decided that it was not in his line, and then added severely, "Young man, your work in the company, for which we pay you, should engross all your time and energy and thought, and we therefore do not look upon these outside activities in engineering with any favor."

This was not an unusual attitude for employers, and Swope was far from disagreeing with it. Besides, he soon was experiencing more of Barton's warm heart than of his cold exterior, and it led to the end of his engineering career as such.

V *The Making of a Businessman*

Years later Swope thought that perhaps he turned readily from the active practice of his profession because he was not a great engineer. He saw that the expansion of the young industry to which he had linked his life, although it had grown from nothing to $100,000,000 a year since his boyhood, required more than the most wonderfully designed machinery and appliances. It now needed intensive and extensive selling.

Plenty of young engineers were becoming businessmen as well, but most of them were starting toward business leadership by way of production rather than sales. Of Swope's M.I.T. friends, this already was true of Sloan with a roller-bearing firm in New Jersey, and Litchfield with Goodyear in Akron. They were learning to apply business methods to their engineering. Swope, four years after his graduation, took his engineering methods into business, specifically into selling and distribution.

Late in 1899 he drafted a plan for a new district sales organization in St. Louis. Barton liked it, but entrusted the management of it to an older man, sending the author along as assistant. Swope was luckier than he knew because, being passed over for the top job, he had an opportunity to learn salesmanship.

One lesson was an exercise in translation. He was sent out of town to bid on the electrification of a Federal prison. He put his case in precise technical terms such as any M.I.T. graduate could appreciate. His was the best offer, too, he was sure. But the order went to a competitor. The disappointed young man returned to Chicago to report and, he hoped, receive from a more experienced salesman an explanation of his failure.

"Did you get the business?" his department head asked as soon as Swope appeared in his office.

"No," Swope admitted.

"That is all," his superior informed him.

It was infuriating as well as humiliating. Nearly fifty years later, Swope's resentment still was plain when he described the incident and added, "That lesson I never forgot—in the handling of men, if they are to grow, they must have an opportunity to tell of their experiences and have someone who is more mature and has had more experience endeavor to point out the weaknesses of their approach and show some sympathy and understanding in the work they are doing."

Actually a little reflection showed him that he had lost his prospect in the complexity of his engineer's jargon. Next time he would couch his proposals in terms which the customer could understand, "and without too much effort on his part," he added.

Consideration for the other fellow's vocabulary led to consideration for the other fellow's point of view. At the turn of the century it was by no means a business commonplace that a deal ought to benefit both parties to it. Swope's acceptance of this principle combined with his technical knowledge and growing facility for intelligible speech made him such a persuasive salesman, although never in a glad-handing, back-slapping manner, that some of his competitors muttered that the engineer Swope "uses his slide rule to cut prices."

More disturbing to him than such gibes was his youthful appearance, for at twenty-seven he had the slight figure and clear skin of a boy, scarcely offset by the strong lines of his facial bones.

"It was difficult to convince customers that I knew what I was talking about," he says with a chuckle.

At the time this was so little a laughing matter that he raised a beard, a decoration which 1900 did not ridicule although the style was going out. Whiskers gave Swope somewhat the appearance of a juvenile preparing for a masquerade in the role of a Civil War general. It probably fooled no one but gave him some extra confidence.

He could use it. The lot of a salesman for Western Electric was not always smooth, neither within the company nor in meeting competition. Sent to El Paso to bid for an order to equip a new power plant against three competitors, he offered the lowest price, but then was informed that the purchaser wanted a deferred-payment plan. Cash was Western Electric's policy, as it was in the industry generally. But Swope figured out a way to give the customer his terms. The Western Electric agents in Mexico were brothers who held leading financial and commercial positions. Swope thought they would be willing to finance the deal if he put it before them in person. He telegraphed his plan to Chicago.

"Use your own judgment," came the reply.

In 1900 it took forty-eight hours to get from El Paso to Mexico City by train. Swope made the trip and won agreement to his plan. But by the time he got back to Texas, the representative of one of his competitors, the Fort Wayne Company, had accepted deferred payments and departed triumphantly with the order.

"I returned home crestfallen," Swope admits, although he suspected that the Fort Wayne Company would not carry out the contract.

Discouragement was replaced by a warmer feeling when the expenses for his Mexican trip were disallowed. The shops and his engineer's drafting board had taught him patience and subordination, but hardly meekness. He promptly boarded a train for Chicago, informed the general sales manager indignantly that this was not his interpretation of the authorization to use his own judgment, and the expense account was approved. His satisfaction was increased when Fort Wayne repudiated its agent's agreement and the El Paso order came back to Western Electric, financed just as Swope had arranged.

It was a "vindication"—Swope's own word—and strengthened his reliance upon his judgment. It also was one of a number of incidents which prompted Barton to promote the aggressive young salesman to the post of manager in St. Louis early in 1901 and entrust him with the organization and presidency of a subsidiary company to handle Western Electric business throughout the territory.

This was a tribute as much to Barton's perspicacity as to Swope's ability, for as yet the younger man had displayed no talent for organization and administration. The subsidiary, which Swope named the Mercantile Electric Company, had 95 per cent of its stock subscribed by the parent; Swope was to find the remaining 5 per cent and the Board of Directors in St. Louis. Cautious in his inexperience, he consulted older heads, including an old friend of the family, David Goldsmith, a successful lawyer whose sister was an intimate co-worker with Swope's mother in charitable work for the needy. Goldsmith, a dry, precise man with more humor than he usually cared to show, was notable for that stern sense of duty and application to work which is attributed to the Puritans. He had formed the highest possible regard for Gerard, seeing in the younger man all the qualities he would have wanted in a son. His admiration was strong enough to overcome a rule of life which he had set for himself, namely to confine association with any business to a lawyer-client relationship. He consented to be a director, and from him Swope learned a good deal of basic corporate law and what in a letter to a friend he called "its ceaseless technicalities." His inquiring mind led him to ask the why of the law as well as what. His mentor brushed aside his searching questions.

"It is hard enough to know what the damned laws are without trying to seek the reason for them," Goldsmith advised his young friend.

The other directors were of the same generation, most of them family friends too, and the company was launched upon a sea of electrical expansion which greeted the new twentieth century. The president of Mercantile Electric had a salary of $200 a month, and this, he thought, was an adequate financial foundation upon which to build a family. Mary Hill agreed, so in August 1901 Swope joined her, her mother and her three sisters on Mackinac Island to be married. His own mother, sister and brother were present too, but otherwise it was a Hull House affair. Jane Addams herself and a Congregational minister who was one of the settlement's "family" co-operated in a special ceremony which both principals always regarded as their real union, although, because the minister was not licensed to marry people in Michigan, they had a civil ceremony before a justice of the peace the day before.

They returned to the St. Louis house in which Gerard had been born. For many months they had it to themselves while his mother and sister were in Europe. His brother, Herbert, grown as tall as their father but curiously like a redheaded, ruddy-faced Gerard in features, was with them briefly. Then he left to take a reporter's job in Chicago on his way to the journalists' Mecca, New York.

Olive Street, like all St. Louis, was changing. It was not just that the city was growing; the homes and factories, streets and shops were being revolutionized by electricity. There were electric lights in quite a few Olive Street homes, although most still used gas, and here and there electric fans mitigated the summer heat. Electric streetcars clanged along Olive Street, symbols of urban expansion. The telephone was entering upon the first decade of its spectacular growth as a necessity for home and business rather than a toy for grown-up children.

The result was a booming electrical industry, but one in which the mortality rate for new companies was high. Swope was well aware of the hazards. He brooded over them with some anxiety, and over his own ability to surmount them. He wondered whether he really had the makings of a successful businessman, and sometimes he was almost sure that he did not.

"Often my consoling thought was that I was in good health and strong physically," he wrote years later, "so I could support my family, if necessary, by digging ditches."

These gloomy reflections were justified if exaggerated. Swope was not born with a mastery of executive techniques and in 1901 was guilty of some fundamental errors of judgment and tactics. For example, he did not naturally or easily delegate to others anything he thought he could do himself, so that when it came time to take the first inventory of his new company, he would allow no one else to handle the job. He wasted hours on it, often after all the others had gone. The result was unsatisfactory, not nearly so good a performance as he had managed in Chicago when fresh out of M.I.T.

At the same time he was wrestling personally with the company's books and could not get them to come out right. He was so discouraged that he felt he had to cancel a long-planned visit to New York although the invitation had come to him and Mary from the vice-president of Western Electric, who was second only to Barton in the administration. Late one night Swope came home, "very blue and discouraged," he recalls, to tell his wife. They agreed that he should turn in their railroad tickets, and mournfully he went down to the station to do it. It was nearly midnight when he started home, plodding through a driving snowstorm with his head down against the wind and a sense of failure as cold as the night. Suddenly two toughs darted out of an alley and pushed against him.

"I thought it was accidental, but on looking up I saw what it was, a holdup, and struck out at one of them," he wrote with relish. "Fortunately, because of the ice and snow, he slipped and fell, and then they both, seeing I was putting up some resistance, started to run. I went home, much buoyed up by my instinctive reaction to such an encounter. The next day we found the 'bug' in the books, and Mrs. Swope and I left for the East that night."

Swope was a quick learner. His faulty inventory and trouble with the books taught him to let someone else have a chance. Before long he did this so well that a Western Electric official visiting St. Louis asked him, "Swope, don't you ever work more than you seem to?"

"No" was the reply. "The work is well organized and is going along in good shape."

Few others got the impression that Swope had extensive leisure. He was so diligent that a quarter of a century later his friend, Goldsmith, still was trying to inspire young men with the tale. Only as an afterthought would the lawyer admit that perhaps ability was an ingredient in Swope's success.

For he was successful, and quickly. He went very far for that day in what came to be called market research. He analyzed his business to find out exactly what he sold, to whom and where he sold it—obvious points of interest, but sadly neglected by most in 1901. He kept account of his proportion of the total market and broke down his costs, translating his statistics into charts—an innovation—and hurling his energies at the weaknesses revealed. He was inflexible in sticking to organizational policies. At the very moment when the books and inventory reduced him to his most discouraged mood, his assistant sales manager presented an ultimatum. The man demanded special conditions of work for himself or he would resign, and the sales manager advised yielding. But Swope, a stickler for rules, thought the proposal subversive of discipline. He called in the assistant and told him his resignation was accepted.

"He immediately changed his tune, and I told him what I thought of such tactics," says Swope with satisfaction, for he always was so prompt to tell subordinates their faults that many thought he enjoyed it.

As obvious as his strictness was his hatred of extravagance. One of his first acts as head of the Western Electric agency was to give up the rather elegant offices his predecessor had rented on the ground floor of an expensive building in exchange for cheaper, less attractive quarters farther up.

"Certainly," he thought, "people are not coming in here to buy machinery from me. I shall have to go out and sell it."

"Then," he adds, "I went out and hustled for business."

He hustled to such purpose that Chicago turned over to him the Cincinnati territory as well as St. Louis. Soon his methodical application of engineering principles and newly found salesmanship lifted that office out of the losses in which it had been floundering. At the same time, he kept on good terms with his competitors, older men such as the Westinghouse and General Electric representatives, younger men such as Franklin S. Terry and B. G. Tremaine, who were in the process of forming an unusual partnership which would make them a power in the incandescent lamp trade. One says "a power" for they operated as a single entity to the point of signing letters "Terry and Tremaine." Starting out as independent manufacturers—Swope's company was agent for Tremaine's "Sunbeam" lamps—the pair found themselves losing business to improved General Electric models. They hit upon the idea of allowing General Electric to finance them in using General Electric's own patents. They organized their own and other independents into a National Electric Lamp Association, the majority of the stock in each bought up by the General Electric Company, which then allowed all members to use its patents. Terry and Tremaine managed the Association, setting up separate research, sales, service, engineering and advertising departments. Each of the formerly independent companies continued to seek out its own customers and manage its own plant, but central direction and service were supplied from Cleveland where Terry and Tremaine set up their headquarters. The pair were so circumspect that at the time Swope had no idea the "Sunbeam" he was handling had become a part of the General Electric system. (In 1911, the Anti-Trust Division took a hard look at this device, and General Electric accepted a consent decree dissolving the Association, which became the National Lamp Works of the company, still under Terry and Tremaine and still with the same operational advantages.)

Terry and Tremaine were following a strong national trend toward amalgamation, although they displayed more ingenuity than most. This first year of the century saw the first billion-dollar corporation, United States Steel, put together around the nucleus of Andrew Carnegie's large holdings. Carnegie himself, safely retired, snickered that "the common stock's mostly water and the preferred mostly air," but a billion dollars had a brave sound. All sorts of other combinations were formed in these years, in ships and railroads, manufacturing and trade, leading up to the "money trust" investigations of a few years later which would teach the country a good deal about its economy.

The trend was scarcely checked by the vociferous opposition of such politicians as the Populists and William Jennings Bryan, nor by thoughtful writers like Henry Demarest Lloyd, who published *Wealth against Commonwealth* in 1894. Early in the new century the public, stimulated by some unusually forceful writers and some highly indiscreet remarks by financial leaders, were losing their uncritical reverence for what was coming to be called big business. People who understood nothing of the industrial economy were sure there must be something wrong with it when great men used colorful phrases which revealed their real views.

"The public be damned," William Vanderbilt's irritated retort to questioning, was the most famous of them.

"A certain number of men owning property should do what they like with it, and act in harmony" was J. P. Morgan's more carefully considered explanation of what he called a "community-of-interest plan" by which the ruinous battles for control of large enterprises in the recent past were replaced by mergers and interlocking boards of directors.

". . . the Christian men to whom God in His infinite wisdom has given control of the property interests of the country," a sentiment expressed by an otherwise little-known coal and railroad magnate named George Baer, aroused the most resentment among people who neither owned much property nor worshiped a God of the Market Place.

A new crop of writers, proudly accepting the unsavory epithet of muckrakers, related this sort of talk to the ruthless suppression of competition by powerful corporations, the unscrupulous acquisition of franchises and natural resources, the scandals in food adulteration just becoming known. At the same time, there was a note of pride in many of the denunciations; the "malefactors of great wealth," as Theodore Roosevelt called them, might be bad but they were big, and their prestige remained high.

Roosevelt's administration saw the first practical steps toward government regulation of business—strengthening the Interstate Commerce Commission, successful anti-trust prosecutions, a new Department of Commerce and Labor, conservation and pure-food legislation. States, notably Wisconsin, experimented with their own regulatory machinery, and the question of supervision over transit and utilities was a hot municipal issue in virtually every large city.

Much of this had been anticipated in the talk to which Gerard has listened at Hull House, and it did not seem so revolutionary to him as to the other young managers among his contemporaries. However, he did not think the arguments of the reformers were the full story of America's industrial economy. There was a lot of truth implied in the words which Mr. Dooley attributed to Roosevelt:

"Th' thrusts are heejous monsthers built up be th' inlightened intherprise iv th' men that have done so much to advance progress in our beloved counthry. On wan hand I wud stamp thim undher fut; on th' other hand not so fast."

Swope saw all around him the fruits of the enlightened enterprise, and he knew that the greed and arrogance of the "malefactors of great wealth" did not motivate the men he met and admired in his own and other companies. A better product available to more people at a lower cost seemed to him a more accurate description of industrial progress. For example, he could see that increased productive efficiency squeezed the water out of

United States Steel to make the stock worth what the public had paid.

His own first venture into the stock market was the result of a tip on the shares of the city's reorganized traction company. Swope put up $100 as margin and sold out with a tidy profit of $1,000. His next tip came from a friend who arranged to have a broker carry the investment. But this time the stock went down, and Swope was called upon for margin.

"I didn't have any," he says, "so I went to an old friend to borrow $500. He lent me the money, but reminded me that I had often said that I didn't believe in such money relations between friends. I took the money, which was hot in my hands, and in a short time told the broker to dispose of my stock, paid my debt to him and my friend."

Swope never borrowed from a friend again. But he liked using other people's money, and he continued to buy stocks, frequently on margin. He raised his loans from banks instead of individuals —"I like to keep these things impersonal," he says—and until late in life almost never was out of debt. He thinks a little debt is "a stabilizing influence," but when pressed admits that the stabilization comes mostly from profits won with the borrowed money. He prefers not to call such successful ventures speculation, and his own have been so generally successful that he feels he really has not been a speculator at all. With such talk a man of strong gambling tastes can conceal himself from himself.

His desire for extra money grew with his family. He and Mary had a daughter, Henrietta, in 1902; a son, named Isaac for his grandfather, in 1904; and a little more than a year later twins, Gerard, Jr., and David. The boys were born in the Swopes' first home of their own, and it was an odd residence for an up-and-coming salesman. Most men in his position live in the best part of town they can afford, partly to associate with potential customers. This represents a philosophy of salesmanship which Swope rejects.

"A good salesman can sell his customers during business

hours," he maintains, and adds reflectively, "I was a good salesman."

In 1903 he was confident enough of this ability to move to a part of St. Louis which few of his colleagues ever saw. He and Mary—Mary particularly—wanted to carry on some of the work they had done at Hull House. But St. Louis had no Hull House, although well-meaning people with vague ideals of social welfare asked the Swopes' advice on starting one.

"The only way to really start a successful settlement is to do it, and not talk about it," Gerard wrote bluntly to one aspiring inquirer, "to go down there and form a settlement by really settling, believing in the effort and not doing it because you want to do good in a vague sort of way. The theory of social settlement work grows out of the doing."

In this spirit, he and Mary betook themselves to one of St. Louis' worst slums—and no city could show worse. There on Carr Square in the midst of crowded, tottering, unsanitary tenements they bought two heavily mortgaged little houses across from a tiny rectangle of trees and bushes. Remodeled into one by Mary's talents as homemaker and teacher, they provided an attractive home for the family and space for the looms on which she gave instruction in a needed craft to neighborhood women, chiefly Irish, Russian and Italian immigrants.

The president of the Mercantile Electric Company had little share in the work. His fifty-six-hour week in the Chicago shops had left time for teaching, but now he thought he was too busy. However, he was struck more forcibly here than he had been at Hull House by the handicaps forced upon slum children; perhaps his new paternity influenced him.

"What these young people need," he wrote of his new neighbors, "is something to lighten the seriousness of their lives, to make them more youthful, more natural."

He wanted the city to provide this as part of its obligation to educate youth, but he would not enter politics to fight for it. (He thinks few businessmen have talent for politics, himself least of all.) Instead he joined a Civic Improvement League and became a guiding spirit in an Open-Air Playgrounds Committee. He and Dwight F. Davis, a future Secretary of War, alternated as chairman. At this time Davis was known chiefly as a tennis enthusiast, recently national doubles champion, whose international cup had been played for only since 1900. Adopting the slogan "A boy without a playground is father to the man without a job," they set up their equipment in an empty Eleventh Street lot. Swope worked hard at it and was pleased with the effect on children, but he still doubted that this sort of private philanthropy was a solution for the problems of slum youth.

"Playgrounds can only be successfully conducted by the city—*by all* the people *for some* of the people," he wrote in one of his reports.

A chance to demonstrate his point came in the spring of 1905 when the Eleventh Street lot was up at auction. He, Davis and a young lawyer bid it in, obligating themselves to pay a little more than a thousand dollars over three years. Davis as the more affluent undertook 6/16 of the cost, the other two 5/16 each, and Swope's share of the first installment was $170.10. He served as treasurer of the group when they turned over the playground as a gift to the city. It proved a stimulus to other civic enterprises in this area, especially after Davis became Park Commissioner.

Despite their residence in the slums, which conventional friends deplored as likely to cut them off from polite society, there were plenty of visitors at the little old house on Carr Square. Anywhere Mary Swope happened to have her being was a pleasant oasis of warm friendship and stimulating conversation. Gerard asked questions and refrained from lengthy dissertation of his own.

The World's Fair in 1904, celebrating the Louisiana Purchase Centennial, brought a large stream of guests. Some were engineers, entertained by Swope as secretary of a St. Louis branch of the American Institute of Electrical Engineers, which he and a few others organized that year. Foreigners dropped in to talk about the experiment being conducted by this young couple in the slums. One who became a lifelong friend was the Danish playwright and critic, Johannes Benson. The Swopes took him to the theater to see Francis Wilson, one of the most popular stars of the American stage. Benson delighted his hosts by declaring that Gerard looked just like the actor, a compliment all the more appreciated because it was so fanciful. Dr. Alice Hamilton spent a day or two with the Swopes at various intervals during these years and thought she never had seen such a warmly devoted couple or one so united in their interests. Not even the care of four small children in a rather inconvenient house distracted Mary from her weaving and her friends.

Dr. Hamilton saw in the carefully researched reports which Gerard drew up for the Civic Improvement League something of the influence of Hull House, bolstered by his training. He produced a series of them in which he argued persuasively for improved streets, more parks, full use of school buildings, especially for adult education. These led to his appointment as chairman of the city's Public Baths Commission. With indoor plumbing and running hot water still a luxury in most homes, the public baths were an important institution, and Swope established several new ones in strategic locations. He believes such administrative work is a civic duty which men like himself can and should undertake. Actual campaigning, whether for an issue or for office, calls for gifts which have no place in the management of a business, he says.

"The man who can direct a successful company loses his taste and talent for compromise, persuasion and explanation, if he ever had any, and these are important and proper in politics," he once explained, and he was getting into the habit of imposing his will without what some colleagues regarded as reasonable regard for their feelings.

His civic duties were cut short. For some time his remuneration had been small in relation to his accomplishment, but he resisted the temptation of better-paying offers elsewhere. At last, shortly before Christmas 1905, Barton invited him to return to Western

Electric's headquarters as assistant supervisor of all branch houses and sales manager of the company's machinery business. A tidy salary increase went with the new job, and a great increase in responsibility. At thirty-three Gerard Swope took a place in the hierarchy of national executives.

VI *The Making of a Manager*

Swope came back to Chicago with immense enthusiasm tempered by just enough diffidence to make him bearable. The enthusiasm was plain to everyone as he tore through Western Electric suggesting brand-new ways of doing things, whether in his department or another. The diffidence was well hidden, operating chiefly as a check upon his urge for even more rapid innovations.

He had a field large enough for his restless energies. Western Electric had become the largest electrical manufacturing company of that day, with annual sales of $65,000,000, well ahead of General Electric. Besides being a supplier of telephone equipment for its parent organization, A.T. & T., or other telephone and telegraph companies, it made and sold a complete line of motors, generators, heavy machinery and appliances to industry generally.

Swope was lucky that Barton, for all his cold caution, liked young men with ideas. Recently he had moved one of his protégés, Walter S. Gifford, who had followed Swope in residence at Hull House as well as in work at Western Electric, into a promising job at A.T. & T. Barton's current assistant, Charles E. Mitchell, was keen, versatile and imaginative, but with a stronger bent for finance than for industry. He and Gerard hit it off well and became very good friends.

It was good to have the encouragement of a contemporary because for a time Swope seemed to be banging into stone walls, bouncing off them only to discover that he had acquired new responsibilities and the dislike of department heads who resented his interfering ways and positive manner. He never stopped barging ahead, though.

He gave fair notice of his intentions to those who paid close attention within a few weeks of his arrival in his new post. At a conference of company officials in January 1906 he read a paper entitled "Keeping the Proper Relations between Sales and Expenses on a Diminishing Business." His thesis was that expenses could be cut simply by changing ways of doing things.

"Although the new method may be no real improvement over the old, it still may be possible to decrease expenses, simply because the work is attacked from a new point of view and with new enthusiasm," he argued.

This belief that change had a value in itself was not allowed to interfere with what he considered other important considerations. At the end of his paper, Barton asked him whether a change of methods wouldn't be equally effective in reducing expenses when business was increasing.

"No," replied Swope, the salesman. "The important point then is to give service."

Although he had been told by Barton that he would not have to concern himself with the plant at all—and so had rented a house on the North Side where Mary had friends—he couldn't keep out of it. In supervising branch houses and selling machinery, he had to know about actual manufacturing and warehousing. He found them, he wrote, "to my mind, at least, in deplorable shape." Cost accounting, without which industry would be lost today, had not yet been invented, but Swope's passion for statistics led him to a very close approximation of it. The mathematics he had learned at M.I.T. as applied to the business principles he had discovered in St. Louis enabled him to make a fairly accurate calculation of the various items of expense in Western Electric operations and the real returns on each. This analysis unearthed some facts that no one in the company had known or appreciated before. One of them was what he thought a very slipshod method of operating by a group of almost autonomous departments with no authoritative central control. He hurried to Barton with this story of waste.

"Young man," said the president, with that stern, cold look of his, "we must assume that this business was run with some intelligence before you came."

Swope admits that he retired "quite crestfallen," but he saw no reason why he had to accept Barton's assumption.

"I got my figures together and went back the next morning and showed him," he wrote.

His reward was to be put in charge of all the engineering, manufacturing and sales of the company's electrical machinery business. This included management of a new big plant in Hawthorne on the western outskirts of the city. One of the brighter moments of the assignment was a visit from his old gruff foreman of '95, who came to apologize for any ill treatment of which he might have been guilty. Swope, who had no memories of being badly used, could assure him quite sincerely that apologies were out of order. But he did not have many such enjoyable moments.

"Again I was beset with doubts as to whether I could make the grade," he says, but he never showed them, for, as one shrewd observer of his methods noted, "he was a remarkable bluffer, putting on the most positive front when he was most uncertain."

Looking back, Swope thinks that Barton agreed with him about the condition of the factory more than the older man would admit.

"He needed me because he was in trouble with his power apparatus manufacturing," says a Swope who has long since dropped any youthful false modesty. "This was just my meat."

It was such tough meat, however, that his time outside of working hours was devoted almost entirely to sleep and not very much of that. He rearranged the machinery in the plant so that materials were handled more efficiently, revised accounting methods, laid out work at the boring mills so as to increase production at reduced costs. He shifted personnel, seeking to give a fresh look at each man's capacity. In one shift he fired the superintendent, a man of real abilities but not for the management of a factory. The judgment was confirmed, he thought, when he heard that the dismissed superintendent had joined the church and risen to become a Protestant bishop. In his place Swope put the assistant superintendent, Gordon Campbell, who had all the flair for machinery which one might expect of a Scot and a liking for work which almost matched Swope's own.

Although he was new to the managerial problems of manufacturing, Swope did not attempt to bolster his inexperience by studying the relatively recent literature on business administration and scientific management. In fact, he says he never even heard of it, much less read any of it. Books on how to direct a business were rather more inspirational than practical in 1906, and he got little guidance from eloquence, so it is small wonder he ignored them. But it is surprising that he missed the stir which was being created in American industry by Frederick W. Taylor, who had capped a career of notable industrial invention by inventing what was called scientific management. "Taylorism" had been a widely debated as well as widely used system since its first extensive exposition in the 1890s. Actually it offered a solution to only a single part of an industrial manager's problems. It was concerned exclusively with men's efficient use of tools, and it was in the process of developing into the modern time-and-motion studies. But even then it was believed by many to be a panacea for all factory troubles, and it had just the sort of mathematical base which Swope enjoyed.

For all his long hours of work and worry, the restless young manager could not resist initiating new projects. He noticed that, outside the industry, no one knew the Western Electric Company existed. Yet demands for electrical products were springing up in all sorts of new and unlikely places. So, early in 1907 he went to Barton again to propose an advertising campaign in magazines of general circulation, an untried experiment for a company which did not sell direct to consumers. Barton quoted Emerson on the better mousetrap.

"I said that might be true," Swope wrote, "but my point was that it would take time for the world to know we were making better mousetraps, that I wanted to discount time and bring it within the purview of his lifetime and mine."

His persistence wore the older man down, and Barton authorized the first institutional advertising in the electrical industry.

Swope went on trying to discount time by taking a room near the factory and going home only for week ends. He got there so tired that he spent most of his time in bed, and the children were kept quiet or out of the way so he could rest. This was hardly the parental companionship he had enjoyed from his own father. But he felt himself either so indispensable to the job or so insecure in it that he sacrificed family life, concerts and plays, reading and friendly conversation to the greater glory of Western Electric. His colleagues began to suspect that he was hardly human, a machine for operating a business.

His reorganization of the Hawthorne factory helped brace Western Electric for the panic of 1907. That in turn gave Swope a chance to test his theories about what to do in a period of diminishing business. One unpredictable element—at least he had not predicted it—was a strike, "the first and last in my experience." As orders dried up or were canceled, men had to be laid off, especially at the foundry. To keep it running at all, Swope obtained a city order for manhole covers, but he had to cut wages, and in a burst of dissatisfaction, the men walked out.

Techniques of strikebreaking were well developed in 1907. There were precedents for starving the men out, beating them down, calling on the courts for injunctions or the police for "order," hiring professional strikebreakers. To a former Hull House resident all of these were unacceptable, but few employers knew much about negotiating with strikers. Swope called on his old settlement friend, Mrs. Stevens. She told him that his best chance for an amicable agreement was to put his case frankly before the workers. Not many of his contemporaries in positions of industrial authority would have listened patiently to such advice. Swope did not even think it odd. He followed it so well that, for the first time, he experienced the thrill of winning over an audience that was not friendly to begin with. He had a convincing manner, and his speech, though rapid, was clear. He told the men that in the current market they had a choice of making manhole covers or nothing. But he also had a possible solution to lay-offs and pay cuts. He offered to organize a special sales drive to bring in more orders of the same kind, so that as many men at as near full wages as possible could be employed. The strikers returned, and Swope carried out his end of the bargain so well that by the time the electrical business picked up, the foundry was running at nearly normal capacity.

By now Swope was working as closely with Harry B. Thayer, the vice-president who had invited him and Mary to New York, as with Barton. In 1907 Thayer took over a good many of the president's duties, adding "general manager" to his own title. A Vermonter of strictly New England lineage—the most recent immigrant in his family landed on American shores in 1650—he had the qualities which are popularly supposed to go with such ancestry. His integrity would have been almost ostentatious if he himself had not treated it so obviously as a matter of course. He was a cultivated man, a keen wit, and a lover of beauty, but these traits were so rigidly subordinated that only those who knew him well appreciated their existence. "A lovely character," Swope has summed him up. In 1907, Thayer was a vigorous forty-nine, a slender man in a stand-up collar that gave his neck plenty of room. His faintly smiling expression was almost hidden by a heavy mustache and pince-nez on his straight nose. After twenty-six years with Western Electric, he was recognized as Barton's logical successor, and in fact was elected president of the company in 1908, the older man becoming chairman of the board.

This event marked not only Thayer's apotheosis but a major turning point in the life of Gerard Swope. For Thayer promptly moved the executive headquarters of the company to New York and invited Swope to join him there as general sales manager for all lines at a salary of $6,000 a year. It was a reward for work well done—the figure looked quite large in 1908 when the President of the United States received $25,000 a year; a rising young steel executive or a good factory superintendent, $4,000; an experienced newspaper reporter, $1,500; and insurance companies were asking Americans to provide $50 a month in an annuity as permanent security for their families.

But Swope had no illusions that it was solely on his record that he won this (or any other) promotion. Speaking once of the three men who had done most for him, he said, "I was a good salesman, and I sold myself to them."

His only trouble was that he had not yet sold himself as thoroughly to Gerard Swope. He still worried about his own abilities, and the only way he knew to overcome these doubts was to work harder. But even his energies had their limits. For several years he had not slept much because he was too busy. Now he couldn't sleep at all because the problems of his days chased each other through his brain at night. The result, of course, was inevitable. Hardly had he got his family settled—in Highland Park on the Raritan River across from New Brunswick, where Mary had been born, where her mother and sisters still lived, and where she had her youngest child, John—than he had what appears to have been a full-sized breakdown, "a nervous depression," he called it. Sidney Schwab, who had attained a considerable reputation as a neurologist, considered the illness so serious that he ordered his friend to take six months of complete rest from business.

This was inadmissible on two counts. In the first place, Swope argued, he couldn't spare the time. Secondly, and more fundamentally, it was not in his nature to yield to anything so irrational and inefficient as illness. He prided himself on his rugged constitution; it mustn't let him down now, just when the key to top management, for he had no doubt that his new position was just that, had been handed to him.

The classic fate of men in the situation in which Swope now found himself is ulcers. Such men eat out their stomachs, in the graphic phrase of the psychosomatic experts, by gnawing away at the gap between their accomplishments and their ambitions. They do it often enough in business to give rise to a belief that the peptic ulcer is an occupational disease of executives. (The highest incidence is among taxi and bus drivers.) That Swope escaped this familiar pattern was not mere luck, nor even good medical advice. He lacked the emotional conflict between dependence and individuality which modern medicine finds to be a cause of ulcers.

"It is his desire to escape from his own fear of being a clinging vine which causes him to reach out for responsibility and gives him the appearance of a go-getter—and often causes him to climb quite high on the ladder of worldly success," says Dr. Flanders Dunbar, a leading psychosomatic specialist. ". . . The ulcer patient's ambition and activity are merely a cloak for his dependent pull."

In the twin desire to achieve something on his own and to seek refuge in the strength of a colleague or employer, wife or mother, the ulcer victim cannot escape a constant fretting over possible mistakes. Even when he learns that worry acts upon his system so as to pour acid into the sore place of his stomach, he can't help it. The difference between such an executive, even when successful, and the real tycoon is that the tycoon has no dependent pull, is so single-minded there is nothing to block his ambition and activity. So he never gets an ulcer.

Swope proved himself a tycoon. Because his drive to succeed was strong and uncomplicated, he could perform the rare feat of transforming himself by a deliberate act of will from a worrier to a fatalist. From that time dated a characteristic which his colleagues found either wholly admirable or wildly exasperating. He made up his mind swiftly and decisively, and showed no sign of regret if he was wrong. It was said of him that he preferred any decision, even a mistaken one, to no decision at all. It was also said that he never admitted an error, but this was true only to the extent that he would not brood about the error.

"An organization needs *prompt* decision," he once wrote, "no doubt or wavering, otherwise the *esprit de corps* is seriously and deleteriously affected. If the executive making such decisions is right in the majority of instances, he gets by; if not, he is given the go-by."

In his new mood he offered Sidney Schwab a pledge of moderation but refused to quit for six months. He would take it easy by going to the office only five days a week—men who had Saturday afternoons off were considered a leisure class then—and he took home on Friday night no more than most executives would regard as two days' work. He also promised to seek relaxation, which to him meant a fairly leisurely inspection of Western Electric factories and offices around the country. He had planned to visit them anyway, but now he did it more slowly, interlarding side excursions which actually completed his recovery and stimulated his taste for travel.

He revisited Mackinac, the scene of his marriage. He took a short cruise alone on the Great Lakes. He spent a couple of days in Yellowstone Park and went as far west as Salt Lake City, summoning his San Francisco manager to meet him there. He crossed the Continental Divide in a coach hauled by six horses and felt so thoroughly restored that as they strained uphill, he got out for a walk. With a long stride learned from his father, he was well ahead of the lumbering vehicle in the first mile, and noted that he covered it in fifteen minutes. His heart was pounding so hard, though, that he decided to ease up for the next mile. It is typical of his notion of slowing down that he made the second mile in fifteen minutes, too. But his heart no longer thumped abnormally and he kept going until the coach finally caught up with him six miles from where he left it.

"The other people in it thought I was crazy," he wrote, "but I felt in fine shape."

He proved his fitness by joining Gordon Campbell and two other Western Electric men on a Canadian canoeing trip. He came back with a strong taste for outdoor life, great admiration for Campbell's woodcraft and a new skill. He had learned how to pick up a canoe only twenty-five pounds lighter than himself and the even more delicate trick of setting it down again without damage. He was ready to plunge into any or every problem the company might have.

Neither he nor Thayer supposed that a general sales manager named Swope would confine himself to selling. As he had done in Chicago, he ranged over the other departments, a sort of general utility executive called in for any chore so long as it was difficult. He enjoyed every minute of it, and it crystallized firmly his ideas on the obligations and opportunities of management. In less than two years, 1909 and 1910, he carried out these six assignments:

1. He negotiated with two General Electric vice-presidents the sale to that company of all Western Electric's power machinery business. The department had been growing in size and profits, thanks largely to Swope's work in the past two years, and it was sold because of that fact; A.T. & T. was uneasy at the increasing share of its subsidiary's business which was not strictly for the telephone and reluctant to expand the manufacturing plant, which increasing machinery sales would require. The men with whom he negotiated were a good deal older, more experienced and better known in the industry. They were Hinsdill Parsons, a suave, adroit gentleman who was general counsel as well as vice-president, and Anson Burchard, whose large frame and big, bold, handsome head would have graced a Roman senator's toga. He was Coffin's long-time assistant and was regarded by his colleagues as a financial genius. They wanted to take over the machinery business with no strings attached. Swope's task was to keep two strings. One was a contract for General Electric to supply power apparatus needed to make telephone equipment for the Bell system. Another was an agency agreement under which Western Electric acted for General Electric in selling generators and elec-

trical control machinery to others. Swope persuaded the General Electric pair to accept both points and did it so impressively that Parsons urged Thayer to let the deal include the negotiator as well as the business.

"I answered indignantly that I wasn't chattel," said Swope.

2. In the same year he negotiated another contract with General Electric covering the incandescent lamp business. This gave Western Electric the benefit of new improvements in a field basic to the expansion of electrical home appliances, since the use of more and better lamps not only offered possibilities of lower rates for current but gave householders more interest in acquiring fans and irons. The contract also set prices which Western Electric charged for lamps, and on the whole was so satisfactory to both companies that Swope never tried to change it when he became head of General Electric.

3. He investigated the virtues of the Hope Jones electric organ which A.T. & T.'s president, Theodore Vail, was keenly interested in buying. Thayer recommended him for the assignment, and Swope went to Ocean Grove to hear a performance. He was not much impressed and liked the Hope Jones factory in Elmira even less. His decision that the company would be a poor buy gave Thayer additional faith in his reliability, although both knew the verdict was frowned upon in the head office.

"I don't think Mr. Vail ever quite liked this advice," Swope once wrote, "but he followed it."

4. He worked out and put into effect a plan for salesmen's bonuses which was something more than a straight extra commission on volume of sales, and in one respect a serious mistake. He argued that men should be encouraged to work on those items which were most profitable to the company but perhaps hardest to sell. So he took into consideration the profit on a man's sales as well as the total volume. His incentive plan was regarded with some suspicion by older executives, and this turned to outrage when one of the best men turned in a record which entitled him to the equivalent of his year's salary.

"You're not going to pay him this sum, are you?" they demanded.

"Certainly," Swope replied. "We have to; we said we would."

He sent a check, and that was the mistake. The salesman, unaccustomed to such sums, blew it all in one tremendous spree and never was much good again. But this, Swope held, pointed to only a minor flaw in his system. He amended it to pay the bonus in Western Electric securities, not cash.

His incentive plan was linked to a program of studies which he required each salesman to make of his district and customers—studies of the electrical business in general and of the individual firms in particular. Few salesmen then possessed the technical knowledge needed to carry out such assignments satisfactorily, but Swope persisted in an innovation which eventually turned the industry's salesmen into engineers.

5. He negotiated in 1910 the purchase of patents essential to the automatic telephone; he had been drafted again by A.T. & T. for this assignment. His skill had been sufficiently demonstrated that he received a free hand with full authority to spend millions, although A.T. & T.'s patent attorney told Thayer that he was making a mistake "to send a child to market." Swope thought this was the most important deal yet entrusted to him, and he had with him one of the leading patent lawyers of the country, Charles Neave, with whom he was speedily on terms of intimacy and mutual confidence. The owners of the patents turned out to be "get-rich-quick" types whom Swope so instantly mistrusted that he called them (privately) "highbinders," an unusually strong term for him. He therefore demanded an option which would give Neave and the engineers a chance to investigate the patents to be sure they were all that was claimed for them. The owners flatly refused. Swope insisted, and suggested that they think it over and meet again in the morning. That night Neave, as an older hand at this game, read his young colleague a little lecture.

"He feared that I had put the entire negotiations in jeopardy," Swope wrote.

But in the morning the "highbinders" gave in; the option was granted; the investigation was made, and A.T. & T. got the patents.

6. In 1910, at Thayer's request—by now he was the Vermonter's favorite trouble shooter—he inspected Western Electric's foreign business and completely revised it. Over a period of thirty years, it had grown rather than been built, principally in making and supplying telephone equipment, and had spread widely if haphazardly. Swope prepared himself for the trip by interrogating the heads of other large corporations with substantial foreign interests, especially George Eastman of the Kodak Company and Clarence Woolley of American Radiator. Then he studied his way through eight countries in ten weeks—England, France, Belgium, Holland, Germany, Denmark, Switzerland and Italy. He appraised the worth of government operations, which were common to most of them, and reached an unfavorable conclusion, although he admitted that the German system was adequate and efficient. He prowled through the basements of hotels and large office buildings with their maintenance engineers to learn how they bought electrical supplies. He amassed statistics on wages and hours of work, inquiring into unemployment, sickness and old-age insurance for workers (which most of his colleagues at home dismissed as socialistic nonsense). He analyzed the backwardness of European telephone service, interviewing his own company's representatives as well as customers. Of the gaieties of the continent he saw little, for he declined invitations to gaudy night spots. When his evenings were not devoted to reports, however, he attended concerts or plays, and spent Sundays in decorous sight-seeing.

The organization of Western Electric in Europe struck him as thoroughly unsatisfactory. Its head since 1880 was Frank R. Welles, an undersized, energetic, old-fashioned gentleman who was remembered by oldtimers in the Chicago office as operating its first typewriter. In thirty years Welles had acquired fluency in a number of languages and adapted himself pleasantly, not to say luxuriously, to European ways. He kept most of his business in his head, to the methodical Swope's dismay, and he had no taste for his visitor's proposal that the company build or buy factories in many countries instead of concentrating its manufacturing in one or two.

Swope came back to New York with a mass of data scribbled on odd sheets of letter paper or memo slips, and a plan. This latter called for strict central control of the European business, for expanding Western Electric in more countries to meet an increasing demand for goods manufactured domestically, and for agreements with foreign companies, especially the English and Germans, to share patents. His reward, as he might have expected, was to be placed in actual although not nominal charge of all foreign operations in addition to his other duties. A man he chose was dispatched to Europe to replace Welles.

These new activities did not prevent Swope from riding herd on his sales staff so closely that some of them thought he must be twins. His first trip to Europe whetted his appetite for travel, but even before that he was dashing from one office or factory to another, inquiring briskly and with disconcerting insight about men and methods. His sharp, severe manner won a great deal of respect but less popularity.

He instituted a series of salesmen's conferences which were more like college seminars than gatherings of good fellows. He set his men to work preparing papers on subjects which required study, usually leading to more information about consumers. (This is all such an inevitable part of selling techniques today that it is hard to realize what an innovation it was nearly fifty years ago.) Alert, very erect in his chair, Swope kept the meetings in order with a strong hand. One imaginative speaker, proposing to demonstrate a psychological quirk of human nature, held up an open vial and asked how many could smell the perfume. He smiled at the forest of up-raised hands and said that there wasn't any perfume. But he never got a chance to explain his point, if any, for Swope called the next speaker. He did not care much for tricks. On the other hand, he knew the value of a little fun and horseplay. Some of his conferences were enlivened with quite elaborate monkeyshines—skits and songs and parodies. One of them, to the tune of "Captain Jinks of the Horse Marines," indicated how Swope looked to his subordinates, for they sang:

> *I'm Captain Swope of the Sales Commit',*
> *I run this good electric ship,*
> *I drive my men with crack of whip,*
> *I'm Captain Swope of the Western.*

There are those who hate to be driven, and those who glory in it, bragging about what a tough guy they work for. Depending upon which type was talking about him, Swope was a ruthless machine with no human compassion or a great leader of men. But unlike many severe taskmasters, he never ranted or swore or abused people. He never lifted his voice at all, although it was pretty loud anyway, as it had been in elementary school. The manners which Ida Swope had taught him as a little boy were part of his nature by now. Such punctilious courtesy as his was rare, even in the first decade of the century. But courtesy is a help in delicate negotiations as well as a social asset.

In Swope's case it made an indelible impression upon at least one girl just out of school about this time, so much so that she still (1957) speaks of him with admiration although they have not met for more than forty-five years. She had been in the office just long enough to hear that the sales manager was a positive demon for speed and accuracy. Then one day when his secretary was away, she was sent in with instructions to be prepared for the worst since Mr. Swope had a lot of mail and one hour to dispose of it before he caught a train.

She hurried into his room, not exactly scared because she is not the type to frighten easily, but a little apprehensive. She saw the pile of letters on his desk, looming up like a mountain, before she even noticed the man himself. Then he got up—a slender, hawk-like person, she thought him, with wings of dark hair parted in the middle—and actually held a chair for her! She wasn't used to such gallantry in business offices, and when he asked her how she liked her work, would she prefer a pencil to her pen, she thought the people outside must have been fooling about his character. But then he picked up the top letter and began talking.

"He dictated eighty letters in sixty minutes," she says, and after nearly fifty years there is still a little awe in her voice.

Swope's impatience sometimes led to less pleasant first impressions. A great hand for reports and documents, he kept the top of his desk heaped with papers. Their mass and the glances he kept directing at them made visitors nervous, his interviews with them unsatisfactory.

"I learned that if you wanted to get the other fellow's point of view, you mustn't be too hurried," he has confessed. "I adopted a plan of keeping papers relating only to one subject on my desk, so that when people came in to see me, I had a fairly clear desk. They took more time to tell their story, and I took more time with them."

An admirable bit of self-discipline, but it did not put all callers at their ease or completely satisfy the young man in a hurry that he was a model executive. Every year he spent at least one full evening reviewing with Thayer the events of the last twelve months. On one of these occasions he asked the older man to tell him frankly how he might improve himself.

"Swope, so far as energy and ability are concerned, there is nothing the matter with your work, and I don't think it can be improved upon," Thayer replied. "But the motto I would like to give you would be *suaviter in modo, fortiter in re*" ("Gently in manner, strongly in deed").

It was good advice, and Swope knew it. He tried to follow it, too, but admits he slipped often. In pursuit of Thayer's ideal, however, he went so far as to attempt to carry into his everyday behavior the one thing he ever learned from golf, a game which had no appeal for him. He took it up about this time for exercise and spent boring hours hitting at a little white ball while a pro with no more patience than himself explained all the things he did wrong. The main one was to tighten up in every muscle as he swung.

"Relax, damn it, relax!" the pro would roar.

Swope couldn't, and he gave up golf after a few lessons. But for years afterward, when his impatience was running away with him, he would repeat to himself, "Relax, damn it, relax!" Sometimes it helped.

He turned to other forms of exercise. His more ample means—his $6,000 salary doubled in two years, and his speculations (although he did not apply the term to them) helped—warranted the purchase of a home. In 1909 he bought a place of four acres in Highland Park, the grounds extending to the Raritan. There, since he allowed himself more time with his family after his breakdown, he began to derive from rural life that joy which only a child brought up in the city can know. A vegetable garden, cows and chickens made him feel quite the countryman. He acquired a pony for the children, and then learned to ride himself so he could teach them. Because he likes to do well anything he does at all, he became an accomplished horseman, and riding remained his favorite exercise ever after. He also enjoyed swimming and took pride in being the first one to brave the cold water every spring.

"I played tennis with the children until they defeated me," he recalls. "Then I retired and let them play with each other."

His time for sports, for wrestling with his sons, for swimming or boating, was strictly limited by his concentration on work and his travels. He was at once studying the business of the Western Electric Company and reorganizing it. He applied the new mathematical equations of cost accounting to sales and learned from them some things about overhead and profits which had not been suspected. One was that Western Electric's high-profit but low-volume items, which had been credited with much of the company's success, actually lost money. The company made all its money from the low-profit orders. The fact was discovered because Swope's formula analyzed distribution costs accurately for the first time.

These equations were not especially difficult for a mathematician, but they never had been applied to merchandising. Yet they were as essential to the efficient operation of new mass-production methods as the belt line techniques of which Henry Ford was the outstanding pioneer at this time—the Model T went on the market late in 1908. What Swope did was to work out the methods by which mass-production industries could gear selling and distribution to the enormously increased output of their factories and keep track of the relation between all expense factors.

On the basis of the market research which he organized, it was possible for the first time to chart for a year in advance the probable volume of business, the costs of doing that business and profit from it. Swope insisted on knowing not only what the predictable orders were going to be but what proportion of them his company would get, where they would come from and why the others got away. He then set what he regarded as a realizable goal for the year—the percentage of business he would get from old customers, the increase in that percentage which might be possible from better work with them, the increase from new customers. He used to say that whenever this "R factor" (as he called the realization total) was 90 per cent or better, there was nothing to worry about. If it fell below, then he knew where to concentrate next year's efforts.

Before he was forty, Swope had established a reputation for managerial skill which was recognized throughout the industry. He also had reduced the essentials of successful management to four words which he used frequently thereafter. The phrase he liked was *Analyze, Organize, Deputize, Supervise,* "which," he once wrote, "is clear and needs no elaboration." Fortunately he often elaborated it so that the exact meaning he gave the words was plain.

In the first word, *analyze,* he included all the market studies upon which analysis was based, and the establishment of the goals which it must be the object of the company to reach. *Organize* was more than the administrative task of building up a staff, locating plants, warehouses and sales offices efficiently, and providing a system of co-ordination among them. It included creative planning of new and improved methods of doing business and expansion into new fields, as well as a willingness to make prompt, firm decisions. *Deputize* involved the selection and training of men, and careful, clear agreement as to the deputy's exact responsibility and authority. *Supervise* meant to Swope a very active operation. He not only liked to visit offices and factories to see for himself what went on, but he made it a point to know at least as much about the essentials of each as any of his subordinates. To a phenomenal memory for figures he added an ability to amass overnight a great quantity of miscellaneous information which he could put out of his head as soon as it had served its purpose.

In the years in which Swope was developing these principles, the structure of American business was coming under increasingly close and mostly unfriendly scrutiny from public and private critics. The wildly unregulated operations of the stock market, which had shocked the public concepts of morality at intervals ever since the first exchange met under a tree on Wall Street in 1791, represented for many Americans the standards of the business community in general. Investigations and anti-trust actions during Theodore Roosevelt's second administration, continuing under Taft's, focused attention upon the abuses rather than the uses of corporations. It is significant that the bestsellers of these years included such books as Gustavus Myers' *History of Great American Fortunes,* a monumental narrative of public and private corruption as practiced by acclaimed leaders of finance and industry, and Upton Sinclair's *The Jungle,* exposing horrors of packing plants. Stories of the powerful crushing smaller competitors by rebates, discriminatory rates or practices, price wars, intimidation, even outright sabotage, were discussed in detail in the popular press. Orators and writers told exactly how Roosevelt's "malefactors of great wealth" mulcted the public.

Incredibly, those who were most bitterly attacked armored themselves in the technicalities of the law and offered in rebuttal to serious charges only an indignant, arrogant protest against government regulation. Industrial leaders who were not denounced themselves preserved a dignified silence which did nothing to keep them from being bracketed in the popular mind with the plunderers.

Gerard Swope read this unfolding of contemporary history with no more than average interest. He cannot remember that it influenced him at all, or that he related the exposures to his own business in any way. He knew that he himself, or Barton or Thayer, would no more countenance a shady financial deal or the wrecking of a competitor's machine than they would rob a till. He would have agreed with Roosevelt that there are good trusts and bad trusts, except that his precise mind would have rejected the word *trust* because it had lost its original meaning of a special form of corporate combination. Some people used it as a synonym for monopoly, and others as a term of opprobrium to cover unethical or illegal business practices. But Swope wanted to know what was being monopolized before he condemned, and as for unethical or illegal practices, these were not confined to the wealthy and the powerful.

He had watched the decline of competition in the telephone business, for example, had helped to speed it, and thought the results highly desirable. One of his few failures had been an attempt to persuade the Kinlock company, a St. Louis independent, to merge with the Bell system. The inability of competing, often duplicating lines to serve the public adequately accomplished a year or two later what his logic and eloquence could not do. Kinlock joined the long list of departed telephone companies.

A little coil invented by Michael Pupin at Columbia University and acquired by the Bell system in 1901 made the long-distance telephone practicable and dictated A.T. & T.'s national monopoly rather than a network of independent local monopolies. But the mergers, Swope thought, were on terms beneficial to Bell, to the independents and above all to the public. Monopoly, some said, prevented the introduction of the newest improvements when these would result in scrapping expensive but still adequate equipment. Monopoly in telephones, Swope would reply, was the only possible way to bring more people more instruments at lower rates, and it was doing so all the time. Still, he recognized that monopoly of a public service called for regulation by a public body, a point on which not all his colleagues agreed. He himself did not like to operate under such restrictive rules as regulation must impose. That was one reason he preferred Western Electric to the parent company.

Nevertheless, as his administrative improvements made themselves felt in increased business, the question of monopoly or of discrimination tending toward monopoly inevitably arose as to Western Electric, too. Swope had introduced a system by which Western bought and warehoused telephone and other equipment which it did not make for all Bell companies, giving them the benefit of better prices for larger orders. Although he himself had negotiated Western Electric out of the business of making generators, he was planning to expand the company's operations into the sale if not the manufacture of all sorts of electrical appliances for shop and home, dreaming of a market of millions of families instead of thousands of companies. To do it, he wanted to make Western Electric a household name, as well known as any brand of soap. In 1911, he ordered his advertising manager to spend in national magazines within two months the then enormous sum of $100,000, saying, "We'll put WE's name on everything electrical going into the American home, whether we make it or not, through our buying power."

But when it was suggested that this buying power and Western Electric's favorite-son relationship to A.T. & T. gave the company an unfair advantage, Swope demurred. Of course, Western Electric had an advantage, but not an unfair one, he argued. He pointed out that its prices for cable, instruments, switches—all the supplies a telephone company uses in common with many other industries—were the same to everyone, whether in or out of the Bell system, and actually more business came from outside. The advantage, he maintained, was the perfectly legitimate, even laudable one of making a better product at a lower price. A large, expensive organization was necessary, as he saw it, to bring in the business and give the service which alone could justify mass production. Only if the people who used the equipment or appliances and the workers who made them were deprived of their share in the benefits could the advantage Western Electric enjoyed be criticized.

His acceptance of a certain amount of government regulation in business was demonstrated by the enthusiasm with which he saw the nomination and election of Woodrow Wilson in 1912. Hitherto he had been a Democrat by the usual sort of conviction—"My father was a Democrat," he says with a smile. Now he was attracted strongly by the philosophy, leadership and eloquence which the former president of Princeton brought to national politics. Swope took no active part in the campaign, but mere expressions of approval for Wilsonian policies which resulted in the Federal Reserve System, the Federal Trade Commission, exemption of labor from the Anti-Trust Laws, an eight-hour day for railroad workers, marked him as a radical to colleagues who looked upon these overdue reforms as the beginnings of socialism.

Swope's own political activities were strictly local, and in accord with what he thought a businessman's proper role. As an executive and as one who had observed some of the worst municipal government in St. Louis and Chicago, he was attracted by the city-manager idea. He joined a small group who put it into effect in Highland Park a little later, paying the manager's salary themselves until the town got used to the system.

By this time, the broad scope of his operations for Western Electric was earning a steadily rising income and new opportunities not only to get things done but to get them done his way. Although he had been directing the foreign business since 1910, Thayer did not put him in charge officially until 1913. The next year he organized a subsidiary to handle it, International Western Electric, with himself as vice-president and general manager. At the same time he became a vice-president and director of Western Electric. His plan was to establish the European business on the same orderly, centralized basis as the domestic.

"Conditions and competition were bringing changes, and the old methods were no longer appropriate," he explains.

The chief competition was German, the chief competitor the Siemens & Halske Company. In the struggle for European telephone markets, Western Electric by 1913 had the advantage of factories in every major country, while the Germans insisted on manufacturing at home to discourage industrialization elsewhere, a shortsighted policy, Swope thought. Siemens & Halske had the advantage of being prepared to push the new dial phones, which Europeans wanted, while A.T. & T. hesitated to tie up the capital necessary for these expensive installations. Swope's first task was to convince Thayer that, as an associate said later, "Siemens & Halske would have run Western Electric off the continent." Then in 1913 he negotiated an agreement with the Germans on use of patents and exchange of engineering "know-how." While he was engaged in these talks, Thayer cabled that the directors would have to approve before a contract would be considered binding.

"I went no further," Swope says. "I came home and asked him to send someone else in whom he had more confidence. Next year he asked me to go over and bring back the signed contracts, which I did."

He reached Berlin for the final negotiations on June 28, 1914, a Sunday. Business talk being impossible that day, he went to the race track—when he can't ride himself he sometimes likes to see horses run—and was surprised to see one of the very rare Sunday extras of the Berlin newspapers. The news, the assassination of an Austrian archduke whose name was barely familiar, in a place called Sarajevo, of which he never had heard, hardly warranted the fuss, it seemed to him.

While the last days of peace went by in fruitless diplomacy in the chancelleries of Europe, Swope was completing his contract with the Germans. By the time it was signed in mid-July, the importance of the Sarajevo murder was plain to everyone. Swope moved on to Switzerland, where he prudently changed all his money into gold, then to Italy, where the talk was all of ways to avoid honoring the alliance with Germany and Austria, then to Paris on July 26, 1914, "where things were in a turmoil."

He had scheduled a conference of his European managers for

the end of the month at Ostend. He decided one had to act as if disaster could be averted, as of course many thought it would, although he was not surprised that some managers failed to appear. Belgian troops were mobilizing and Western Electric's factory in Antwerp had been taken over by the government. On Saturday, August 1, Swope watched the troops, enjoying a display of small field guns drawn by dogs, and then drifted into the Casino, noting that play was exceptionally high, with many Army officers participating. He slept late and came down in the morning to a lobby buzzing with the news that war had begun, that German troops were pouring into Belgium in violation of the country's neutrality. His conference had dissolved, and he managed to get passage for England on an overcrowded little sidewheeler. There was an exciting moment when a shot from the Dunkirk batteries halted the vessel, which lay tossing violently in choppy seas while a patrol boat came out to investigate and permit her to proceed to Dover with her seasick cargo—people were packed in too tightly to consider themselves passengers.

For three weeks, Swope remained in London, grappling with the manifold problems which obviously would face his company and trying to prepare for many more which no one could foresee. Then he sailed for home on a ship crowded with tourists, businessmen and families of expatriates escaping from the war zone.

He returned to one of the most gratifying honors he ever would receive, election as alumni trustee of M.I.T. (At the end of his five-year alumni term, he was elected a life member.) He flung himself with enthusiasm into making his old school worthy of its splendid new site in Cambridge, the munificent gift of a mysterious "Mr. Smith,"who turned out to be George Eastman of the Kodak Company.

"I had many ideas on modifying the curriculum," Swope wrote, "but when it came to their being applied, I found it very difficult indeed."

The difficulty did not discourage him. He supposed the academic community no more resistant to change than certain business elements he knew, but it took time to learn how to achieve it in the environment of learning.

"Close and cordial co-operation with the faculty, the Corporation and particularly the president gave me a clearer insight into the educational problems, and possibly gave them a little of my experience in the twenty years that had elapsed since my graduation," he explained.

He found his ordered, fully occupied days thoroughly satisfying, and one of the satisfactions was the joy which his success gave to his mother. She had come east, dividing her time between her two sons and bragging about both unreservedly, for Herbert had confounded gloomy St. Louis predictions to become one of New York's leading newspapermen, a star reporter, city editor of that newspaperman's newspaper, *The World,* and engaged at this time in winning the Pulitzer Prize for his notable war correspondence.

As the United States became the only major neutral in a world at war, the problems of administering a world-wide business became more and more complicated. Swope was in London in the spring of 1915, listening to bombs dropped by Zeppelins at night and arranging war orders for Western Electric's British factory by day. He was there when the sinking of the *Lusitania* in May sent a wave of anti-German feeling through his country and led him to sail for home to wrestle with the problems of merchandising electrical equipment amid the doubts and hesitations of a period of reluctant, halting preparedness for war, a 1916 election campaign won on "he kept us out of war," and a winter of inexorably disintegrating relations with Germany.

Swope was on the West Coast when he heard that Enos Barton had died on May 3, 1916, at the age of seventy-three. Memories of his cold exterior had faded long ago; the impression of a warm heart and much kindly encouragement remained. Swope missed him even more later in the year when his old friend of the General Electric negotiations, Anson Burchard, suggested for the second time that he join that company. This time Burchard offered management of General Electric's foreign business.

It was tempting. Swope had been obliged to push his reorganization of Western Electric abroad against a good deal of inertia. Some of his colleagues thought he had suffered from it, although he took internal opposition pretty well in his stride as one of the normal executive hazards. He consulted Thayer, and the Vermonter was very frank with him. A.T. & T., Thayer explained, held to a policy with which he thought Swope disagreed and which would not offer the younger man fullest opportunities. Although sales on that part of Western Electric's business which remained after the machinery deal with General Electric had trebled under Swope's regime, the parent company favored contraction of anything not strictly related to the telephone. This was not exactly news to a Western Electric vice-president, but twenty-one years in a company which on the whole had been good to him and was now paying him $20,000 a year had forged a tie which it was not easy to break. Swope told Burchard he was complimented by the offer, but he would stay where he was.

In the early part of that winter, while the last hopeless efforts were being made to keep the United States out of war, Swope planned a trip to the Far East to expand business, which would be strictly a telephone enterprise. He was still in New York on January 22, 1917, when Wilson made his last great peace appeal—the one which contained the famous phrases "peace without victory" and "not a balance of power but a community of power." Like millions of others, Swope hoped against hope that such reasonable counsels might yet prevail. Then he was off for Japan, unaware that the effective German reply to Wilson's appeal was an announcement of unrestricted submarine warfare, or that the President's first words on reading it were:

"This means war."

VII A Manager in the Army

While the attention of most Americans was concentrated on the European war front early in 1917, Gerard Swope was traveling in the opposite direction. Telephone expansion in the United States obviously was halted for the duration of the war; Europe was even more tightly closed; the Far East remained as an outlet for his energies.

He proposed to expand Western Electric's business in Japan and even in China, still reeling from the revolution which had overthrown the Manchu Dynasty five years earlier. He had no idea how long he would stay, but his curiosity was strongly aroused even before he started. The prospect of seeing great, sprawling, disorganized China and tightly ruled, rapidly modernized Japan appealed powerfully to his imagination. Sailing across a providentially mild Pacific, he jotted down notes on questions to ask, conditions to study—such scribblings as:

"The well-being of our people is the well-being of ourselves. How is the well-being of a people to be measured? What is the effect of Occidental civilization on this problem? Japan gives a good way to measure this. Here is a people of about 50,000,000 who have emerged into the family of nations—indeed into the first rank of the Powers and all within fifty years. As a result, is the well-being of the people of Japan greater, better, more comfortable today than fifty years ago? Is their life easier? Do they get more out of life now than then?"

His search for answers led him into explorations which foreigners seldom undertake. He started with officials of the Nippon Electric Company, Western Electric's subsidiary. He learned that the telephone system, government-owned, of course, was sadly inadequate to serve the people. Expansion was so slow and delays between application and installation so long that existing lines were transferred for as much as $500, some said even $1,000. Within the company there was room for a great deal of Swopian improvement, tighter accounting, more comprehensive studies, better use of space and machinery.

He studied the country as carefully. Through his Japanese directors—a large minority interest was owned locally—he met editors, engineers, teachers, high officials and plain citizens. He visited schools and courts, police stations and factories, temples and parks. The venerable Marquis Okuma, one of the three surviving Elder Statesmen who were reputed to rule the land, explained to him the growth of constitutional government as he had seen it, and he could remember Perry's visit which opened the country to the West. Okuma, looking as if he had been carved from old ivory, told him it was "Japan's duty to lead China kindly into stable government."

Filling pages of assorted paper with notes on interviews and impressions, Swope accumulated much admiration for Japan's accomplishments, a healthy doubt that she was as far along the road to parliamentary government as many of his mentors said, some reservations on Japanese industrial abilities and many warm Japanese friends. Despite his unfamiliarity with the niceties of

Japanese etiquette, the Japanese liked him, recognizing his genuine courtesy. They were flattered, some Americans in Tokyo thought, that a man of Swope's prominence in a big American company took so much interest in their ways. The fears of his associates that he bruised Japanese susceptibilities were proved groundless in his dealings with the Mitsui Company, the dominant financial and industrial institution in the country. Swope, seeking stronger local support for the Nippon Electric Company, proposed to the Mitsuis that they invest some millions of yen and be represented on the Board of Directors.

"But," he wrote, "they mentioned a much smaller sum, and I said if they would only take that amount I should be disappointed. When we came out, one of my Japanese associates said to me: 'Well, the transaction is all off. Such an expression, to their minds, is an affront and they won't do business with you.' 'Oh,' I said, 'they can't take me that way; they will realize I come from Missouri and the uncivilized West, and they surely will make allowances for my lack of politeness, if that is the way the matter is handled in Japan.' And sure enough, in this instance I was right and the Mitsui's officers were broad-minded enough to overlook my crudities, became interested in our company and had a representative on the Board."

Swope believed that on the whole the people had benefited from modernization, certainly in education and health. He was impressed by the excellent order maintained by few policemen. But he noted that the dominant influence in higher learning, technology, the military and government was German. The Prussian model, with its tradition of feudal discipline, was more acceptable to the ruling class than democracy, he thought. Then he saw that technological lessons had not been as well learned as first appearances indicated.

"Jap. making bad mdse. now—don't think they can hold trade even in China after war," he scribbled after some study of Japanese factories.

He was careful not to apply American standards—"comparisons with US absurd," one of his notes reads. His judgments, good and bad, were reached only after a stay long enough to give him an intense and abiding interest in the Orient.

This was strengthened when he went to China. Although disorganization here was both thorough and traditional, he found much to admire. One of his first impressions, however, was that government had only a precarious hold on the people. When he reached Shanghai from Japan in midsummer, China was a republic. By the time he got to Hankow, he heard that a northern war lord, Chang Tso-lin, had re-established the Empire in Peking. When he got there after a twenty-six-hour train ride, Chang had fled and the country was a republic once more.

Despite this exhibition of instability, Swope decided to form a Chinese manufacturing company, a task obviously so time-consuming that he sent for Mary and their two older children, and the family spent some months in the comfort of a modern Peking hotel. The usual pattern of local capital joining with Western Electric was out of the question; the only possible partner was the Chinese government, shaky as it was. Although Swope's experience of such negotiations was small, the China Electric Company was duly organized to manufacture telephone equipment in Shanghai, Western Electric and the Republic each owning 50 per cent. Swope was as curious about China as he had been about Japan. He traveled a great deal, and everything he saw suggested additional points on which he wanted information. One of the American managers, insisting he had enjoyed Swope's stay immensely, added, "My knowledge of China automatically increased with my efforts to satisfactorily answer the many questions machine-gunned at me. I had no idea that my knowledge of China was so limited until I found there were so many questions that could be asked to which I was unprepared to give an answer."

At the end of seven months, weighing all the evidence he had collected, Swope set down an estimate of each country. It reads:

J—ceaseless activity
wonderful organization
governmental efficiency
limited opportunities

Ch—unlimited opportunities
rich but undeveloped resources
ceaseless industry
hopeless inefficiency
inability to organize or administer

Swope celebrated his forty-fifth birthday in December by sailing for home and what he supposed would be supervision of Western Electric's general business. But he had been back only a few weeks when Edward R. Stettinius, another St. Louisan who had become a leader in New York's financial community and was serving at the moment as Assistant Secretary of War, asked him to come to Washington. When Swope arrived, Stettinius turned him over to General Goethals, who headed the Army's Service of Supply. George Washington Goethals was one of the authentic heroes of his country, builder of the Panama Canal, a bluff, forthright soldier keen on discipline. By the beginning of 1918 he had to wrestle with a supply problem which dwarfed previous American military experience as the Canal dwarfed a drainage ditch. He wanted Swope's help, and asked him to talk to another general, Hugh S. Johnson.

Swope and Johnson spent all that evening together, with the soldier doing most of the talking. Johnson, a red-faced, choleric fellow, was the Army's youngest brigadier, only fifteen years out of West Point. He proved himself this evening to be full of ideas and picturesque talk. His first idea was that Swope should work on supply statistics as a captain. Swope replied mildly that there were better men for that sort of job. Johnson dropped the point and went on talking until, about midnight, he said, "Oh, hell, come down and help me in the organization of the Service of Supply and be my associate."

Apparently this was Goethals' idea too, for the General repeated the invitation, making it a specific assignment to survey the setup and draft recommendations. Swope agreed, although kind friends advised him against it. An impressive array of successful businessmen had come to the capital to win the war, only to retire defeated or embittered or disgraced—or all three. They and their friends, citing instances, argued that Swope would not be permitted to succeed.

The vice-president of Western Electric was not impressed. He knew that able men had failed in the very job offered to him—John D. Ryan of the Anaconda Company among them. But he knew, too, that other businessmen were doing excellent work in Washington. Besides, as he pointed out to objectors, this was no time to shrink from a personal risk. He resigned from Western Electric, although he supposed he would get his job back after the war, and entered government service as a dollar-a-year man. The company accepted his resignation but continued his salary.

His survey of how the army bought, stored and moved the innumerable objects it needed disclosed a more chaotic system than Swope expected. In peacetime, the military establishment consisted of ten bureaus or corps, each of which decided its own requirements. Each then ordered the items according to its own procurement procedures, struggled for its own transport and paid its own bills. This system, which had ten buyers competing for scarce supplies and railroad cars without regard to duplications or the relative importance of the materials, had been continued into wartime. The only modification was that, after the War Industries Board was set up late in July 1917 the ten had cleared through the new body. In October, Bernard M. Baruch, an immensely tall, tough man with hitherto unsuspected abilities for smoothing industrial-governmental relationships, had been appointed to the chairmanship. It was apparent that more and more authority over the entire economy would be vested in this Board, and Swope drew up his plan accordingly.

An entirely new system that would be ideal on paper was not a very difficult task. But Swope had to draft one that could be used by men trained in the old methods. He must also avoid the pitfalls of which his well-meaning friends had warned him.

One of the chief objections to the businessman in government was "conflict of interest," the temptation to favor the company or the industry from which the businessman came, especially when he still drew his former pay. There was plenty of this going on, but

Swope did not believe that it was a factor which need worry an honest man. He himself explained to Secretary of War Newton D. Baker that he expected to return to Western Electric, and that he still received his salary. Baker, a former reform mayor of Cleveland who was surprising even his friends by an outstanding administrative performance in the War Department in spite of pacifist views, was perfectly satisfied. He suggested only that Swope be careful not to concern himself with any government contract to which his former employer might be a party.

The real explanation of the failure of executives new to government, Swope thought, was a fundamental difference between public and private business. Years later, and after a good deal more experience of both, he put it this way:

"Many men who had been outstandingly successful in business came to Washington in this war emergency to offer their services, but they failed because they endeavored to follow the same methods they had found successful before. They were not flexible enough to adapt themselves to different conditions and different personnel. They insisted on doing things the way they had done them in private business.

"I was satisfied if I could get the same results which I obtained in private business. Therefore, I studied the way government did things and tried to adapt the program I recommended to those ways. Whether it is right or not—and I am inclined to think it is—more people must be consulted in establishing a government enterprise than is necessary or even desirable in private business. The hard-driving methods which can and do succeed in such a business simply will not work in the public service."

This was especially true when the government operation was of such a magnitude that it compared to even the largest industrial corporation as that corporation compared to a village garage. World War I put the government of the United States into operations of that size.

Swope's proposal was sufficiently revolutionary to unify the Service of Supply for efficiency and leave the various branches enough autonomy to prevent demoralization. In essentials, it was the system used to maintain the much larger, more widely scattered armies of World War II. In outline, the plan provided that, without disturbing the basic Army setup, all data on supplies needed, when needed and where needed funneled upward to a single director, Goethals, whose office was organized into five divisions to buy, store and transport for the whole Army. Besides avoiding duplication and competition, it left only one Army spokesman to deal with the War Industries Board.

Swope sat at Goethals' desk while the General read through his proposals, looked up and said as decisively as Swope himself, "This is just what I want. I am going to recommend it to General March, the Chief of Staff, and if he accepts it, I want you to be Assistant Director."

Swope smiled the rather winning smile which unexpectedly breaks up the severe lines of his lean, long-nosed face.

"General," he said, "I am naturally pleased that you should ask me, but you don't know me very well. Maybe you can get someone to do that job better than I can."

Goethals leaned his substantial frame back in his chair and did not return the smile.

"I am sixty years of age," he replied grimly, "and in my life I have had to make decisions as to men as I have met them—I confess I have looked you up and asked about you. On the whole, in my lifetime, in making such selections, I haven't made many mistakes, but when I have, I have never forgiven myself or the man."

He emphasized that word *man,* and looked hard at Swope, who since has commented, "This was true, especially the last part of his statement."

Back in his own office, Swope told Johnson of his interview, and the young general, never one to conceal his feelings, "showed great dismay and disappointment." Johnson, too, had worked on the problem, and Swope had come to have a high regard for his ability and the quickness of his mind.

"So I went to General Goethals and told him that General Johnson, who had been working on the project long before I was, should be appointed.

"'Swope,' Goethals replied, frowning, 'I am not accustomed to being told whom to appoint to my staff.'"

Barton could have told him that Swope was not accustomed to being shut off when he wanted to expound a point.

"After talking it over further," Swope wrote, "he finally decided to appoint us both."

Officers in the Service of Supply were left in little doubt as to the source of orders that flowed in steady streams from the new office, although the civilian camouflaged the fact that he was carrying out the program he had drafted. Swope, refusing a brigadier general's commission, partly because he didn't like the idea and partly because he would be dealing largely with major generals who would "pull rank" on him, got results by using government methods, with modifications. He could forgo the symbols of authority, but he retained the habit of command. General Robert E. Wood, one of the new division heads, a future president of Sears, Roebuck & Co., was in Swope's office one day when the head of Ordnance dropped in to say he had an order from Peyton March, the able, irascible Chief of Staff, which contradicted one issued by Swope. Which should he obey?

"Why, General, I am surprised you should ask," Swope replied banteringly. "Follow mine, of course."

The General went away satisfied—he had experienced the easy way in which the Assistant Director could assume responsibility even when it was not rightfully his. But Wood, a man rigid in his thinking and never noted for a sense of humor, was shocked.

"Do you know what you have done?" he demanded. "You have laid yourself open to a court-martial. Don't you know that an order of the Chief of Staff cannot be countermanded except by the Chief of Staff?"

"No," said Swope, "I didn't know it, but I know their order is wrong, and we will have it countermanded."

He explained to Goethals, who explained to March, and it was as he desired. He proceeded more diplomatically most of the time. At a meeting of the War Industries Board he listened without protest while Goethals accepted a suggestion that, to save steel, some of the methods of France and England be adopted in American machine shops, but as soon as they were outside he asked, "General, do you know what you have done?"

"What do you mean?" Goethals demanded testily.

"You have made a decision to change methods in machine shops which can't be done by fiat. Our material is relatively lower in cost and our labor relatively higher in cost than in France or England. So we endeavor to save our labor and possibly are more wasteful of material."

Goethals saw the point, and Swope explained the facts to the original proponent of the idea so that the matter never was heard of again.

He was seldom so silent in Board meetings. The scope of his job, ranging over the entire industrial scene, brought him to his feet on almost any subject that could come up, and he was not the only Swope whose voice was heard here either. Baruch had brought Herbert in as one of his principal assistants, and he too was concerned with over-all problems rather than any one industry. One day—steel again was before the Board—the brothers held the floor for so long that James Farrell, president of United States Steel, who thought he had some knowledge of the subject but had been unable to get in a word edgewise, finally snapped, "Young man, did you ever hear the old adage, don't Swope until you're Swopen to?"

He never offered to say which brother he meant, but he did not silence either appreciably. The elder was talking the Army into liking as well as accepting his system, and Thayer would have been proud of his *suaviter in modo*. For example, he had a good deal of trouble finding an officer he thought fit to consolidate the hitherto wildly divergent accounting practices of ten bureaus and corps. Finally he selected General Herbert M. Lord, an officer of twenty years' experience who learned in this post much that later made him an extremely able Director of the Budget. Walking back from luncheon with Goethals one day, Swope remarked casually, "You will be glad to hear that General Lord has agreed to accept the job and do the work along the lines we outlined."

Goethals stopped dead in his tracks in the middle of Constitution Avenue and glared at his assistant.

"Agreed, hell!" he barked. "That was an order!"

"Yes, General," Swope replied smoothly, "I know it was an order, but I didn't tell him so. I thought it was better if he would understand and agree with us than if I told him he would have to do it."

"Swope, you beat the Dutch," was Goethals' only comment.

Swope's system soon operated so smoothly that he began to feel his main job was being an apostle of the obvious. Officers and civilians alike kept bringing him problems which required no thought.

"They asked me simple questions, like how much is 2 plus 2, and I would quickly and definitely give the answer 4," he wrote.

He mentioned this to Goethals, who leaned across the desk and whispered in conspiratorial tones, "Swope, I have been fearful that people would find me out, too."

Goethals was a martinet, but Swope was finding him not only just but downright lovable. With their superior, March, his relations were less friendly. He deplored the Chief of Staff's habit of sending an orderly to summon a subordinate with orders to wait until the subordinate came along. On one such occasion, March was concerned about newspaper charges that the Army was piling up more goods than it could ship to France, benefiting troops not at all and needlessly depriving civilians. Since one of Swope's jobs was to prevent just this, he had made an exhaustive study of exactly what tonnage was and would be available, and how the supplies would be shipped for a year ahead. He produced this for March, and they went over it together, Swope pointing out the more pertinent items.

"We became interested in the discussion, and I forgot all about his dignity and his four stars," Swope wrote of the incident. "At one point, I said, 'General, do you understand that?' "

In Peyton March's tradition, a subordinate assumes that four-star generals are omniscient. The Chief of Staff, in fact, often behaved as if he thought so himself. But this time he looked up in mild but genuine surprise.

"Yes," he said, "I do understand it, and it is the first time I have."

The new Service of Supply reached its peak of efficiency just before the war ended on November 11, 1918. Immediately the whole ponderous machine had to be stopped, industry demobilized, orders canceled. In five days, working himself and his staff at top speed, Swope had the necessary orders drafted in detail, and when Goethals asked him about them on the Sunday morning after the Armistice, Swope replied cheerfully, "They have gone to the printer, General, and here is a copy."

"But I haven't seen or approved them," Goethals protested angrily.

He calmed down when Swope assured him time was being saved, that changes could be made in proof if necessary. Whereupon he read and approved them as written. Gerard Swope's war service was over as soon as he could find someone to carry on the routine of the office during demobilization. He selected an Ordnance general and remained to help the new man familiarize himself with the work.

"He wasn't given any word of preparation or request," Swope wrote disapprovingly. "He was simply ordered to appear at our offices on a certain day."

In the wonderful, heady world of Washington celebrating a victory that supposedly banished war forever, Swope prepared to return to private life. He shared the hopes but not the optimism of his fellows. Even when he went to the gallery of Congress the day after his forty-sixth birthday to hear Wilson inform the opening of the "lame duck" session that he was going to negotiate the peace in person, Swope listened "with a heavy heart and foreboding of what his going to Europe might mean."

He left Washington late in December 1918 with no such doubts to mar his personal satisfaction. Goethals, confessing that "I am not an adept at kind words," found quite a few to pay tribute to his assistant's ability and loyalty, adding the flat statement that the Division's success was due to him. A Distinguished Service Medal citation agreed. And at this time, Thayer sent him a letter in which Ernest Hopkins, president of Dartmouth College, who was serving in the Secretary of War's office, had written:

"It is a comparatively rare thing in Washington today for a wholly capable man to come into the situation and to work with good temper for maximum accomplishment without too much fretting over obstacles in the way. This Swope has done, however, meanwhile breeding on all sides complete confidence in himself and his mental processes, as well as liking for himself. The effects of his thinking are now being felt throughout the whole organization of the War Department."

It was something to have won the friendship of such men, of the hard-hitting, hard-drinking Johnson, of the gentle but astute Baker. It was more gratifying to have shared in work which he knew had been a major factor in the success of the biggest job of industrial organization the world had ever seen.

VIII *International Industrialist*

Swope had hardly settled into his home—it had seen him only for fleeting week ends throughout his Washington service—than he received a call from Anson Burchard of General Electric, who wanted to renew his company's 1916 invitation on behalf of its ruling spirit, Charles A. Coffin.

"You'll have to talk quickly," Swope told him. "I'm planning to sail for Europe right after the first of the year."

Burchard and Coffin talked so rapidly and to such purpose that on the first of the year, 1919, only a few days after Burchard's call, Gerard Swope went down to 120 Broadway as the head of all General Electric's foreign business at a salary of $25,000 a year. Coffin had been attracted to him chiefly, he thinks, by his administration of Western Electric abroad and his skill as a negotiator. He proved the latter point in the terms on which he accepted his new post.

Coffin's idea had been that Swope should be a vice-president in charge of the foreign department. Swope's idea was that he should be president of a separate, although wholly owned, General Electric corporation to handle independently all business outside the United States and its possessions. He also wanted a free hand in selecting both his staff and his Board of Directors. Coffin agreed to these conditions, the first time he had not had his own way in a matter of internal organization since General Electric was formed.

Both men enjoyed their first contacts, recognizing underlying kinships of soul despite great surface differences. At seventy-four, the baldish, white-mustached, deceptively gentle founder of the company was slightly shrunken in physique from his vigorous middle age, but Swope thought he retained the keen analytical mind which had given him a reputation for being a manager's manager, a genius at organization who could win the most varied types of subordinates to accept his administrative edicts.

A lover of books and flowers, an enthusiast for education, Coffin had the look of a dreamer when he discoursed on his cherry trees and violets, but a subtle change of expression made his gaze very sharp and penetrating when the subject came back to business. He had run General Electric with a firm hand for nearly thirty years. As creator of the fourth largest industrial organization in the country, he was a man of enormous prestige in the business community and virtually unknown outside of it. Even his rare ventures into public service were unpublicized. He had organized a notable war relief project, a clearing house which added immensely to the efficiency of Red Cross work in this field, but few in that organization itself ever heard of him. In his day he had displayed an energy equal to Swope's own; in his middle seventies he slowed up a little, although not so much that anyone in General Electric thought of challenging his authority.

In 1913 Coffin had exchanged the presidency of his company for the chairmanship. He had placed one of the industry's pioneer engineers, Edwin W. Rice, Jr., in his old office, but Coffin remained the executive head; he alone signed reports to stockholders just as he had when he was president. Rice, who was a scholarly type and looked it, with a round face, round spectacles and a tiny imperial ornamenting his round chin, devoted himself almost exclusively to problems of research and engineering, in which he displayed great imagination and took much responsibility. But he was barely consulted on such matters as the new subsidiary for foreign business.

Swope's characteristically swift decision to make a change was not quite as sudden as it seemed—his lightning calculations usually had some solid study behind them. The circumstances which had led Thayer to tell him in 1916 that he might have more scope outside the increasingly regulated A.T. & T. system had not changed. Western Electric's increasing absorption in the telephone to the exclusion of other equipment and appliances would cut him off from these fields. The fact that he would have more money in his new post was genuinely a minor consideration; he had been earning as much as he and Mary wanted, and more than either of them ever thought about in their days at Hull House.

"After twenty-three years of service and association, however, it was not easy to sever the ties," he wrote, so he refrained from telling Thayer of his plans until "I had come to a final and definite conclusion."

He had an uncomfortable few minutes when he did break the news to Thayer, for there was a real affection between them, and the older man obviously was distressed. Swope insisted on sending a check for salary received during his Washington service. Thayer insisted on giving it back, and got his way.

This interview behind him, Swope plunged into the analysis and reorganization of General Electric's foreign business. The International General Electric Company was duly incorporated with Charles Neave, Swope's patent lawyer friend who also had been a wartime associate, as chairman. Stettinius, returned to J. P. Morgan & Co. from the War Department, was among the financiers and businessmen who agreed to join the Board. A six-story building to house the new company was started in Schenectady, symbolically just a little apart from the rest of the plant but on a site which architecturally dominated the whole.

General Electric's foreign relations were not in the chaotic condition in which he had found the Service of Supply, but Swope thought they had been badly co-ordinated, and the war had disorganized them seriously. Foreign factories had been damaged or allowed to deteriorate; contracts in former enemy countries had lapsed, and since IGE was a new entity, all agreements would have to be renegotiated anyway. The very variety of General Electric interests abroad made careful organizational plans essential.

First of all, his new company would be responsible for a big export trade, mostly General Electric products but also those of other manufacturers, in a world where trade had been dislocated on a scale never known before. Secondly, all over the globe there would be subsidiary companies, some wholly owned by IGE, some with local capital as well, to make and sell electrical goods. Thirdly, IGE would invest in other companies, mostly in highly industrialized countries where it would not be able to compete successfully. Finally, it would contract with major foreign corporations for exchanges of patents and "know-how," with IGE supplying engineering skills to speed electrical development wherever profitable arrangements could be made.

All this called for extensive negotiations in many countries, a job which Swope proposed to do himself. He calculated that he would be out of the country more than half the time, so he would need more than usually able deputies to manage headquarters while he was away. Within three months he had set up the machinery of his new corporation, a performance which Coffin for one observed with noticeable approval. But he attracted the attention of others too, for there was a good deal of interest among company officials as to how the dynamo from Western Electric—such was his advance billing—would handle himself in the new environment.

"Your short three months with us has confirmed the admiration which we vaguely felt before," one of them wrote in a friendly, penciled note. "You have won the entire confidence and affection of everyone with whom you have come in contact . . . we have that comfortable feeling of assurance of success."

The author of this was Owen D. Young, vice-president and general counsel, who six years before had succeeded Swope's old friend, Parsons, killed in an automobile accident. Swope had met him for the first time in 1913 under such casual circumstances that neither remembered them. They had hardly seen each other since, but as soon as they were thrown together in the early months of 1919, they formed a mutual admiration society which no future differences ever marred.

Young was a year younger than Swope, an Upstate New York farm boy who had managed an education in the law through the same sort of family sacrifice and personal ambition which put Gerard through M.I.T. Admitted to the bar, he had scored an almost instantaneous success, and soon was specializing in the new electrical industry. His legal triumphs for the engineering firm of Stone & Webster, some of them over General Electric, had led Coffin to seek him as Parsons' successor.

Where Swope was short, slim and brisk, Young was tall, with deepset eyes and a pipe that never stayed lit, and so gangling and languid that admirers thought he resembled Lincoln. Swope did his best thinking while walking fast or busily turning over papers. Young's mind was most active when his long body was sprawled at rest, the back of his neck supporting a surprising share of his weight. Both spoke well and clearly, but while Swope's staccato words were effective as he spoke them, they were likely to be awkward reading when transcribed. Young's casual conversation had a literary style. Swope's intensity often fooled people into thinking he had no interests outside of business. Young's detachment fooled them into thinking he had no interest in business at all.

Swope, wasting no time after he had his headquarters in shape to operate without him, was on his way to Japan when he read Young's cordial note, and in his rapid scrawl while the train roared west, he replied, "I only hope I am not too old or too confirmed in my ways to profit from association with you—whom I so much admire, and now more than ever before."

He was pleased to be opening his new work where he had left off in the old—in the Far East. He carried an assignment to look into the status of Shipping Board shipbuilding contracts for the Government, but for the rest he was on familiar ground. His negotiations in Japan and China followed closely the pattern he had set for Western Electric. In fact, this was true of all his contracts as well as his organizational plans.

"Read a Western Electric contract with some foreign company and it is the same as the IGE contracts," says Clark H. Minor, who had been Swope's manager in Antwerp before the war, was sent by him to China in 1917 and now joined the new company, of which he eventually became the head.

The general pattern provided: Experts from General Electric would be on loan to the foreign company as needed; IGE would furnish assistance in designing buildings, machinery layouts or detailed manufacturing plans; employees of the foreign company might receive training in General Electric plants in the United States; exchange of inventions and improvements would guarantee the foreign company the benefit of General Electric progress and give General Electric the fruit of developments abroad.

Swope was accompanied on this trip by the general counsel to his company but did all the negotiating himself. Those were the days, some of his contemporaries sigh, when a corporation executive could tell a lawyer what he wanted and have legal papers drawn accordingly instead of having to check with a lawyer to find out what it was possible to do. The older method served Swope so well that the contracts resulting from this trip and another series negotiated in Europe later the same year drew from Coffin expressions of surprise as he confided to Young that this new man had exceeded his expectations.

"Swope hasn't missed a trick," he was quoted by others as saying.

Actually, Swope thought, Coffin valued his work "far beyond

the merits of the contracts themselves" because the older man did not fully understand the foreign market and its potentialities. He himself was inclined to attribute his success largely to his bearing in mind the fact that a good agreement for any long-term relationship must benefit both parties to it.

"It was comparatively easy to determine what we wanted, but more difficult to determine what would be the basis for a contract fair to both sides," he explained. "To do this I tried to put myself in the place of the other party to see what I would ask for in his place."

His habit of analyzing a situation enabled him very often to present the first draft of a program so obviously advantageous to all concerned that the men across the table would accept it as their own.

He was in New York only a month between his Eastern and his European trips, but in that time he heard from Young about a complicated radio deal in which the lawyer was a prime mover. It promised to have important international as well as national significance. Young gave him a mass of papers about the problems involved to read on shipboard, and Swope found them a fascinating story.

Wireless had made tremendous strides during the war, and because of the war. The Navy, pooling all patents regardless of who owned them, had built a communications network which rivaled cables and enabled Washington to communicate easily with armies in France and negotiators at the Paris Peace Conference. Wireless put Woodrow Wilson's Fourteen Points before the German people—although radio as yet carried no spoken words but only code messages. A lot of people thought that one speech had shortened the war by a year. The President was very anxious that the United States keep its advantage in the new medium, and in the midst of the most difficult of his Paris talks, he had ordered the Navy to see to it.

The very day after Swope left for Japan, Admiral Bullard, head of Navy communications, and the chief of his radio division called on Young. General Electric owned the Alexanderson alternator, essential to long-distance transmission, and was negotiating to supply several million dollars' worth to the British Marconi Company. Bullard's first request was that the sale be stopped lest Great Britain add mastery of the airwaves to her control of most of the world's cables, and Young readily agreed to withhold the alternator.

Replacing the wartime patent pool so that the United States could keep in peace as good a wireless system as the Navy had built for war was a more difficult problem. General Electric, Western Electric, A.T. & T., Westinghouse, United Fruit and the American branch of the British Marconi Company each owned essential patents. After exploring several alternatives, Bullard and Young agreed that the first five of these firms should assign their patents to a new company which they would own jointly and which would buy out the Marconi Company to preserve the exclusively American character of the enterprise. The government, including the Department of Justice, not only approved but urged the arrangement as being in the national interest. What Swope was reading on shipboard was the history of these talks and a plan for the organization of the Radio Corporation of America.

"I have read with delight the record of the great work you have done in the wireless, which I hadn't really appreciated before," he wrote to Young before he reached Cherbourg. "I bow down before you with even greater respect and more humility than ever."

He added that he had little hope of accomplishing much in a Europe still torn by war and suspicion, and he closed with "Pray for me."

Actually on this trip he reorganized the British Thomson-Houston Company, negotiated new contracts on his favorite model with French, Belgian, Netherlands and Italian companies and made a good start on a deal with the German counterpart of General Electric, the Allgemeine Elektrizitaets-Gesellschaft (A.E.G.).

The aftermath of war, while the peace conference lingered on in Paris long after the chief negotiators had left, made all business difficult. Travel was slow and uncomfortable, accommodations a bit primitive. Swope had to stand up in a train corridor nearly all day and half a night to get from Holland to Berlin, and then found as a bed nothing better than a mattress on the floor of a hotel bathroom. He could overlook such discomforts, but the disruption of industrial life which they symptomized and of which he saw far more serious signs was distressing.

One obvious difficulty was the uncertainties created by German reparations and interallied debts. Swope talked about these problems a good deal with Louis Loucheur, the French Minister of Reconstruction, one of the few French political figures of his generation who dared to take a realistic look at them, and Walter Rathenau, son of the A.E.G. founder, who was Germany's leading economic statesman. Before the war, Swope had enjoyed the company of this astute, cultivated industrialist and now renewed the acquaintance with pleasure. Like Swope, Rathenau had headed his country's service of supply in the war, but Swope thought he was more inclined toward politics and possessed abilities in this direction which might have saved the Weimar Republic if he had not been assassinated in 1922.

Over the next two years Swope drafted plans—admired in high places but not acted upon—for using preference shares in German heavy industry and utilities to pay reparations and funding Allied debts on a basis bearing some relation to these reparations. He saw the evil of these twin economic incubuses at close range, for he spent most of 1920 and 1921 in Europe, basing himself in Paris, where his family joined him, but traveling almost constantly. More contracts, covering the Continent, were the result, "all of them difficult in a way," he wrote, "as we in America were the only points of contact between these various countries and companies, and the antagonisms of the war were still in evidence."

Back home, a wartime boom was slumping into depression, and Swope found the ascetic, aging Coffin worried by the prospect of increasing General Electric's debts—$45,000,000, or two years of the company's total net income, was owed to banks alone. Coffin was thinking of counteracting the shrinking domestic business by selling the preferred stock of IGE on the open market. It was a poor time for such an offering, with blue-chip shares falling every day on the exchange, and he did not like the idea of seeing any of the subsidiary's capital held outside the parent company, but more borrowing from banks would be expensive. Swope solved the dilemma for him by negotiating an $11,000,000 loan on easy terms with Eugene Meyer of the new Reconstruction Finance Corporation, "later paid with interest and without any difficulty," the negotiator wrote.

In the autumn of 1920 he set what some observers thought was the capstone of the admiration in which Coffin had come to regard him. This was an adaptation of his Western Electric seminar-sales conference to a meeting of IGE managers and representatives from all over the world. Men from twenty-one countries gathered for a series of intensive sessions in New York and Schenectady, where the six-story IGE building was now filled with Swope's busy staff. The program, over which Swope labored with infinite pains and which both Coffin and Rice witnessed throughout, pulled together all the facets of the business, giving the branch managers their first fully rounded view of the potential scope of the industry and their own share in it.

Swope himself closed the conference in a summation which some who heard it thought the most brilliant speech he ever made. Its echoes were heard throughout the General Electric organization. In Cleveland a rising young executive in the lamp department was told that Swope had run the most effective symposium on sales ever conducted in the electrical industry. In Schenectady, a young field auditor heard Swope's tour de force admired so extravagantly that some officials were asking, with a hint of truth behind the jest, whether General Electric had now become a subsidiary of IGE.

Swope himself did not linger to savor the triumph. He hurried back to Europe, and during that winter Coffin began to think seriously of abdicating. He was feeling his age; his face had grown thin, and his cane was carried for use, not show. He talked with

Owen Young, whom he had selected long ago in his own mind as the next Chairman of the Board, saying that he never had seen anything like the way Swope pulled the foreign business together. He felt that at last he had found someone who combined the vigor, integrity, administrative talent, industry-wide interest and all-around experience which he believed the chief executive of General Electric ought to possess. Rice was an old friend and colleague, a brilliant man in his own field and still in his fifties. But Young, who knew him well, says that he shrank from decisions dealing with credit, sales, personnel, finance or administration. Coffin, who celebrated his seventy-sixth birthday on December 30, 1920, never had felt that he could leave the reins in Rice's hands. But he did want to relieve himself of some of his burdens, although he never would retire completely. Early in 1921 he informed Young that he had just about made up his mind that Swope should be the next president of General Electric.

"His only worry was whether Gerard and I could get along, could work well together," Young recalls.

At this time Coffin was receiving reports about the president of IGE very much like those sent to a head of state concerning a mysterious potentate with whom an alliance might or might not be desirable. A typical one came from Charles Neave, who thought Swope ought to be put on the Board of the General Electric Company, although only Burchard, of all the old-timers, had been so honored while still active. Neave added:

"He seems to have fully proved his capacity to work in with your organization, and to repeat and follow and carry forward the lines along which your organization has been developed and has been successful. That he would be able to do that was, I imagine, the only doubt that was in the minds of any of us—and that doubt has, I believe, been entirely dispelled, and he has proved himself a real addition to your organization.

"He has had several offers to take up other work in important positions—one of them at any figure he himself might choose to fix. He was not, for a moment, tempted by them, as he is entirely happy in his present surroundings, and in his association with you and your organization. But others recognize his ability for larger things, as we do."

All unaware of this talk, Swope had calmly rejected the lucrative offer of which Neave spoke, one of the most extravagant made to any businessman up to this time. It had come from Clarence Dillon, whose banking house of Dillon, Read & Co. was reorganizing the Goodyear Rubber Company. This firm, caught in a trap of the business slump and large rubber commitments at peak prices, had to accept almost any conditions the financiers cared to impose. Dillon undertook to find $87,000,000 of new capital, but the company paid in effect 14 per cent interest. The bankers insisted on their own choice as president and would keep stock control in the hands of three trustees until the bonds were paid. Young was one of these trustees, but he was not instrumental in the offer Dillon now made to Swope. The banker dangled a bait of $250,000 a year, ten times as much as the presidency of IGE paid, plus "additional emoluments" which, it was testified in a later stockholders' suit, would have amounted to a million dollars in four years. Swope was not tempted.

"I answered at once that I knew nothing about rubber and I did know a little bit about my present job, that I was happy in my associates, and that I thanked him for the offer," Swope wrote.

Returning to New York in March, he received news that the president of his Japanese company had died and there was difficulty in finding a successor. He decided he had better go himself, and he invited Young to accompany him. By this time the two had become close friends on a first-name basis (not so common in 1921 as it would become) and were falling into a lifelong habit of solicitude for each other's health. There is no record that either ever gave his own any thought at all. Swope especially was often accused of taking it for granted that everyone was as rugged as he was himself. But he and Young punctuated their correspondence heavily with exhortations to take it easy, go away for a rest in the sun, take no risks. Reading it, one is surprised not to find adjurations such as "Be sure to wear your rubbers" or "Have you got your muffler on?" In March 1921 Swope decided that a long trip to the Far East was just what Young's health demanded. Young agreed enthusiastically; he told Coffin it would be an acid test of how well the pair could get along in intimate association.

It turned out to be very well indeed. For one hundred ten days they were hardly out of each other's sight. The crossings of the Pacific in small ships, three weeks each way, gave them a chance to talk out their ideas on life and work, business and art, philosophy, religions, people, the past and the future. Among other things, they discovered that their ideas of their company, the industry and themselves were wonderfully compatible.

By the time they had visited Japan, China and the Philippines, toured the Confucius country, bought Chinese porcelain for their wives and sailed for home, their talks had revealed to Swope that he and Young were being groomed for a big role in General Electric, and as a team. They had exchanged exhaustively their views on what their company or any company ought to do, the principles which should govern it, the objectives it should seek, the kind of men who should manage it. The one hundred ten days had enhanced their respect and admiration for each other, and their understanding, too. It was right at the end of the voyage across the Pacific in a lovely August of gold and blue days and tranquil nights that Swope turned to his friend and said, "I will do all the work—I like it."

IX *A Managerial Revolution*

"It was only after my return in August 1921 that the first mention was made so far as I know of my becoming president of the General Electric Company," Swope wrote many years later.

After his long discussions with Young, however, the proposal did not come as a shattering surprise. Nor was he wildly elated, for he was invited to take command of a company suffering more than average depression damage. The war had expanded General Electric's plant, and that of all American industry, beyond the old demands of peace. In 1920 the company received $318,000,000 worth of orders, a record, from delayed machinery needs and a war backlog. The 1921 figure was $179,000,000. A huge plant in Bridgeport, taken over from the government during the war, was running at a small fraction of its capacity. Whether Coffin no longer felt qualified to deal with the resulting difficulties or didn't want to try, the sorry state of business certainly speeded his decision to relinquish power to younger men. One of the difficulties was the sheer size of corporations, with big combinations in automobiles, the movies and electrical gadgets rivaling the older leaders, steel and oil, railroads and machinery. There was a strong feeling in 1921 that corporate growth had passed the point of maximum efficiency, and the depression was cited as proof of it. Even without government intervention, it was argued, a medium-sized company concentrating on one or two products could outproduce and undersell the clumsier giants of the market.

This was one point in history where it might have been possible to mold American business in the direction of limited size. Most Americans had a wholesome fear of monopoly and thought bigness was a sign of it. The trust-busting campaigns of twenty years, while not retarding growth of individual enterprises, had made such growth suspect. The war record of industry, a masterpiece of production, was being marred after the event by revelations of inordinate profit to insiders. Income-tax figures showed that the war had made 18,000 new millionaires. Leading companies had deliberately wasted millions because they were on a "cost-plus" basis which gave them a profit on the waste at government expense.

The situation could have been capitalized by a forceful leadership bent on reversing the trend of industrial consolidation and combination. Such leadership might have steered new industries into a pattern of relatively small independents in keen competition. Airplanes, radio, synthetics and plastics, electric refrigerators and washing machines and stoves and vacuum cleaners were in their lusty infancy. In the next few years they either would give rise to hundreds and thousands of solid new corporations or swell the size of the existing leaders.

From the Federal government no leadership of this kind was to be expected. The Harding Administration was only five months old in August 1921, but already it was clear that so far as it had policies in this area they were designed to further concentration rather than competition. Secretary of the Treasury Andrew W.

Mellon, whose family controlled the Aluminum Company, Gulf Oil, railroads, coal and chemicals, had been recommended to the President as "the only man the big interests will not bluff." But they would never try to bluff him; they could trust him because he was pre-eminent among the big interests himself.

In the industrial world there was no sign of leadership to promote competition. If the best abilities were not already in the service of the biggest corporations, they wanted either to get there or to swell their own corporations into first rank.

Even among liberal intellectuals, the fine old fervor against bigness was fading. A young economist, Rexford G. Tugwell, and an even younger lawyer, Adolf A. Berle, Jr., although little known as yet, were laying the foundations for theories that the finest development of the industrial system was not in breaking it into smaller units but in putting large combinations under social control. This was a point of view which many students thought they could discern in the teachings of the brilliant but difficult Thorstein Veblen, a thoroughly unorthodox economist then at the height of his reputation.

Neither the politicians nor the intellectuals were guiding the actual progress of industry. That was left to the businessmen, and Gerard Swope now was to be one of the most powerful among them. Called to the executive management of the nation's fourth largest corporation after making his career in a subsidiary of an even larger one, A.T. & T., he was beset by no philosophical doubts. He was far from sharing either the pessimism of those who thought the slump was permanent or the illusion of those who believed corporations could grow no larger. But he realized that he was being called upon to perform an emergency operation. Coffin and the Board of Directors expected him to reverse the downward curve of their business. He was quite willing to assume the obligation because he thought one needed no magic gifts to see that a new world powered by electricity in homes, offices, factories and farms was going to open up in the next few years. His task, as he saw it, would be to garner for General Electric the cream and the bulk of the resulting orders.

He foresaw, too, that fears and doubts inevitably would afflict men in strategic positions throughout the forty-two General Electric plants and offices when the new administration should be announced. He made this point rather forcefully as an objection to his appointment, but not so forcefully that he convinced either Coffin or himself that he ought not to take the job.

"Naturally the vice-presidents who had been with the company many years and had given it loyal service didn't feel very kindly that a younger man, only recently in the organization, should become its president," he explained after his retirement. "I sympathized with them, told Mr. Coffin and the directors that I was happy where I was. But Mr. Coffin overcame all obstacles and difficulties."

It took the older man eight months to do it, "from early morning until late at night," Swope remembered, for it involved a real reorganization. Two vacancies on the Board were filled in the autumn by the election of Swope admirers, Stettinius and Dwight Morrow, who was the most tactful and popular of the Morgan partners. The directors were the least of Coffin's worries; they were used to taking his advice on major decisions, as any Board must when a strong executive is in command. Internal relations among General Electric officials presented a more formidable obstacle to a smooth succession.

First of all, there was Rice. It is common for the president of a large corporation to move into the chairmanship to make way for a new chief executive, but Coffin had already settled on Young. Rice was only sixty, hardly retirement age, although he had been in the electrical industry for forty-two years. The post of honorary chairman of the Board was created for him, so obviously as a sop to pride that some of his friends were surprised when he accepted it.

"I never did know how Mr. Coffin persuaded him to give up the presidency," Swope says, but Rice was used to taking Coffin's orders.

The next hurdle was the man who had brought Swope from Western Electric, Anson Burchard. As the only active officer on the Board except for Coffin and Rice, he felt he had a certain seniority—a fourth official, the Bernard E. Sunny who had been Chicago manager when one G. Swope, helper, was hired at $1 a day, was virtually retired. The business community knew Burchard better than any other company vice-president, and he had been very close to Coffin personally and professionally. Young thinks that he would have been reluctant to accept the burdens of president but wanted to be asked. Coffin, however, was far too realistic to humiliate the man he wanted by making empty gestures to the man he didn't want. Burchard was consoled with another presidency, succeeding Swope at International General Electric.

He was not the only one with ambitions. Two vice-presidents, who probably would have received most votes within the company itself, were mollified a little by election to the Board of Directors, which was enlarged from fifteen to nineteen to accommodate them and the two new top officers. This compromise weighted the Board overheavily with General Electric men, eight to eleven. The theory behind such a Board as General Electric's—eminent men in finance or businesses which have nothing to do with the electrical industry—is that the outsiders bring keen, independent judgment to company policies. The independence and the detached point of view are diluted when the Board includes active officers dependent upon the president for promotion or pay. Actually, Swope saw to it that the two vice-presidents very soon were retired from their executive posts, and the precedent was not broken again.

So they came to the decisive day of May 16, 1922. Throughout the company, a terse announcement was conned unhappily by officials who had no pretensions to the presidency but were uneasy at the prospect of having to learn to get along with a new man and his new ways. Coffin had been no angel, but at least they knew him. As they drafted telegrams and letters of congratulations and pledges of co-operation, they asked themselves, "Where will this newcomer start reorganizing?" They asked the question in the manufacturing division, in sales, credit, engineering, accounting.

It was frustrating to end up with no more than "In my shop, I wonder?"

In the financial columns of the next morning's papers—orderly changes in administration of even the largest industries were not then front-page news—Coffin's retirement dominated. The business community, editors of that day thought, was more interested in the old chief than in the new commander. Their preoccupation with Coffin gave them a wrong slant on the succession, too. Young was not very well known outside the electrical world as yet, was in his own words "just a lawyer fella," but the press billed him as Coffin's successor in the management. Only the men worrying about their futures in General Electric knew how mistaken that was. Young and Swope already had agreed that the president was to be executive head of the company, supreme in all matters of production, sales, credit, personnel, prices, research and engineering. The chairman would be his partner in broad policy decisions and take the lead in representing General Electric before the stockholders and the public.

On that morning began a flood of congratulations to the new president. There were warm personal messages from friends he and Mary had drawn to themselves during twenty years and from members of the class of '95 at M.I.T. There were cordial, familiar letters from Western Electric offices all over the world—from Thayer and Mrs. Barton, from engineers and salesmen—and rather stilted expressions of pleasure from General Electric officials. Industrial and financial leaders, old associates in Washington, school fellows in St. Louis, wrote to him so that the pile was the equivalent of a fairly thick book.

Swope was much too busy to savor them at leisure. He knew that he must establish his leadership in General Electric quickly or not at all. It was beyond Coffin's power to stifle all jealousies and disappointments, and they could not be allowed to feed upon themselves. Young, who realized as well as Swope the extent of these feelings, has expressed the view that they did not break through the surface at once because the disgruntled vice-presidents and department heads decided to hold their fire while they sized up the new president, discovered his weaknesses, let him make a few mistakes.

"By the time they were ready to shoot, Gerard had his grip on the company, proved his superiority and was in unquestioned command," says Young, pausing to relight his pipe and chuckle. "What made him such an outstanding executive? He couldn't help it. He just *was* an executive."

The quality of leadership is so difficult to pin down that even men like Young, who have it and have associated with it intimately all their lives, are hard put to define it. But Swope was so precise and specific that Young thought it could be done in his case.

"Starting with his most obvious characteristic," Young wrote, "one recognizable on the instant of a first meeting, is his dynamic personality. He is like a spring under tension always, never spent and never relaxed. The next characteristic is his utter incapacity for ambiguity. He cannot think ambiguously and he could not speak ambiguously if he would. As a result of these two qualities, you have force and clearness, which are as vital to an effective person as they are to effective speech. Together they are an instrument of penetration like the scalpel or the X ray, a tool which nature gave him and which has improved progressively with use. It is a dangerous tool which has ruined many men. It is safe only when coupled to industry and anchored to character."

Of all the men who worked closely with Swope, Theodore K. Quinn is his severest critic. After rising high in General Electric, he not only left but reached the conclusion that such large corporations imperil American freedom and the American economy. He writes:

"Swope was the hardest-working man I ever knew. He seemed to feel that he had few natural advantages and that he could only make up for it by concentration on work—almost to a fanatical degree. He wanted the rules he made to be strictly observed and was autocratically rather than democratically inclined. . . . If you picture Swope as much more than an unusually active, mathematically-minded, boundlessly energetic, single-track-minded man, concentrating on his job to the exclusion of all other interests, ambitious to the extreme and determined to make his mark and get rich—not necessarily for riches, but for power and to win the applause of his fellows—if you make him out to be much more than this, I do not believe it will be an accurate picture."

Neither friend nor critic credits Swope with inspirational qualities of leadership. Neither admirer nor detractor leaves any doubt about his control over the company and the men in it. Both concentrate on those qualities in the man which best exemplify the preconceived picture. There was a coldness, a machinelike impersonality about him which inhibited warmth, whether of affection or dislike. (Both Young and Quinn are exceptions on their respective sides of the fence, but the high temperature of their feelings seems to be induced by their own temperaments rather than by any fuel from Swope's own passions.)

Even when the president of General Electric was most forceful, most unreasonably demanding, the result was not described as "fireworks." Subordinates told no colorful stories of his glee or wrath. His reserve in good times and bad discouraged intimacy. He had no endearing eccentricities of speech or dress or manner. One of his few discernible baseless prejudices was a moral disapproval of obesity. When he used the noun *complacency*, he prefaced it with the adjective *potbellied*, although why he preferred this to *skinny* he never tried to explain. He took a sympathetic interest in few individuals and never pretended to more. His very defects of personality and his singleness of purpose furthered his mastery of the General Electric Company. He established and maintained it by weaving together the strands of his old motto: "Analyze, Organize, Deputize, Supervise." It may be easier to understand if his progress is followed in these four parts.

Analyze

In the first months of his presidency, Swope studied General Electric as it never had been scrutinized before. He read, questioned, traveled to plants and offices until he could disconcert many officials by seeming to know more about their departments than they did themselves. At Schenectady, for example, the assistant manager of the Publications Department, which included an intangible item called public relations, tried to impress the new boss and never forgot the dispatch with which Swope squelched the effort. This was Chester Lang, a cocky, cheerful young fellow whose chief was showing Swope around.

"I tagged along," Lang recalls, "and when we went through a room where we kept files on each catalogue item the company had—some 400,000, each on its own card—I thought it time for me to attract his attention. So I asked him brightly if he knew how many cards we kept here. 'Yes, 368,416,' he said without even slowing his stride."

In those first weeks, Swope also toured one of the company's small factories in Maspeth, Long Island, "a nuts and bolts plant," the men called it because it manufactured a variety of odds and ends such as switches and outlet boxes. The whole shop was "only" two city blocks by one—you can measure the Schenectady plant in miles—and Swope was escorted by Superintendent Bill Ruete, a burly, mustached old-timer in a derby hat, and his assistant, Charles E. Wilson, a big man with the build of a fullback and the slightly battered face of a pugilist who has quit the ring just in time. Swope stopped only once, to watch a punch press stamp outlets into hexagonal boxes which were turned by hand as the press flashed up and down. A big Polish girl with a wrist like steel from snapping boxes around all day handled the machine at a fast clip.

"How many fingers do you lose a day?" Swope asked.

"He'd picked out the one hazardous operation in the whole place," says Wilson, "and right then I realized we had a man who knew manufacturing, not just a merchandiser, as the grapevine had it."

Only a good deal later did the young man know that Swope had noticed anything else about the Maspeth factory, Wilson himself. At this time Wilson was thirty-five years old but had been in the electrical business almost as long as Swope. Charlie was born in New York's Hell's Kitchen in the days when most of its boys who lived to maturity wound up in Sing Sing. He himself left school in the seventh grade at the age of twelve to help his widowed mother earn a living. He got a job with the Sprague Company before General Electric bought it, starting at $3 a week and rising to four. In a year or two he supplemented this wage by appearing in evening bouts around town, for he fancied himself as a boxer. A big youngster with the ability to take as well as give punishment—a requisite for survival in Hell's Kitchen—he liked to use his fists. One day he used them on another lad in a brawl in the shops and was fired. The foreman was sorry, but that was the rule, unless Superintendent Ruete relaxed it. This awesome figure, impressing the boy by his business suit and a necktie ornamented by a ruby surrounded by diamonds, greeted the repentant sinner with a volley of invective about the fate of young bums, ending with a rhetorical question as to what this particular young bum thought he wanted to be anyway. Charlie had not learned about rhetorical questions.

"I want to be a manager," he replied.

"Manager!" Ruete roared in outrage. "Whatcha mean, manager?"

"I want to wear a dark suit and a stickpin and make four thousand dollars a year like you."

"How do you know I make four thousand dollars a year?" the superintendent demanded.

"Well, one day the paymaster was away from his desk, and I looked to see what people made," the boy confessed.

Ruete not only restored the job, but took Charlie in hand. He forbade fighting, for fun or for profit. Then he made sure his protégé would have no time for it anyway by keeping him in night school for the next fourteen years.

"He wanted me to have a Harvard accent, but I balked at that one," says Wilson, who obeyed in every other respect.

One by-product of Swope's analysis was a certain popularity with factory workers who never before had the slightest contact with the president of the company; few knew Coffin or Rice by sight. They thought it remarkable that Swope came among them at all, noticed that they had fingers, asked them questions. When he gathered their foremen together for talks on work, pay and promotions, they approved audibly. They were heard referring to him as "Gerry," a familiarity never imitated by higher officials.

Word got around that he had strange but welcome notions on earnings. The Erie works manager bragged of "a third horizontal 10 per cent reduction in all day and piecework rates, and in addition by very careful time studies, we have further reduced our piecework rates on an average of 12 per cent." The poor fellow, looking for praise, learned that Swope called indiscriminate cuts in the piecework rate "disastrous" and had set his face firmly against the practice of reducing them as soon as men began to increase their earnings.

"I never saw Mr. Coffin or heard Mr. Rice speak, yet this fellow did not wait thirty days before he let us see and hear him" and "I was glad he slapped the Piece Rate Department in his remarks" were typical worker comments.

To Swope, this good opinion was welcome but less important than what he learned about flaws in labor relations. His analysis, furthermore, showed what he thought were other weaknesses. The General Electric Company owed too much money, and its accounting procedures were insufficiently precise. It had too many plants making too few products. There was too little understanding of the whole company, too much emphasis upon a man's own department. Engineers and salesmen considered each other separate races of people. Neither knew nor cared what the other fellow was doing. Management had neglected the training of younger men and the security of older ones, he thought. The virtually complete autonomy of the Terry and Tremaine incandescent lamp operation was an exaggerated symptom of lack of co-ordination at the top which he found deplorable.

Organize

In his first steps to lift the company out of the slump, Swope demonstrated an unorthodox belief that men were more important than buildings or equipment, designs or money. Successful industrial managers of the early 1920s, with Henry Ford as their prophet, were convinced that a plant's efficiency depended upon the design of the building, the wonderful new machinery and "Taylorism" or Charles Bedaux's impersonal "speed-up" system. These devices, they thought, permitted them almost to do away with human skills on the assembly line. Swope bluntly called this a fallacy; he leaned so far to the other extreme that some subordinates thought he reached it.

"Men and the training of men was what mattered to him," says one former General Electric official who went through these first years of the Swope regime. "He proved that the right men could increase production with less elaborate machinery or less efficiently designed plants than improperly trained and led workers with the last word in equipment. He went so far that he finally left General Electric with less plant than it should have had."

By the time his colleagues had become used to this, they had received an answer to the question uppermost in their minds on May 16. "Where will he start reorganizing?" they asked. "Everywhere at once" was the answer.

His passion for precision communicated itself to men who never had been so closely supervised before, and his policies worked toward an actual revolution in the company. Swope believed that sound organization and growth called for expansion into the manufacture of all the electrical appliances which science or ingenuity could devise. He had expounded this doctrine at Western Electric; he was convinced it was even more desirable for General Electric.

He noted that for the corporation's main business, the heavy generating machinery, transmission equipment and motors called apparatus in the jargon of the industry, there were about twenty-five thousand customers. He envisaged multiplying this by a thousand, to include twenty-five million American families. Appliances sold to these people would increase the demand for generating equipment. A business based on the steady needs of all the people would be more stable than one which produced only for the fluctuating requirements of utilities and industries.

Protests that consumer goods and industrial equipment should not be made by the same company struck him as irrelevant. The main thing, from the public's standpoint, was to get products of good quality at low prices. If General Electric could compete in that market, it should not be barred because it did well in other markets, too.

He did not propose to accomplish this part of his revolution overnight. He would need time to select the proper items for a start, arrange manufacturing and selling facilities, pick out the men who could handle an appliance business.

Meanwhile he began reorganizing the financial structure of the company. He was as unhappy as Coffin over the large bank loans, and even more over the bonded indebtedness—a total of more than $80,000,000. In addition, he disliked the idea of preferred stock. He promptly organized the retirement of them all, and accomplished it within four years.

He turned his attention early to the scattered lamp department. It made a great many different brands, none of them identified with General Electric by name, and the president of the company had less control of them than the new bearer of the title liked. He thought that, for all their prestige, progress toward better light at lower cost was sacrificed to jealousies in the various fragments of the department. At Terry and Tremaine's beautiful industrial city, Nela Park in Cleveland, he expounded one day his theory that if all lamps carried the emblem GE, a valuable unity would result. His hearers protested, but after the meeting one of them, a redheaded, aspiring young department head, Theodore K. Quinn, admitted that the company would benefit.

"Then why were you against it?" Swope asked.

"I work for National Lamp, not General Electric," Quinn replied.

The sense of fragmentation implicit in this remark was what Swope wished to overcome, but he only said, "If you were president of General Electric, what would you do?"

"I'd make the GE name well known and well thought of, and then the lamp people would ask for the privilege of using it."

Later Quinn thought that this suggestion started him up the ladder of promotion. Swope, however, already had embarked upon just such a program. He had been in office less than a month when he called a conference of managers of the various operating departments to establish an advertising policy. The company never had had one, so that although there was an advertising manager (who reported to the vice-president in charge of sales as the publicity manager reported to the vice-president in charge of engineering), each executive handled his own advertising quite independently of any others, and often quite contradictory to them.

At the end of a day's discussions, spokesmen for various advertising agencies were invited to present their ideas. Most of them, having some part of the General Electric business, feared to jeopardize their account by urging a change, but also feared alienating Swope by not urging a change. The result was a good deal of clever but meaningless talk from all except two. Thomas Logan, a facile writer but on this day a dull speaker, presented a brilliantly worded, monotonously voiced argument against producing anything that did not bear the initials GE. Bruce Barton, of an as yet little known firm, proposed an institutional program to promote General Electric as a whole. He won the majority—fifty-five to two favored his plan over Logan's—and Swope's vote was among them.

"When Barton, Durstine and Osborn was a fledgling agency . . . our acquisition of this very desirable account was literally a bombshell in the agency business and unquestionably hastened our rise to major status by months if not years," Barton wrote a generation later, recalling that he thereupon bought a horse so he could casually meet Swope riding in Central Park early in the mornings—and grew to like riding himself.

In line with his belief that men were the major factor in a corporation's success, Swope devoted a good deal of his attention to the relations between workers and their jobs, and workers and their immediate superiors. His attitude was summed up by a bewildered elderly works manager who had acquired a new superintendent named Bond for one of his departments. Swope made a whirlwind tour through the plant and, just before leaving, asked, "How's Bond getting along with the men?"

"Why, all right, I guess," the manager replied a bit uncertainly, for the form of the question puzzled him. "In fact he gets on well with them."

"Good, I'm glad to hear it," said Swope.

He walked away briskly, while the manager looked after him, scratching his head. Then he turned to another official to remark, "Things have certainly changed around here. Why, before Mr. Swope, if a superintendent got along well with the men, he'd be fired. They'd say he couldn't get enough work out of 'em if they liked him."

Before he had been president for five months, Swope was telling a meeting of foremen that part of their job was to "let the management know what the men want," and adding, "Usually in our factory management we jump on the foreman to speed up his production and complain that his costs are too high. Almost the last thing our foreman will remember is the relations with the men who work for him, but that, as a matter of fact, is the most important consideration."

Swope thought the piecework system the fairest method of payment ever devised, if the rate is properly set and not reduced as soon as workers become more skilled. He told the foremen nothing is more disastrous than such a cut, nothing better for the company than high piecework earnings because they mean "greater production for the same amount of floor space and equipment."

He realized that, for all his urging, foremen were hardly the natural spokesmen for workers, but alone of the major corporation heads of 1922, he saw that someone inevitably would speak for the men, and contemplated the prospect without any rise in blood pressure. Dealing with the spokesmen was going to be one of a manager's jobs, and he accepted the idea without any sense of outrage. In his analysis, he had found that the aftermath of a particularly bitter strike in the big Lynn works in 1918 was a "Plan of Representation" set up by the War Labor Board. It was a company union, with the bargaining for labor done by employees of the company elected by their fellows, but it was better than no bargaining machinery at all. When Swope talked to the worker representatives at Lynn, he found that they had been the leaders of the strike and were no longer bitter.

"I believed then and I believe now," he says, "that misunderstandings between men and management arise because there isn't any good way of discussing difficulties and grievances as they come up, that if you know what is in men's minds, the problem already is half solved and it is easier to come to an understanding."

However, when he proposed the Lynn plan to the workers in Schenectady, they turned it down.

Swope was more immediately successful in establishing a plan of representation for executives. It was called an Advisory Committee, which had existed for years, but he gave it new meaning. It now became a forum for the exchange and discussion of ideas concerning company policy and a channel through which his authority reached into the essential operations of every department. In 1922, it was composed of twenty-one chief officials of General Electric. Meeting once a month, it helped Swope fasten what Young called his grip upon the company and also gave an opportunity for what he himself called "frank discussion and understanding" of policies and details of company management. As chairman, he saw to it that each man got his say, but also that he kept strictly to the point. If a member were absent, Swope would "rattle off operating results with the same familiarity that the vice-president would have shown," one of them remembers, "and generally with fewer words." In the inevitable disputes he reserved to himself, of course, the final decision.

"I have thought from time to time," he wrote once, "that no question could arise on which there could not be differences of opinions, sometimes so diametrically opposed and evenly balanced that your executive must make the final decision."

Under this system, all lines of authority led to his office on the twentieth floor of 120 Broadway. They were held in his own hands, too, for he did not organize a personal staff with aides to act for him. He relied upon secretaries for details—"we were his memorandum book," one said—for protection against nonessential interruptions, for orderly presentation of papers which crossed his desk. For ten years before he came to the presidency of General Electric, this work had been done for him by Amy Marratt, a quick, efficient, tactful, self-effacing woman who obviously thought that the career of Gerard Swope was the only worthwhile interest life could hold. Rather above average height, with dark hair and eyes and very neat in her appearance, she was so much a part of his background that men and women who saw her every day were hard put to it to describe her, and rather surprised to remember that she had been quite nice looking.

Because she loyally liked work as much as he, she had handled all his secretarial needs up to now, but the president of General Electric has a more complicated office life than even a Miss Marratt can manage singlehanded. As her colleague, Swope recruited a young man, chosen primarily to be secretary on his travels, James Harris, who at twenty-one was fast, alert and accurate. He proved to be resilient enough to retain a sense of humor in spite of his intimate association with a mind he likened to a buzz saw. Thirty-four years later, after serving under three General Electric presidents, Harris remembered that almost the first thing Swope said to him was "I don't care what else you do, but don't waste my time."

Up to that moment Jim Harris had supposed the president of a big corporation drifted into the office about ten-thirty in the morning, read and dictated a few letters, held a couple of conferences before and after a leisurely lunch and left early for a round of golf. His disillusionment was complete. Swope was behind his desk at nine o'clock, "and if he didn't get his mail out of the way in the first half hour his day was spoiled." It was seldom spoiled. Any letter he dictated of more than six lines was almost an occasion. Any letter he received that ran to a second page went into a folder for week-end reading.

"Anyone who has something important to say, says it in less than a page," he informed Harris dogmatically.

The secretary never observed that he ever curbed his impatience or reminded himself to relax. He had a habit of pausing in his rapid dictation to refer to an instruction he had given perhaps fifteen minutes before and ask, "What's being done about that?"

Harris quickly learned not to reply that there hadn't been time to do anything. Instead he would say, "That's being taken care of outside."

"He would be satisfied with that," Harris adds, "but I went out and saw to it that the people outside damn well were taking care of it, because he'd be sure to ask again before eleven o'clock."

Deputize

"I feel very strongly," Swope once declared in elaborating his favorite motto, "that when you deputize with responsibility, you must see to it that there goes, with that responsibility, adequate authority."

The first essential in deputizing, of course, is a deputy. Swope's choices were so sudden and often so unorthodox that they seemed to be intuitive. Asked once how he judged the capacity of a man, he said, "Do you mean do I have a gimmick? No. I have a talk with him. I watch his face; I like a man with a frank, open look. And I make up my mind."

He was not without system. Once a year at promotion time he perused the records on everybody in the company who made $10,000 a year or more—"Two whole days it took us," says his secretary, who obviously thinks anything which required so much of Swope's time was a monumental task. It was popularly supposed that he did this because he didn't trust anyone else to decide salary raises. But it also served to keep him abreast of the abilities and work of men he seldom met.

After the event, of course, his choices seemed logical. Perhaps the one that startled company executives most was the appointment of William R. Burrows to head manufacturing. The job always had been held by a veteran of the big-apparatus business. Burrows, gruff and tough, with craggy features and a biting sense of humor, had come to the old Thomson-Houston Company as an apprentice, before General Electric was born, and had grown up in the lamp department. He had devised some of the machinery which made mass production of lamps at lower costs possible, but makers of the custom-built heavy equipment scoffed at the idea that such experience qualified him to deal with their products. Before long some who had raised their eyebrows the highest were admitting that Burrows was the best manufacturing man they ever knew. His outstanding quality? "He liked to work," says Swope.

When it came to picking a man for a labor-relations job, he was equally unorthodox. On his first visit to the Schenectady works, he met a turbine engineer, Charles E. Eveleth, who had the frank, open face Swope liked and was "full of imagination and charm," the ideal type to put the men in a mood to accept the Plan of Representation. Eveleth was appointed assistant manager at Schenectady (later manager); a workers' council was formed, and then similar plans were introduced at the other plants, too.

Just how much authority Swope gave along with responsibility has been a subject of dispute. Some complained that he told them not only what to do but how to do it. One man to whom he assigned a knotty sales problem quotes him as saying, "I want you to use your own judgment—work it out your own way. Here's a little book I wrote at Western Electric which may be helpful."

The little book was an account of a conference which Swope once conducted on this very subject.

The harshest remarks by any of Swope's former deputies are made by Ted Quinn, who writes:

"In all my years with the General Electric Company, Swope never *gave* anyone a free hand. He was the directing boss. When he failed to give orders it was only in those cases where he didn't know. . . . If Swope had had any idea at all, he would have insisted upon it, in my opinion."

On the other hand, Charlie Wilson thinks that Swope backed his men to the hilt.

"He always gave you a free hand once the decision had been

made," Wilson says. "In fact he insisted that his subordinates do the job themselves. He wasn't averse to needling a fellow along the way—he'd say, 'Make those engineers get the lead out of their pants' [the words sound like Wilson although the idea is very Swopian]—but once you had the green light, you could roll."

Wilson, however, warns the listener that his affection and admiration for Swope are so great that allowances should be made for anything he says. A more objective note is struck by Dr. Whitney, that same chemistry instructor of 1891, who now joined the General Electric Advisory Committee. He had founded the research department in 1901—some historians credit it with being the first professionally scientific one in American industry—at Rice's invitation, and it had achieved notable triumphs under his direction. Research and engineering had been Rice's major interests in the company, but Whitney says that Swope gave the laboratories even more support, although following scientific work in less detail. Furthermore, he never even hinted that there ought to be a practical result.

"The only thing he ever asked me was 'Have you got everything you need?' " Whitney says.

Finally, there is the testimony of Jim Harris, who, as a sort of guardian of the portals, says almost his hardest job was turning away company officials who were sure that if they could just have a few minutes with the big boss, he would make So-and-so change his ways.

"I never could convince 'em that Mr. Swope never would overrule a man to whom he'd assigned a job," says Harris, who had an unrivaled opportunity to know, "nor listen to details anyway."

Supervise

In Gerard Swope's vocabulary, this is a very active verb. He himself described it as measuring by as many yardsticks as possible the extent to which his goals were being achieved. Most of his standards were expressed in mathematical terms. He liked figures; they conveyed images to his mind which mathematical illiterates do not comprehend, but in the simplest forms his yardsticks were the amount of return on an investment, a percentage of cost or time reductions, the rise or fall of sales, calculations proving the worth of a design.

"In this work of supervision," he once added, "you must constantly be asking the questions."

One of the more irritating features of Swope as supervisor was the early hour at which he turned up to ask questions. It was not at all unusual for him to appear at a General Electric factory by eight in the morning. The workers, who had to punch a time clock, thought he was eccentric but keen. The managers, who could have slept an extra hour if Swope had not come to town, were, as one of them put it mildly, "a little annoyed." They found, too, that usually he knew the answers to his barrage of questions before he inquired. They did not know of the hours he spent studying to achieve this advantage, and they would have been surprised by the celerity with which he dismissed information from his mind. He was likely to call for a comprehensive report when he really wanted to know only a single item in it, which made a lot of extra work but, he thought, kept his people on their toes. He added to their uneasiness because, as Jim Harris put it, "he wanted everything done right away or maybe sooner."

On the other hand, plenty of executives liked the challenge. It was a pleasure for Charlie Wilson, he says, to watch the way Swope, thin-lipped and severe, could skim through a lengthy profit-and-loss statement, put his finger unerringly on the one weakness or mistake, and snap, "What happened here?"

"There was no use trying to fool him," Wilson adds admiringly. "If there was a clear explanation, okay. If not, just admit it was a mistake and promise to fix it, also okay. But you'd better be pretty sure you did fix it."

His liking for work was contagious, a good many of his aides have testified. "You didn't mind working so hard for him because he worked twice as hard" is the way Jim Harris remembers it.

So within a matter of months Gerard Swope worked a managerial revolution in the General Electric Company. It was a revolution in method of administration, fitting managerial techniques to the revolutionary machinery of production. There was very little that he had not devised or adapted in Western Electric. Much of it had been foreshadowed or urged by other men. His distinction was to put into effect in one of the biggest businesses in the country practices which only had been proposed in theory or used on a small scale.

In doing so he answered the questions which had been in the minds of his subordinates when he took office. But some larger questions remained—How well will these innovations work? Can a corporation as complex as General Electric be supple enough to keep pace with change? Will its hurrying president be fast enough on the turns to keep from skidding into the ditch? Will the company grow so strong that it dominates the whole industry?

X *A Hot Pot of Tea*

To an influential section of American public opinion, industrial management always is an object of suspicion. In the last analysis, leaders of this school observe, heads of large corporations are accountable only to themselves as long as they show a reasonable return on investment. They comprise a self-perpetuating dynasty, too, as they have the power, not to say duty, to select their successors, as Coffin selected Swope and Swope was to pick Wilson.

Stockholders, numbered now in the hundreds of thousands, have neither time nor ability to interfere in policy and are organized on serious issues only by rival managerial hopefuls. Directors in a company like General Electric are chosen more directly by management than by the stockholders who actually elect them. There is no public body with control over strictly administrative matters. So, it is argued, there are no checks on the essentially arbitrary authority of men in the seats of power. The fact that in these days they are employees—Henry Ford was the last owner-manager of a great corporation—is an added objection.

As is so often the case, there is less debate on what the facts are than on what they mean. Swope, for example, does not dispute them in this instance. He agrees that directors and stockholders provide no practicable curbs on management.

"Yes, management today does define its own responsibilities," he has said. "It depends on the personal factor of the president in each case. It depends on whether he is selfish and narrow or broad and has a sense of stewardship. It is a matter of free will. The president and management can take either of two courses. He or they have the freedom to choose how they will define their responsibilities."

The public interest in industrial facilities which produce most of our goods, then, is at the mercy of men over whom the public has no control, who are held in check only by their own consciences. Furthermore, it is said, the qualities which carry men most surely to the top of the industrial hierarchy are selfishness, narrow-mindedness and ruthlessness added to ability, rather than public spirit and generosity.

Swope says that the record does not bear this out, at least not recently. He holds that managers of large corporations have demonstrated as much intelligent concern for the general welfare as heads of smaller firms, or any other group in the population for that matter.

Both sides in this debate can point to notable examples. The obligation of industry, as Swope defines it, is to produce more and better goods for more people at relatively lower prices, while preserving for those who work in the industry and those who invest in it an adequate return for their contributions. His opponents accept this objective. But some of them think it would be attained more surely by men accountable to the public. Others would achieve it by replacing a few big corporations with a large number of small or middle-sized firms to sharpen competition.

Swope was less concerned with the theory of industrial economy than with its practice. Throughout his working life, the trend had been toward increasing size and hired managers. He was content to make his career under these conditions, and if he delved into the philosophy, it was to assert the value of continuity rather than argue about bigness. He once had a study made of corporate mortality, compiling figures on business organizations which had come and gone since the General Edison Company was founded in 1878.

"I was amazed at these figures myself," he said. "Twenty million companies have come into being, and almost the same number have disappeared."

Only twenty companies older than General Electric were still in existence, the chief ones being Du Pont, 1802; Western Union, 1851; Waltham Watch, 1854; Wanamaker, 1861; Pullman, 1867; Western Electric, 1869; and Singer Sewing Machine, 1873. The study seemed to him no argument for reverting to a larger number of smaller companies; he preferred stability. Nor did he agree that the figures were proof of little fellows being put out of business by bigger ones. A far more important factor in the longevity of a manufacturing enterprise, he thought, was the flexibility and ingenuity with which it could adapt old products or devise new ones to meet the changing needs of the market.

He was as well aware as any critic of the danger that efficiency might suffer as size increased. He devoted much time and attention to avoiding this peril. He also knew that for a company like General Electric, rectitude was not enough; it was important that the public be convinced of that rectitude.

In this, as in much else, he and Owen Young were an effective team. In his early days as general counsel, Young had been eager to win good will for the company through publicizing the man who had made it.

"Not in my time," Coffin rebuffed him firmly. "I won't have anything to do with it."

Young thinks Coffin's distaste for anything smacking of personal publicity had been intensified by some rather saccharine attempts to beatify Judge Elbert H. Gary after this paladin of

United States Steel had won a grimly reactionary reputation with his expressed belief that steel workers liked a twelve-hour day. Young had to settle for Coffin's consent to playing up Steinmetz as a General Electric genius. So the chairman was ready to fall in with Swope's ideas, to suggest some of his own and to personify the company before the nation so well that in General Electric offices it was said that he was "Mr. Outside" and Swope "Mr. Inside."

Both recognized that one good place to start a public-relations program was the twenty-eight thousand people who owned the company. An attitude of "treat 'em rough and tell 'em nothin' " had been adopted by most corporate managements toward stockholders. It was beginning to be felt that this was improper for stewards and shortsighted for salesmen. In October 1922, five months after they had taken office, Swope inaugurated a system of quarterly reports to shareholders signed by himself and Young. Between them, they cautiously expanded the amount of information in the annual report. Soon they included pictures! They were quick to see the value of quantity in stockholders. At a time when new ones usually were sought only if new stock had to be sold, they divided General Electric shares two for one to get the price from around $100 to $50 so more people could afford it.

For those of the shareowners who attended annual meetings, Young proved a delight. His easy, gracious manner was a perfect foil for Swope's brisk summary of the state of the company. It was almost impossible not to feel that with two such men in his employ, a stockholder had nothing to worry about. However, at every meeting there were a few hecklers. Swope seldom attempted to answer them, although sometimes irreverent aides noted gleefully that his neck grew red with anger. Young's courtesy never failed. He had a gift for the soft answer to an angry question and the sensible answer to a foolish one. When an owner arose with a paper which obviously contained a long list of objections and incautiously voiced a very complex one first, Young blandly asked his assistant to escort the gentleman to the files and get out the figures. By the time they got back, the meeting was over.

Swope's forte in this sort of game was being heckled by employees. When he appeared at their meetings, he welcomed questions, anonymous or otherwise. Before long, people knew he meant it, and very searching inquiries as to company practices and policies would be put. But they were never impolite, as a stockholder might be, and he took pride in having ready answers. He was such a good "communicator," as Young calls him, so brisk and informative, so obviously glad that you had asked him that one, that his hearers seldom noticed that sometimes his reply strayed from the point.

If stockholders and employees were a good nucleus for winning friends, the cultivation of the rest of the population was a major preoccupation of both top officers to an extent unknown among industrial leaders of their eminence up to then. With Swope this was a matter of sufficient moment that when a woman sitting next to him at a dinner one night gushed to him about how nice it was that a young man she knew was in charge of public relations at General Electric—he wrote press releases for one of the departments—Swope said earnestly, "I beg your pardon, but *I* am in charge of the General Electric Company's public relations."

The key to successful public relations is a good story to tell. Inefficient operations, faulty products, high or unfair prices, are sorry passports to popularity. Efficiency, therefore, was the goal Swope set. For all his agreement that modern management fixes its own authority, there were limits to his power and he regretted them. There is a hint of envy in his story of hearing Henry Ford tell how, having decided to shift from his ubiquitous Model T to a new Model A, he closed down all his plants for six weeks and spent $130,000,000 on new tools and equipment.

"I told him I admired his courage in doing it," Swope says. "We in big companies with many thousands of stockholders could not do it that way."

"I don't have that embarrassment," Ford replied. "I had the money to do it. I thought it was the right thing to do, and I did it, and enjoyed doing it."

Neither mentioned the hardships of 120,000 men thrown out of work for six weeks without any unemployment pay or the many thousands of Ford dealers whose incomes shrank alarmingly that year while they waited for a new model. Yet these by-products of the change-over could have been avoided if Ford had been able to listen to advice. His own son had advocated the more orderly and humane procedure of advance planning long before the father had reached his decision. But Swope was dazzled by the display of authority. When he talked about it, he ignored the unnecessary individual tragedies which it had caused.

Much as he might have relished Ford's freedom of action, others were glad then, as he was himself later, that he had to observe some restraint. He needed only months to make up his mind what he wanted to do with the company, but the doing took years, and was the better for not being hurried.

By the time a man is fifty, his basic ideas are pretty well set, and Swope's program for General Electric was implicit in all that he had done before. He still wanted to put the company's monogram "on everything electrical going into the American home," only now it would be GE, not WE. He wanted an organization that would grow as fast as the industry and last as long as Du Pont. He wanted better training for the men in that industry, and more security for them (and for their less skilled fellows) in every sense of the word. That meant to him a much bigger company, more tightly organized, more efficiently operated. Idle facilities, virtually autonomous operations, all activities which did not further the ultimate goal, would have to go.

The first step was the easiest. He eliminated all but fifteen lamp factories and concentrated their work, along with such "nuts and bolts" operations as that of Maspeth, in the largely idle Bridgeport plant. He restrained his impatience to do it all at once when Charlie Wilson offered, if given a year, to design and set up the machinery so as to treble production. Thanks to these changes, and to a general recovery from the depression, General Electric plants during 1923 employed thirteen thousand more workers than they had in 1922, and the average pay was 13 per cent higher.

The second step called for a little more finesse. Terry and Tremaine's "National" lamps were about half of the General Electric total in this field. "Edison" was the other half, and almost equally independent, but Swope brought the Edison department under his wing with no difficulty. Then, as one official described it, "he infiltrated and surrounded" the little empire of Terry and Tremaine. Thirteen months after he came in as president, the team was broken up. Tremaine, a great hand with a balance sheet, was elevated to the Board of Directors, and Terry, a wonderful manager of men, was placed in charge of the consolidated lamp department as a vice-president.

The third step was delicate, for it involved a basic policy disagreement with Coffin, one of whose brilliant strokes had been the formation in 1905 of a subsidiary to finance new power companies, primarily in small communities where it was especially hard to sell stock. The aim, of course, was to create customers for General Electric apparatus, and in doing so the offshoot, the Electric Bond and Share Company, had become an exceedingly profitable holding and management concern with a large voice in the nation's utilities. By 1923, Swope decided that it was bad business and hardly ethical "to own our own customers and be in two businesses at the same time," as he bluntly expressed it.

Young agreed, and added that it probably was illegal, too. At this time, halfway through Harding's term, few worried about anti-trust action from a government so friendly to business that its enemies called it sycophantic. But Young, like Swope, was a Democrat, and his previous experience of the Sherman Act had made him suspicious of such Republicanism as was represented in the administration.

He now told Swope in detail about the situation he found when he came to General Electric in the beginning of 1913. Some months earlier, as the presidential campaign of 1912 opened, Taft's Attorney General, a pillar of corporation law and political conservatism, George W. Wickersham, brought an anti-trust suit against the company. Only a year before, General Electric had accepted a court decree to abolish Terry and Tremaine's National

Electric Lamp Association, within which, the government complained, the fact of a single ownership of many brands was concealed. Wickersham now charged that this agreement was not being carried out, and he went so far as to institute a criminal rather than a civil prosecution.

The consternation among directors was pitiful. Hitherto the Department of Justice had handled these things in a gentlemanly way. Criminal prosecutions under the anti-trust laws usually were reserved for labor leaders. Meantime, the election had taken place, and a horrid radical, a wild man from Princeton, Woodrow Wilson, would be inaugurated in a few weeks. If General Electric directors could be indicted by their friends, what was going to happen when their enemies took office? Young felt genuinely sorry for men as scared as this and decided to try to learn the new administration's intentions. He obtained an interview with the President-elect, put the case frankly before him, and never forgot the resulting lesson in political science.

"Your directors are frightened," the ex-professor told him, "because they do not understand that a progressive administration is the only one that can be fair to business. A reactionary administration never can be. Before an election they will make some demonstration such as this one because they know they have incurred suspicion and they wish to show that they are not dominated by business. A progressive administration can be fair because it is under no such suspicion."

In 1913 Young had thought the company wrong to conceal its ownership of a score or more of ostensibly competing lamp companies, although not criminally so, as Wickersham had contended. At his recommendation, the concealment was completely abandoned, and the directors were able to sleep nights.

In 1923, Young said, the situation was similar except that there was no progressive administration in sight. This was an added argument for Swope's position, but he hardly needed it, because when he made the best case he could of the relationship between the parent and the subsidiary, it sounded hollow. In answers to questions, he had pointed out that Electric Bond and Share owned no more than 5 per cent of utility stocks and bonds, and besides, he would add wryly, it is often more difficult to sell someone in the family than a stranger.

Of course, ownership and control are not the same thing in the corporate lexicon. Young has pointed out that the 5 per cent ownership enabled General Electric to control about 60 per cent of American utilities. That was a mark of the subsidiary's success, and it always is difficult to argue with success. Furthermore, Coffin had originated Electric Bond and Share himself and had a founder's fondness for his brainchild. Swope found himself in the position of wanting to give someone else's baby out for adoption over the parent's anguished protest, a baby valued on the books, which means very conservatively, at $25,000,000.

Coffin was on the spot to object. He kept office hours almost as regular as those of the active head of the company. He dropped in on the new president to chat about current business or his garden or a book he had read until Jim Harris was amazed by Swope's patience. Actually Swope did not resent the older man's intrusions. He liked a martinet—he was one himself—and his deference to Coffin was sincere, but not to the point of obedience. Someone once asked him who had given him the most trouble in all his years at General Electric, and he replied in some surprise that he never had any trouble with anyone. What about Coffin in the Electric Bond and Share matter?

"Why, I never had the least trouble with Mr. Coffin," he objected, and paused. "Oh, if you mean that he came into my office one day and said, 'Swope, you can't do this,' and another day, 'Swope, you must be crazy,' why, of course, that happened. But there never was any *trouble*. I had decided to dispose of the Electric Bond and Share Company, and I did."

Obviously if anyone had trouble, it was others who had it with Swope. In this case Coffin eventually was reconciled to the inevitable; the stock of Electric Bond and Share was distributed to General Electric shareholders as a sort of bonus, and the big utilities financing firm was on its own.

The incident eradicated the last bit of doubt among General

Electric officials as to where authority now lay. Even Edison, who at seventy-five was the grand old man of the electrical industry, seemed to notice an aura of command when he encountered the new president in 1922. The benevolent "wizard" chatted amiably for a time and then, with a quizzical look, remarked, "Well, you have the nose for the job."

Edison didn't know it, but Swope had acquired a reputation for poking that nose into every corner of General Electric operations. He irritated a great many subordinates who were used to being let alone. They saw the dynamo at work and some of them were a little scared of getting their fingers caught; only later did many of them appreciate the power which had been generated. Swope's routine had for these people the fascination of fast-moving, unfamiliar machinery; the sight of the wheels going round was so absorbing, the watcher sometimes forgot what the machine was doing. Thomas Logan, the advertising man with the facile pen and dull voice, thought Swope was getting rid of "the fine old crinoline standards" of the whole industry and irritating competitors who "long for the good old days when an executive could take a nap in the afternoon." Logan added, "It took some of the older boys quite a while to realize that when Mr. Swope mentioned the neck of the bottle, he was not asking all hands to have a drink but was referring to a production problem."

Hardly anyone got used to his precise use of time. He set up two-, three- and five-minute appointments, and his subordinates learned that he really meant it. Miss Marratt saw to it that everyone came for these interviews on the dot; an appointment scheduled for three minutes lasted exactly one hundred eighty seconds, so she always had the next man on hand. In Swope's neat but never very elaborately furnished office—his one luxury was a working fireplace—the visitor would find the president with a folder before him and a few penciled notes. "Some of us would have given a lot to get a peek at those notes," says Chester Lang, who saw many of them at a distance on his way up to a vice-presidency. The folder would have been taken out of a right-hand desk drawer, where Miss Marratt and Jim Harris arranged a pile of them in the order of the day's appointments. After a courteous greeting, the visitor would be regaled with a terse, rapid flow of advice or suggestion or order. Then, five or six seconds before the time allotted for this interview had expired, the folder would be closed and on its way to a left-hand desk drawer while a crisp voice inquired forbiddingly, "Is there anything more you want to discuss?"

Sensible men were on their feet as he spoke—that is, assuming they had bothered to take a chair. One department head remembers that he never sat down, not so much because he was awed but because he knew he wouldn't be there long enough to make it worth while. So their answer invariably was "No," even if they had gone in with every intention of speaking about what they thought was an important subject. Harris used to hear their colleagues ask them if this time they really had done it.

"Well," a typical reply would run, "just as I was about to tell him, I found myself outside with my hat on."

"He was a hot pot of tea, all right," says Harris admiringly.

Swope's idea of brevity as the soul of business became a habit. Thirty years later his notion of the time which should be allowed to this sort of thing was brought home to a younger man who had telephoned for an appointment, explaining that he had an engagement some dozen blocks away at eleven.

"Glad to see you," Swope assured him cordially. "Come along from your appointment, say eleven-fifteen."

"But my appointment is for eleven," the other repeated.

"That's what I thought you said," Swope explained mildly. "Five minutes for your appointment, ten minutes to walk over here, eleven-fifteen."

"Well," was the doubtful reply, "I'm not sure I can get through with this fellow in five minutes."

"Oh, I'm sorry," Swope apologized. "I assumed it was business."

Charlie Wilson, to whom this story was repeated, whooped with pleasure—he is a man who can take a minute or let it alone.

"Ha!" he exclaimed, beaming. "Mr. Swope hasn't changed a bit." He paused, then added reflectively, "You know, I think I was Executive Vice-President before I ever got five minutes."

But he hastened to explain that if a fellow really had a lot on his mind, and it really was important, Swope would give hours, all day if necessary. But not in the midst of a lot of other appointments. Requests for time to explain in detail would be met with. "Very well, be at my house at nine on Saturday."

It would not have been politic, Wilson says, to mention a golf date, but in his study Swope would listen, ask searching questions, perhaps continue after lunch and then—this was the best thing about it—reach his decision then and there. "Go ahead" or "Forget it" were the alternatives, never "Let me sleep on it" or "I'll let you know on Monday."

The house to which such pilgrimages were made was one which Swope's new position made possible, and it was a symbol of independence, too. The president of the General Electric Company is bound to become a rich man—not that the salary and "extra compensation" ever were up to Clarence Dillon's Goodyear offer—and would be able to afford, even ought to have, an estate in the country.

Swope's salary ranged from a low of $69,000 at the depth of the depression to $110,000. The extra compensation varied (none at all in the early thirties); the first year of published figures, 1936, his total was $146,500. At the time, he and Young, who always received the same amount, were forty-seventh and forty-eighth from the top of all salaried people in the country. The number one spot then went to Alfred Sloan with $561,311 and, altogether, nine General Motors officers were paid more than Swope, as were ten entertainers, a variety of industrialists and financiers, even one editor and one writer, both Hearst employees.

In 1922 Coffin suggested that Swope buy on Long Island, where Coffin himself and a good many other company executives then lived. Swope replied politely that he preferred a place away from his associates; he wanted to invite them to break in on his week end, not have them drop by casually because they were neighbors. So he selected Westchester, and left the rest to Mary.

She found a very pleasant English-style country house, The Croft, with one hundred ten acres of woods and garden, a lake big enough for boating, and trails linked with those of other estates to offer many miles of unmotorized riding for the horseman. As the years passed, they increased their property by nearly three hundred acres more, another lake and a dozen or so other houses for their children or staff or to rent, and for a time there was a substantial farming operation.

The family was augmented frequently by long visits from Mary's sisters and, until her death in the summer of 1925, Gerard's mother, "Grossie" to the children and less a stickler for punctuality with them than she had been with her own. They received more of Swope's thought than of his time. His trips, his frequent Saturdays of conferences in his study and evenings of paper work separated him from his children even before they went off to school and college. But when he was with them, there was no shop talk. The household never heard him speak of the General Electric Company or its problems.

Gerard did draw up regulations for their behavior, very much like those he had established for Herbert in the eighties. But these were administered, except for corporal punishment, by Mary. Discipline was strict, but enforced more by the force of the father's personality than of his hand. Spankings were incurred for only two offenses, lying and eating Aunt Sal's wonderful fruitcake (very rich in brandy, it was), nor was there any appeal from such penalties to the higher court.

"That is your father's department," Mary would explain.

Actually the success of Gerard's system was due to her administration of it rather more than any intrinsic merit in the rules—one has the feeling that she would have made a success of her family by any set of regulations, or none.

Of even greater importance were the pleasures of living, whether at The Croft or a large duplex apartment in the city, which had nothing to do with rules. They all have remembered that their own personalities and careers were sacrosanct. Neither Mary nor Gerard ever tried to influence them; if they wanted to go to college, well and good; they selected their own institutions and their own subjects. If they didn't want to go to college, that was all right, too. There was no more praise for Isaac when he chose M.I.T. than for Gerard, Jr., when he selected Dartmouth and Harvard Law, or for David when he decided against college altogether.

Their father's prescription for rearing the young, therefore, is of more interest for the light it sheds on his attitude toward life in general than as a handbook for parents; he once took the trouble to commit it to paper.

"In bringing up the children," he wrote, "I believed in these fundamentals:

"HEALTH—ABILITY (methods of work)—CHARACTER

"I encouraged exercise and athletics—riding the pony, swimming—later boating, training them in running and in competition with each other, wrestling with me and standing up to each other. I encouraged them in their work always to finish everything they started. Corporal punishment was meted out for only one offense —*lying*. [They remembered Aunt Sal's fruitcake better than he.] I used to say, if the children had *ability* we could thank God, but as to *health* and *character* we could contribute something. Later on they were given an allowance with specifications of what the allowance should cover. Still later on an irrevocable trust was established with the Bankers Trust Company in New York. The capital of the trust could not be touched by them, but the income was theirs to do with as they liked, but it had to suffice for their needs as to: 1) food, 2) shelter, 3) clothing, 4) education, 5) traveling, and 6) pleasure. Each January each child made a budget for the coming year, and at the end of the year, the actual expenditures were compared with the estimate. Any savings were then invested in their own name, and then the income and the principal belonged to the child without limitation. Not one of the children ever spent more than their income, but when they wanted to make a larger expenditure than usual, they would come and talk it over, and if approved, I would advance the money, which was to be repaid, and in every instance this was done, and with the further agreement that no loans or debts would be made with anyone but me.

"Indeed their savings and investments thereof constituted in each case a very sizable fund."

The onerous features of these domestic rules were complained about with more or less fervor at the time, depending upon the temperament of the complainer. But this feeling faded so completely that each of the sons adopted them with only slight modifications for his own children.

Just as his family never heard him mention business, so most of Swope's associates knew almost nothing of his private life. Some who were close to him in the office never heard of his interest in settlements and playgrounds, in music and drama, nor anything much about his family background. At least one of them took it for granted that his parents had been wealthy, stating positively that "only a rich man's son would have that much thrift without being greedy." Another supposed that he seldom read a book or saw a show because he did not digress in business discussions to say that he was reminded of what some author said or of a scene he had enjoyed.

It was a quirk of this methodical, impatient man that he never drove a car. Some of his friends thought he knew he would be a menace on the road. As a pedestrian he never took any notice of wheeled traffic or red lights, and it was not supposed he would deign to change his habits if he sat behind a wheel. He himself offers another explanation. At Hull House, he had spent a lot of time fixing everybody's bicycle because he was an engineer. When his friends began to buy automobiles, he decided he wouldn't expose himself to such tasks any more. If he didn't learn enough about a gasoline buggy even to drive the thing, no one would ask him to make repairs.

This version is typical of the way in which he had stripped his routine of living, at home and at the office, to what he deemed the bare essentials. And, in fact, there was no time to lose if General Electric was to consolidate its position in the electrical world and move ahead to the leadership which he envisioned. He had achieved a great deal in the way of internal reorganization in a matter of months, but the effects were not yet obvious to outsiders. Keen observers in the industry expected him, on the basis of his reputation, to do great things with the company—what and how they did not say. As early as July 1922 a writer in one of the trade papers summed up the question in a great many minds when he asked, "How soon will Swope call out this muscle-bound Hercules and start the setting-up exercises?"

XI *Men and Motives*

"Any woman who does anything electricity can do for her is working for a few cents a day."

A series of advertisements on this theme in 1923 for Bruce Barton's new account served notice that policy was changing at General Electric. But Swope's plan to put the GE monogram on every electrical appliance the housewife used did not begin to mature for two years more. For all his impatience, he wanted to be sure he started out with a sales leader, a basic feature of the home of the future. The interval would give him time to develop a new system of distribution, since an organization which sold heavy machinery to industry and electric-light bulbs to dealers was hardly geared for selling to individual families.

To select the first item, he ordered one of his careful market studies. This indicated that the most likely leader in the appliance field would be an electric refrigerator, although when he began his survey in 1922 there were no more than forty-six thousand home refrigerators in the country. Several makes were available, and by 1924, while ice wagons were still a feature of city traffic and icemen standard characters in off-color jokes, new apartment houses were being equipped with mechanical refrigerators. General Electric was far enough behind the procession that Swope wanted something more than another box indistinguishable from its competitors.

He learned that the company had owned for years a patent on just what he was looking for—the delay in developing it was later pointed to as one of the dangers of letting a big, successful corporation fool around with products outside the main scope of its interests. This particular patent, covering hermetically sealed working parts for a refrigerator, had been taken out some twenty years earlier by a mechanically inclined French monk, the Abbé Audiffren. The obvious sales talk was that it never could get out of order. The obvious manufacturing problem was to make a machine that would justify the sales talk.

The company had experimented with the Audiffren principle for several years, but not until Swope demanded that it be put on a mass-production basis were the mechanical difficulties approached in earnest. Then one of Dr. Whitney's inventive geniuses corrected the flaws in a motor which was sealed against repairmen and the curiosity of its owner. The designers were so proud of it that they put it on top of the box in the early models, making a GE refrigerator easily distinguishable and getting in the housewife's way.

Swope's role in this development was typical of his relationship with the scientists in his company. As an engineer turned businessman, he displayed greater interest than knowledge. Rice never let his presidential duties interfere with his concern for what the men in Dr. Whitney's laboratories were doing. But then Rice was a better engineer than Swope and had assumed fewer executive responsibilities. Swope never failed to visit the laboratories when he was in Schenectady, which was often. But at the time of his earliest trips the talk of Steinmetz (who died in 1923 before Swope got to know him well) or Alexanderson or Coolidge already was beyond the grasp of an engineer who had done little technical reading since the nineties. The literature on electrical science was so vast that no one with nonscientific work to do could keep up with it, and reading was not enough anyway.

"As soon as a man loses his daily intimate contacts with the men doing the actual work in the laboratories, they get beyond him," says Whitney, "no matter how much he reads. As president of the company, Gerard would give us problems to solve but he could hardly follow the steps by which we did it. He was even more interested in the problems we set ourselves, but essentially as a layman. The big thing was that he appreciated to the full that a big industrial company like General Electric could not progress without very extensive research. He was a good listener when Christian Steenstrup explained what he had done to make the sealed motor a practical matter, but I doubt that he understood it thoroughly."

As the man to merchandise this first in a long line of GE household appliances, Swope selected the redheaded Cleveland lamp salesman, Ted Quinn, who had told him he worked for National Lamp, not General Electric. It was 1925 before the refrigerator was in mass production, and a nation-wide network of distributors recruited and indoctrinated for their task, but at last Swope had a product for his twenty-five million customers.

Diversity brought with it new threats to efficiency. Swope, however, looked upon the tendency of large, complex institutions to become cumbersome as a challenge to his organizing talents rather than as a reason for fragmentation.

"Much is sometimes made of the advantages of small organizations," he said, "with the implication that a large company cannot have them. That is not true. We can have them. . . . I think we tend to dwell too much on the advantages of small concerns and the disadvantages of large ones without taking effective steps to minimize our disadvantages and play up our advantages."

The chief disadvantage was the relatively high overhead, especially supervisory and clerical costs, necessary, he once informed a questioner, "because as human beings we do our work mighty poorly." He used to contrast the expenses of General Electric with those of a small competitor doing a business of about a million dollars a year. The main differences in the way the two companies spent each dollar they took in were in profits and salaries. General Electric, in these early 1920s, paid 41.7 cents of every dollar for wages and salaries; the small competitor, 36.2 cents. General Electric put 8.7 cents into dividends or surplus; the small competitor had 12 cents for these purposes. Many such small firms, therefore, had a couple of cents to knock off the price of their products and were operating at full speed, he observed, while the large General Electric shops were working well below capacity.

It became, therefore, a major administrative problem to enable General Electric to make the most of the advantages of size, which Swope listed as continuity, stability and the strength to absorb losses on a new or changing product that would bankrupt a smaller concern. Of course, it is argued that this strength of big corporations bankrupts smaller competitors sometimes. But Swope retorted that this was irrelevant so far as the public was concerned, and of the large corporation he said, "It can give service through continuing to produce and distribute some lines at a loss, and make up those losses through its other lines of business."

As was his custom, he tossed in figures to support his contention. At the time he spoke the company had eighty lines, and in a typical "bad" year thirty-eight of them were losers, each for a relatively small amount, while the others made up for them threefold. In a typical "good" year, only half as many were losers—but still nearly one quarter of the whole—and the losses half as much, while the profits made up for these tenfold.

"Not many companies can do that," he said proudly. "Diversification helps to make this result possible year after year."

To his way of thinking, the public, the workers and the industry are all better off when losses can be absorbed in this way rather than by eighty separate companies. If there had to be a company for each line, either one fourth of them would go broke even in good times or they would have to charge higher prices. True, the others might be able to charge somewhat lower prices, but not very much because total profit represents a small fraction of sales price, in the electrical industry especially.

Only if the eighty separate companies were managed more efficiently than the one would there be any likelihood of avoiding the losses or the higher prices. Swope, therefore, not only preached the gospel of efficiency but tried out some practical devices for achieving it.

One of his earliest was to open to the whole company a highly successful institution which Terry and Tremaine had originated for their lamp executives. For fifteen years they had been holding "summer camps" on an island in Lake Ontario near its junction with the St. Lawrence River. Since they bought the sixty-five acres and named it "Association Island" after their National Electric Lamp Association, gradual improvements had been made, but campers lived in tents and roughed it. The men who came there for a few days at a time were not expected to spend all of it in play. They discussed business problems on an informal basis—"adult education disguised as a picnic," someone called it.

Such gatherings helped overcome the difficulty, inherent in all large organizations, of knowing what other people are doing. In the prearranged as well as the spontaneous sessions, salesmen, executives and technicians who, in the normal course of their work, never saw each other, exchanged ideas and anecdotes. Swope added five other camps to the one for lamp people, one each for the major departments of engineering, manufacturing, commercial work and merchandising, and a general camp for men drawn from all departments.

He himself attended whenever he could. It was a good place to spot promising human material, and even better as a forum for presenting his own ideas. But chiefly it gave the men from scattered offices and factories an acquaintance with each other and the work of the whole company which comes in smaller firms from the normal day-to-day association.

On the island and at General Electric meetings elsewhere, Swope developed his own special brand of eloquence. He would give a short summary of what he considered important company operations. This would be replete with figures, for he never lost his illusion that this most precise language is as intelligible to others as it is to him. Then he would ask for questions. He took them from the floor or from written slips sent in ahead of time, anonymous or signed. His replies, an extemporaneous virtuoso exhibition covering the industry in general and General Electric in particular, were regarded by nearly everyone as the high light of any session.

In rapid, animated but often incomplete sentences he would explain policy or practice on prices, plant conversion, research, selling, advertising, labor, salaries, bonuses, vacations, new products—anything. If he had "crammed" for the examination the night before, it was not apparent. Men who elsewhere regarded him as cold, reserved, the nearest thing to an inhuman machine of which flesh and blood is capable, have borne testimony to his warmth and sparkle in these appearances. His pleasure when a verbal exchange with some anonymous workman in the audience ended with the man's withdrawing a charge of injustice was infectious. Sometimes he flatly denied a bit of unfair treatment, only to find out that it was true. Then he took pains to correct the situation; he did not waste time informing the same audience of his error.

"There wasn't any question about his sincerity in wanting to give you the facts, all the facts and nothing but the facts about the company," one of these listeners has commented. "It was like watching a machine come to life. You felt that he was having a high old time for himself, for there wasn't a bit of hypocrisy about him. He would have scorned to waste the time hypocrisy requires."

Swope keenly enjoyed pitting his prodigious memory and the quickness of his perceptions against all comers. But he never forgot himself in the contest so much that he lost sight of his aim —to increase his men's understanding of the company.

Along with an innocent vanity in his verbal facility went a

realization that this game of trying to stump the president was a valuable administrative device. It sharpened wits which might have rusted if their owners had thought that in such a large organization brilliance might go unobserved. Here was an opportunity to show how clever they were or offer suggestions and impress the big boss—if they were careful.

"A lot of fellows were sorry later that they'd asked smart-aleck questions," says Wilson.

Wilson was only one among many who found it exciting to indulge in this give-and-take with their president, unheard of in their experience. The way the man rattled off figures and percentages was a major factor in his rapidly growing reputation for knowing more about any phase of the business than the men who worked in it. Gordon Campbell, whom he had brought over from Western Electric and who knew him better than almost anyone else in General Electric at this time, used to tell aspirants for jobs: "If you do come to work for the company, and Mr. Swope ever asks you what you think of anything, you tell him just what you think because he'll usually know the answer before he asks. If you tell him what you think he wants, he'll drop you."

And a veteran of the Coffin regime who found that Swope took some getting used to told a newcomer: "I've been around longer than you have and I'll give you some advice. If Swope ever asks you something and you don't know—say 'I don't know but will look it up.' Never guess. I did. I guessed one day. Three months later he came to me and told me I had told him the wrong figure."

With stories like this going around, there soon was very little temptation to try to fool him about a fact, a situation or an individual. He got the kind of figure-filled, accurate reports he liked. More important, he got more careful and conscientious work from his subordinates than they might have given another, even someone they liked better. He didn't know all the answers, of course, but no one in the company ever found out just where the limits of his knowledge ran.

Some of his ablest aides never did work out to their own satisfaction just what made them struggle so to win his approval. It wasn't for praise; they agree that he seldom offered any. It wasn't for money; General Electric was not noted for extravagant salaries. It wasn't that they were afraid for their jobs; most of them could have got better-paying ones elsewhere. It wasn't that he exalted them by inspirational leadership; they thought him too cold and precise.

Some of them suggest it was the contagion of his conviction that a man's business is worth his last ounce of energy and brains. Others think that his ardent desire to excel roused their competitive spirit and drove them on to show him they were as tough as he. Still others say it was the force of example, their knowledge that no matter how hard they worked, he worked harder. A few admit frankly they were just scared, not of being fired but of his displeasure.

Dr. Whitney, his old teacher, gives a more scientific explanation. Swope filled men with wonder because he could pull desired data out of his mind at will. Now the brain, says Whitney, is simply a fine recording device which begins to accumulate its impressions at birth. As the stored records pile up, it is increasingly difficult to find anything.

"Gerard," he concludes, "has a fine filing system in his head."

For all his insistence upon intense concentration on business, Swope knew that the electrical industry did not exist in a vacuum. When he had some really hot inside information on general conditions, national or international, he would impart it at employee meetings—his impressions of a visiting British Labor delegation, unpublished figures on world trade, the results of a new economic survey, a letter from a friend on the spot who had a novel explanation of a political situation. When Young served early in 1924 on the Dawes Committee of experts who were trying to find a way out of the impasse of German reparations, Swope told his audiences about the splendid contribution their chairman was making to world stability.

Young was the leading figure in the Committee, appointed during one of the most difficult postwar crises after France had marched troops into the Ruhr to hold that industrial heart of

Germany hostage for payments due. The Germans responded with passive resistance, demonstrating that bayonets are the least effective of mining tools. One of the chief aims of the Committee was to get the French troops out. The only deal acceptable to all was based on a loan which would have to be floated in the United States, and Young asked Swope to sound out "anybody whose advice you may think helpful" on the terms American financiers would impose. Within two days, Swope met half a dozen leading international bankers for a joint discussion—Thomas W. Lamont of Morgan's was the one he most admired—and had individual interviews with Clarence Dillon and his old Chicago friend, Charlie Mitchell, now president of the National City Bank.

"Very complete and exactly what I wanted," Young wrote gratefully of Swope's summary of their remarks.

The so-called Dawes Plan was hailed a few weeks later as solving the world's knottiest problem—"even the farmers of Westchester County think you have done a wonderful piece of work," Swope radioed to his friend. (Actually it only postponed bankruptcy, if it did that, but at least the French went home.) It was the subject of one of those rapid-fire summaries at a General Electric meeting. It marked the beginning of a long period of notable public service by Young, of which Swope was as proud as if he had done it himself. Young was thinking of this period when he said years later, "There never was the slightest jealousy between us. I think that with almost any other men this would not have been so. He might very well have been a little piqued at one time when I was getting a great deal of publicity, but on the contrary, he was genuinely pleased. I might have been a bit jealous of the way in which all the men in the company looked to him as the executive head, but I never wanted to be."

The habit of looking to Swope as chief did not stem entirely from his speeches, his organization of camps and new lines of manufacture, his improved distribution methods, his forceful, driving personality. A big factor was his active concern for the security of everyone who worked for the General Electric Company. He wanted them all, from the porter to the president, to have savings, life and health insurance, a chance to own their homes, protection from unemployment. Blind admirers, judicious appraisers of his role in industry, bitter critics of his policies and methods, men he promoted and men he fired, agree on this: Swope's employee benefits programs were not only a service to the thousands directly affected but a salutary lesson to industry in general. Within the company, these programs cemented a loyalty to him and the organization among many who might not have felt so warmly about "the most machinelike person I ever knew," as he was called by one who deplored almost everything else he ever did.

"Swope's greatest contribution was in teaching industry how to treat people," says Dr. Whitney.

In Young he had an enthusiastic collaborator, and he needed one. The ideas he advocated were common talk among his old friends from Hull House, but most leaders of finance and industry, including some who sat on the General Electric Board of Directors, regarded them with dark suspicion. Young, like Swope, had been influenced by people who were not the usual associates of business executives. Both were regarded by otherwise admiring colleagues as tinged with a dangerous radicalism.

"Perhaps," Young once wrote in cheerful retrospect, "you and Mary were discolored a little by your rather intimate contact with Jane Addams of Hull House and Lillian D. Wald of Henry Street. Perhaps I had gained a little understanding of color from Ida Tarbell and Lincoln Steffens. I mention them not as excuses for our behavior but in gratitude for their help to us both."

Wherever they had got their notions, both were going around in the early 1920s asking people, in preparation for an improved pension plan, what was the most useful age of man. Whitney remembers that he stubbornly refused to say. He wanted to know what man they were talking about. But his former pupil was not relying upon casual questions. In his first year as president, Swope assigned the general auditor and an eager youngster, who later would be the company's secretary, to survey employee benefits generally and submit recommendations. On the basis of this and other studies, he reached the conclusion that on the average men were at their peak at thirty-two and down to about half their best productivity at sixty-five.

"So let's take half away from the old fellow and give it to the young one," he told Whitney. "If we retire the older men at half pay, we make not only their pay but their places available to the young."

Before these studies were completed, Swope had moved on homes and savings. The first was fairly simple; he put the company's guarantee behind a second mortgage, and 2,760 employees took up the offer in building or buying houses in the next few years.

For a savings program, he reviewed the history of one which Young had tried in 1920 with Coffin's approval—allowing employees to buy stock through pay-roll deductions. When the stock went down in a bad year, many, through fear or need, sold at a loss or canceled their subscriptions. When it rose, most of the rest grabbed a quick profit. It didn't strike Swope as a sound savings plan. In 1923, he presented to the employees a prospectus drafted by himself for a General Electric Employees Securities Corporation, an investment trust. The company owned the capital stock and took the risk of market fluctuations. The employees subscribed for bonds, up to a maximum of $500 a year each, since the plan was meant for those in the middle and lower salary brackets. Thirty thousand invested; the corporation became one of the largest investment trusts in the world, and the biggest single owner of General Electric stock.

Swope made a few false starts in his proposals for life insurance. A great believer in it himself, he assumed that all men would grasp eagerly at the opportunity to acquire some. Young had helped institute a system of free coverage up to a modest amount for all employees after a certain length of service. Swope thought help in getting larger policies was better than a gift of small ones—"things should be done *with* people, not *for* them," he explained. So he announced that free insurance would go only to new employees who took out some for themselves. It was a flat failure.

"I was surprised," he admitted, "to find that new employees said to themselves that they weren't going to die or weren't going to stay with this company all their lives, and so did not take the insurance."

He applied pressure, and at the same time modified the plan. The insurance was offered to employees of forty-five or younger after five years' service, along with a message from the president that the company wanted men who recognized their obligation to their families and society. This hint plus the attraction of limiting the offer did the trick. General Electric had twenty-one thousand employees in this age and service bracket, and every one of them joined the insurance plan. Then it was opened to older men, and 85 per cent of them signed up, too. Swope limited it to men because he doubted that the sixteen thousand women the company then employed would consent to pay-roll deductions for this purpose.

"Frankly," he confessed, "our theory had been that women did not recognize the responsibilities of life, for they probably were hoping to get married soon and leave the company."

He couldn't have been more mistaken. When they got the chance, nearly twelve thousand of them took out the insurance.

He made one more wrong judgment of employee reactions when he tried to win adoption of an unemployment insurance plan which he worked out in the belief that sensible people fortify themselves in good times against the hazards of bad. By 1925 employment and wages were at an all-time high in General Electric plants. He proposed, therefore, that the workers and the company together build up a fund from which men who might be laid off in any future slump could draw up to half their normal earnings. A factory pay-roll deduction of 1 per cent of wages would be matched by the company, and the fund would be administered by a board drawn equally from representatives of workers and management. The fund might provide emergency loans as well as unemployment benefits. If unemployment in the plants grew beyond the limits of the fund, the 1 per cent contribution and matching company payments would be extended to the clerical and executive personnel, all the way up to the president and chairman.

It was something new in security for the employees of a large corporation, and the men were suspicious of it. In one plant after another they turned it down by very substantial majorities.

"They said business was good and this was just another scheme to deduct something from their wages," Swope wrote regretfully.

Disappointed as he was—ever since Hull House he had known that benefits for the jobless were a sound idea—he turned to other security measures and was consoled for the unexpected failure of his unemployment insurance program by the equally unexpected success of a pension plan. He thought the men would need a great deal of education before they consented to a pay-roll deduction for it—he proposed 1½ per cent of earnings. But when he put it up to them, a large majority voted for it right away, and on the decisive test only one man held out against it while seven thousand who were not eligible asked to be taken in.

The universal practice up to this time was that, if pensions were provided, they were a gift from the company. Their purpose was the very practical one of keeping useful men. General Electric had had such a program since 1912. But Swope was keen for an employee contribution, arguing, "When a man dies or retires and his family is in want, and he has been associated with you, if you take the corporation's assets to alleviate suffering, it may be a good deed, but it is unfair to the stockholders and his associates in office or factory."

Retiring the old men is a fine way to clear the road for youth. But a problem in any organization, increasing in complexity with size, is how to find the young men who should be pushed ahead. Swope spotted some in his rounds of factories and offices or at the island camps. He instituted a systematic search for more by ordering every officer of the company to submit to him the names of promising young men. This "PYM List" reposed in his desk drawer, and he drew it out to ask about their progress and be sure he met them on his travels. He was jealous of their careers, too. In his own retirement he was asked if he wasn't proud of men who, trained in General Electric, went on to make their marks in other companies. His highly selective memory had rejected the idea that men as good as all that ever left. He couldn't remember a single one.

For all their appreciation of Swope's character and abilities, the men who rose to high positions in General Electric felt for him more admiration than affection. Many of them called Young "Owen"; the president was always "Mr. Swope." Both men were born to a generation which used first names sparingly, especially by a younger man to an elder. But it was much easier to warm up to the chairman, if only because of that quality in Swope which his friend has described as "a spring under tension always, never spent and never relaxed." More apprehensive officials in the company, noting the man's ceaseless activity and razor keenness, thought that being around him was like working with a buzz saw.

"You can't get cozy with a buzz saw," one explained.

The rank and file of workers, however, continued to regard Swope with favor unmixed with fear. Take the matter of health. He never was sick himself, or wouldn't admit it if he was. Jim Harris remembers with mock terror the day Swope had a cold, and thinks the only day's work he ever missed was once when he was thrown from a horse. In the office, he seemed to have as little sympathy for the ills of others as for his own, unless he was worrying about Young, whom he was quite capable of "ordering" home to his mother, to obey her as if he were again a boy of ten and be careful of himself. He seemed to his other associates to regard their lapses from perfect health as a reflection on their efficiency. His attitude toward a company executive under the weather was one of his most unattractive traits.

But for men and women in the shops, he had a genuine concern. He demonstrated it by retaining Alice Hamilton annually for a number of summers to inspect General Electric plants and recommend measures for the health and protection of workers.

Dr. Hamilton by this time was one of the nation's leading authorities on industrial diseases and pre-eminent in the field of industrial poisons. The employment of such experts to eliminate work hazards was unusual in the early 1920s; to give them a free hand was unique.

"Gerard always was greatly interested in whatever I had to report," she says. "He never tried to defend the company or explain, but saw to it that whatever I suggested was done."

She had a lot to suggest, too. General Electric used only a few poisons—she recommended harmless adhesives in place of poisonous ones and better safeguards in working with lead and mercury. But many of the works were old; Swope's emphasis on men rather than machines had cut down on new building programs, and industrial architecture had not been notable for catering to health. Dr. Hamilton sent in long lists of recommendations for improved sanitation, better dispensaries, different chairs or stools or benches to reduce fatigue, rearrangement of machines or the handling of materials to eliminate accident hazards. In her rounds, she was struck by the affection with which men at the machines spoke of the company's president; she wasn't used to it in other factories she visited.

Of course, Swope's concern for workers was a matter of efficiency, but one may doubt that it would have been so steady or inspired such a warm response if it had not been genuine.

XII *Secrets of Management*

"Success or failure of an enterprise depends usually upon one man, upon the quality of one man's judgment and, above all things, his capacity to see what is needed and his capacity to direct others," said Swope's old teacher, Louis D. Brandeis, in one of the statements of his economic philosophy to which was given the title "The Curse of Bigness."

Brandeis held that it was impossible for anyone to know enough about a really large, complex organization such as General Electric to have informed judgments on all the problems on which its chief executive must rule. Bigness, he added, fosters "yes-men" to a dangerous degree.

"There is a limit to what one man can do well," he argued. ". . . you will find, in the first place, that the man at the head has a diminishing opportunity of exercising a careful judgment upon them. Furthermore—and this is one of the most important grounds of the inefficiency of large institutions—there develops a centrifugal force greater than the centripetal force."

Brandeis's former pupil concurred, but added that the damage could be repaired if the one man got other men to take some of the burden of judgment. Lesser executives, agreeing that in Swope's administration success certainly did depend upon one man, have noted that when he made a mistake, he ignored it because he expected his aides to turn it into a triumph.

"What do I have you for?" Wilson remembers he would ask more than one subordinate.

"He said it jokingly," Wilson adds, "but there was a lot of truth in it. It was up to us to get him off the hook."

Swope once bought a small company which continued to operate as a separate enterprise but under Wilson's department. He told Wilson about it after negotiations were complete, mentioning that the price had been about a million dollars.

"Too much," the younger man commented.

"What do you know about it?" Swope demanded.

Wilson admitted that he was not familiar with the company but doubted that an inventory would show General Electric got a very good deal.

"It's up to you to make it a good deal," Swope told him.

For months the new acquisition was Wilson's major headache. Not only had Swope paid $150,000 too much, but there was a mysterious leak of another $150,000 which remained unaccountable after exhaustive checking of the books. Further detective work directed suspicion at a salesman, whose boss proceeded to beat a confession out of him, although Wilson had urged that the man be watched without hinting at any lack of confidence. Wilson, dashing down the hall at the sound of smashing furniture and anguished howls, was just in time to save the salesman from being kicked to death. Between clearing up this mess and setting the little company on the way to compensating for the excessive purchase price, Wilson put in many anxious overtime hours. But he did not mention his troubles to the president, even when he got the best possible opening.

"That deal didn't work out so badly now, did it?" Swope remarked one day when the company was comfortably in the black.

"No" was Wilson's only reply.

Of course, the fallibility of human judgment was not Brandeis's only objection to corporations the size of General Electric. As a one-time scourge of "the Money Trust," he knew more of the abuses than the uses of corporate management. He had been intimately acquainted with pillars of respectability and philanthropy who also were pillagers of railroads, banks and industrial companies. He approved highly of state laws which limited the size and activities of corporations. Sheer size, he thought, sometimes was able "to dominate the state." He feared "the rule of plutocracy." The Boston lawyer, appointed to the Supreme Court by Woodrow Wilson, was now, in the 1920s, a part of that judicial team to which the country looked for some fine social and economic leadership in opinions introduced by the phrase "Holmes and Brandeis dissenting."

"Ownership has been separated from control, and this separation has removed many of the checks which formerly operated to curb the misuse of wealth and power," he once said, and even earlier: "Large dividends are the bribes which managers tender the large investor for the power conferred to use other people's money."

Brandeis thought he saw ample evidence that these corporations were destroying companies managed by owners, not through added efficiency, but through sheer financial power which permitted them to compete at a loss until the smaller firm was forced either to sell or dissolve. As an active advocate of collective bargaining before his elevation to the bench, Brandeis had been struck by the readiness of large corporations to resist unionization, often with intolerable brutality. He had listened to steel and textile representatives argue for a high tariff to protect living standards of American workmen. But few American workmen were as miserable as those in steel and textile mills.

Swope, too, knew something of these evils, but he denied that they were an inevitable feature of corporate management. He believed the increasing managerial problems which accumulate in any human institution as it grows larger could be handled by his pet methods of "analyze, organize, deputize, supervise." He believed that the abuses which Brandeis described accurately enough were the work of shortsighted or conscienceless men, not essential attributes of bigness. After four years in his General Electric post, he summed up his views in a speech on "The Responsibilities of Modern Industry."

"It isn't necessary to be big to be successful," he said, "but it is absolutely essential to be successful to be big."

Success, he conceded, meant a profitable business. But he thought that responsibility increased with success, and he startled businessmen who hadn't already heard him philosophize in private by his appraisal of where the manager of a corporation like General Electric owes his duty. For he put the public first and the stockholders last. In between came the workers and the industry as a whole, in that order. (Later in life he put the workers ahead of the public, too.)

The primary obligation, as he saw it in 1926, was to provide "more things for more people at lower cost." This, he said, summed up the history of civilization—"the great difference between ours today and that of the Greeks is not that the Greeks didn't have some people who enjoyed all the comforts and conveniences but that today more people enjoy those comforts and conveniences." He could always find plenty of examples in the electrical industry, for as the quality of its products improved and sales swelled, the prices went down.

This was not, however, an automatic operation of a natural economic law, so that the public could not always count on reaping the benefits of improved techniques and processes. During the early 1920s there was the interesting example of aluminum. In 1923, the Aluminum Company of America set a price of 26 cents a pound, production cost then being figured at 18.25 cents. A few years later the cost of manufacture was down a cent and a half, but the selling price rose 2 cents. Of course, Alcoa enjoyed what the Federal Trade Commission in 1924 characterized as complete monopoly. Its officers would not have agreed that management owes an obligation to the public ahead of that to stockholders, perhaps because the Mellon family of Pittsburgh owned 40 per cent of the shares and were not known for subordinating anything to their own incomes.

Swope offered no special humanitarian arguments for putting corporate responsibility to employees second on his list. He simply said it was good business, because highly productive workers were well paid and secure. In one of his first speeches as president of General Electric, he had told an audience of foremen that they should see to it "that men are making good money" and should worry about the one who was making too little, not one who was making too much. Now he said, "Nothing we can do will compensate for inadequate earnings on the part of the working man."

Adequate wages, he pointed out, were achieved by putting the power of modern machinery at the man's disposal. The big reason why Americans took home more pay than Englishmen or Frenchmen or Italians was "the much greater power we put in back of the workingman." This made it possible for a manufacturer to fulfill his obligations to public and worker because with power "high earnings on the part of the workingman are not inconsistent with low costs of production." But he did not think management should stop with high wages. He listed help to employees in their savings, better homes, insurance and protection against unemployment as other sound business procedures.

Responsibility to the industry itself, he defined as exchanges of information and ideas which would enable each unit to fulfill its obligations more completely. Only through common agreement could items be standardized, so that a GE lamp would fit a Westinghouse socket, uniform codes of electric wiring be obtained, fire protection be co-ordinated and so on. He thought industry could do a better job here than the state. Shortly before making this speech, Swope had been the leading figure in preliminary negotiations to form the National Electrical Manufacturers Association, and shortly afterward, in October 1926, he became its first president, so he had been devoting a good deal of thought to the practical uses of such an organization. It was, he pointed out, a partial answer to those who said competition was dying. There were two hundred eighty-eight member companies, dividing a business of about a billion and a half dollars—General Electric got 23 per cent that year with its nearest competitor doing half as much.

Stockholders, Swope noted, want "a fair, regular and uniform return." Management, therefore, can consider them last on the list because they will get their desire only if the public is served, workers well paid and the industry itself sound. He thought that management did owe the owners clear reports on earnings, orders, shipments and other pertinent activities—he was rather more inclusive in his ideas of which were pertinent than many others—and he thought that "those who put their lives in the business" (the workers) were as much entitled to the information as those who invested money.

On the basis of this philosophy, Swope considered General Electric safe from the perils of which Brandeis spoke. But fear and suspicion were not dissipated by his logic, and at the time of this particular speech, Swope had been involved for nearly two years in the company's defense against a government attack.

It had started in a manner which could have been predicted on the basis of Woodrow Wilson's explanation of the trends of reactionary administrations. The scandals of the Harding regime, spreading from veterans' hospitals to oil to prohibition to alien property to liquor and pardons, had reached as far as the Attorney General, Harry M. Daugherty, early in 1924.

"The political situation is fearful," Swope wrote on February 21 to Young, in Europe with the Dawes Committee, and added that he thought Daugherty would have to resign.

A month later to the day, General Electric was named defendant in an anti-trust suit, along with Westinghouse. The grounds were not the most serious which might have been cited, since

Electric Bond and Share, whose disposition was being argued in the office, was not mentioned.

"I am relieved and think you will be," Swope radioed to Young, explaining that the suit "involved only the question of our method of distribution of lamps and resale price and our license agreement with W. in connection therewith."

The government objected to the license under which Westinghouse used General Electric patents to make its own lamps, pledging itself to limit production. General Electric's contracts with its own lamp distributors set prices, and this was held to be a combination in restraint of trade. The company's defense was that it licensed Westinghouse on the same terms as any other producer, large or small, and that, unless stability in industry was illegal, its contracts with distributors were valid since they barred only cutthroat competition. Swope could, and did, point proudly in and out of court to the fact that electric-light bulbs were one of the few items an American could buy at a better quality and lower price than before the war, while the wages of workers who made the lamps had increased a good deal faster than the national factory average. He was very proud that after his reorganization of the lamp department and four years after he took office, the cost of the better lamps had gone down 45 per cent although the cost of living generally was up 10 per cent.

The suit had been brought too late to purify Daugherty's reputation. A week after the papers had been filed in court, Swope emerged from a long meeting of his Board of Directors and its Executive Committee to hear that the Attorney General had resigned at last, and Swope immediately conveyed the good news to Young, saying, "I am chuckling with joy . . . and I want to share my pleasure with you."

However, that did not end the case. Many in Washington were inclined to regard it as one of Daugherty's few good deeds, and his successors allowed it to stand. In 1926 the Supreme Court rendered its verdict, a unanimous opinion that General Electric had not violated the law, and Brandeis was one of those concurring.

Meanwhile a Senate resolution in February 1925 instructed the Federal Trade Commission to investigate monopoly or control of utilities. Two months earlier the company had distributed Electric Bond and Share stock among its own thirty thousand shareholders. The question, therefore, was whether this was a bona fide separation. Swope explained that the thirty thousand owned Electric Bond and Share "both legally and morally" before the distribution. He continued: "Now, you might say that the thirty thousand stockholders who control the General Electric Company also own and control the Electric Bond and Share Company, and rightly so. But you must note that transactions of sale and purchase in these securities are going on constantly. Such selling is bound to go on, and as the years pass, there will be ever greater and greater diffusion of the stock."

The FTC agreed with him. Its report of "no monopoly of either power companies or supply of electrical equipment, nor control thereof in restraint of trade," coupled with the unanimous Supreme Court decision in the lamp case, was a green light for the distribution setup which was being expanded to take care of General Electric's growing line of household appliances. These decisions and the company changes Swope had introduced won the accolade he most appreciated among all those that were possible in the business world. On a late June evening in 1926, he spent a few hours with Coffin on Long Island. The founder was eighty-one years old, still keen and observant, still visiting the office, still giving advice "whenever I asked for it." As the younger man was leaving, Coffin put an arm around his shoulders and said, "Gerard, you have made me very happy in the way you have been running the company."

Two weeks later Coffin died. There was more than the average sincerity in the tribute which Swope wrote. For all his regimentation of time, he missed the unannounced visits of this man who could probe gently but incisively into managerial progress. They had shared an interest in education—the retiring chairman had been vastly pleased when, as one of his first presidential acts, Swope suggested to the Directors an appropriation of $400,000 for a Charles A. Coffin Foundation. The income was used, in addition to awards for distinguished contributions to the industry, for fellowships to encourage postgraduate study. In his last years, too, he had enjoyed through Swope an intimacy with the theater which gave him a pleasant sense of accomplishment, for at The Croft he met Francis Wilson, one of the early presidents of Actors Equity. The founder of General Electric was intrigued by some of the administrative problems which confronted this struggling group, and he gave Wilson a good deal of help.

"Of course," says Swope, smiling, "he never understood that Equity really was a labor union. Mr. Coffin didn't like unions very much."

Coffin had known and approved of his successor's work in forming an industry association. He was mercifully spared a project, undertaken immediately afterward, to organize the workers as well as the manufacturers. Swope waited only a few weeks after the first meeting of the National Electrical Manufacturers Association in 1926 before he undertook to spark the formation of a nation-wide union of electrical workers which, far from being a company-dominated institution, would be an affiliate of the American Federation of Labor.

No president of a large corporation such as General Electric ever had welcomed unionization, much less gone out of his way to invite it. Swope knew that he was exploring uncharted managerial paths, and he had yet to learn that it is easier to organize bosses than workers.

Most of his colleagues in industry would have called his proposal radical if they had known it. Many would have added "betrayal." Their hostility to unions—active or passive according to the strength and bitterness of the individual's feelings—was an accepted feature of the nation's economy. At this time Pennsylvania's coal and iron police were at the peak of their armed power to intimidate workers. A union contract was considered so far outside the pale of business ethics that Richard B. Mellon, chairman of the Pittsburgh Coal Company, a brother of the Secretary of the Treasury, testified before a Senate Committee that after a year of operating under a three-year contract which set a fixed wage, he and the other directors decided, in 1925, to close up for a few months, then invite the miners back on an open-shop basis at a reduced pay scale. Although he later took it back, he also testified that it was necessary for the private police to have machine guns—"you could not run without them." There were steel and aluminum mills still operating on two twelve-hour shifts in 1926, and a union delegate who attempted to organize these workers was lucky to escape with a jail term; usually he would be beaten, too. Company unions existed in some other mass-production industries, and their managers for the most part seemed to think it a mark of generosity that they bargained with their workers on any terms.

Although the nation's industry was halfway through a decade of shrinking union membership, due in part to violent suppression, Swope thought the trend was likely to be reversed.

"It still seems to me," he said long after collective bargaining in the mass-production industries was a matter of course, "that, given the sort of labor relations existing or clearly predictable in 1926, it was simply good sense for a man in my position to take the first steps. It might make the difference between an organization with which we could work on a businesslike basis and one that would be a source of endless difficulties."

In this frame of mind, he asked William Green, president of the American Federation of Labor, to a meeting. He hoped that his good will toward labor was well enough established to eliminate doubts as to his sincerity. Green knew that the president of General Electric had been an admirer of Samuel Gompers and the only major industrial leader to attend that labor chieftain's funeral in 1924. Since the discussion might revolutionize his company's labor policy, Swope asked Young to accompany him.

He had no illusions that introduction of outside negotiators into General Electric's relations with its workers would make management's task easier or more pleasant.

"Oh, we knew well enough that we'd have our troubles when it came to bargaining with them," he said matter-of-factly.

Some facts of life and human nature might as well be faced without repining; it does no good in the long run to pretend they do not exist. They only confront us later, perhaps in more menacing form. The essential fact in this instance was that labor unions in the mass-production industries were inevitable, a corollary of the principle that these industries could find their proper market among all the people only if workers were well paid. Many who accepted this last part believed that well-paid workers would have small incentive to join unions, whereas actually good pay makes for strong unions. Organization is sought more eagerly and defended more fiercely by those who have something to lose than by those who merely hope to gain. This is true of the whole economy, not just labor. Bar associations were built into powerful forces by leaders of the profession who already commanded high fees. Medical societies established their closed shop for doctors only after the rewards of practice based on skill lifted physicians above the status of vagabonds to which they used to be consigned. Trade and industry associations generally are strong or weak in proportion to the prosperity and size of the companies which comprise them. Similarly, men who work at machines or on assembly lines band together more eagerly if they have a high standard of living to protect as well as the hope of better wages and shorter hours. The fact that well-paid workers can afford dues sufficient to finance hard-fought campaigns has been another factor in their growth.

Analyzing this future of labor relations, Swope put unionization into the same category of managerial problems as increasing costs of an essential raw material or the rise of an efficient competitor in a national market which never had had domestic production of its own. It was a condition, not a theory, and could not be argued or fought or bought out of existence.

"I was sure—and still am—that the best way for management to deal with unions is in a businesslike spirit free from either hostility or paternalism," he explains. "Labor relations born in an atmosphere of reason should be more harmonious and efficient than any child of strife or charity."

He was adapting with modifications the politicians' saying that if you can't lick 'em, join 'em. Sometimes it makes sense to join 'em without trying to lick 'em because the fight itself may be worse for all concerned than either victory or defeat.

Young shared these sentiments—he had been making speeches about a "cultural wage" which would provide food for the intellect as well as the body, and he predicted a day when workers owning their companies would buy capital as a commodity. So there was no trace of pugnacity in their meeting with Green early in December 1926.

"We talked with the utmost cordiality," Swope recalls.

At this time, fifty-three-year-old Green had been the head of the AFL for two years. A Middle Westerner, he looked like a prosperous man of business; strangers often took him for a successful merchant. His round smooth face easily mirrored geniality and good will. In his youth he had been a coal miner, and gained his first prominence in the labor movement as president of the Ohio Mine Workers. Except for the two big unions of garment workers, the miners were the only large body of labor then organized on an industrial basis. It might be presumed, therefore, that Green would be more sympathetic to industry-wide unionism than a leader from one of the strictly craft members of the Federation.

The cordial talk consisted largely of Swope's pressing gently for AFL initiative to organize electrical workers and Green's resisting any commitment although expressing cautious interest. A reporter, if one had been present, might well have supposed their roles reversed. Swope, wiry and hard-muscled, with his positive manner of speech and his strong features, resembled the popular conception of a labor leader far more than did his guest. Green, plump and bland, was a cartoonist's model of the corporation executive. Of the actual conversation, Swope remembers:

"I began by explaining the methods of industrial relations which we had developed in the General Electric Company. I described the Plans of Representation, which so far had worked well. I thought that this offered a good foundation for a union. I suggested to Mr. Green that he endeavor to enlist the Plans of Representation of the General Electric Company. The first step, I proposed, was that he should seek to win from the membership of our plants a small contribution to the AFL to be used by the Federation in efforts to improve conditions for the workers throughout the electrical industry. This, if successful, would have led to the formal organization of a single union of workers not only in the General Electric Company but in the plants of all electrical manufacturers."

Swope spoke with his usual conviction when he told Green what his men wanted. His certainty was based in part on a source of information he was careful not to reveal. For some time he had been on cordial terms with John J. Leary, Jr., labor reporter for *The World*, of which his brother, Herbert, had been executive editor for a couple of years longer than Gerard had been president of General Electric. They had discussed the difficulties a manager faces in trying to learn what men at the bench really think. Jack Leary, who had been a labor organizer in his day and blacklisted by a company which later became part of General Electric, was interested in a boss who had what he called "an honest-to-God desire to do the right thing by his people." Jack undertook to find a new kind of labor reporter, a man with factory experience who would collect data on what workers thought about their work, their company, their foremen, rules and regulations. Swope liked the idea on condition that he should never know who the reporter was—he left the hiring and the contacts to Leary. They agreed that the man should have $100 a week, his expenses and whatever wages he earned at the jobs he took in General Electric plants. Leary, in his instructions to the man, emphasized Swope's desire for facts and his insistence that reports to him might name bosses but never men. These documents were the source of some of the information he gave to the AFL president.

"Mr. Green seemed to be very much interested," Swope says. "He asked questions, which we answered freely. Our experience in the company, however, was limited. The largest group of union members in our employ was a handful of pattern-makers in the foundries. We dealt with an even smaller number of carpenters, plumbers and so on—too few to offer a precedent for the plants generally, but enough so that we knew we would be intolerably handicapped if the bulk of our employees were organized into different and often competing craft unions. We could and would deal with one bargaining agent but hardly with a dozen or more. The history of jurisdictional disputes in other industries such as the building trades was an obvious warning."

The next move was up to the Federation. Swope had opened a door which could lead to unionizing all mass-production industries—surely success with electrical workers would have been imitated in steel, automobiles, textiles, rubber and so on, and with less bitterness than was the case later. Whether or not Green appreciated the opportunity, Swope never was quite sure.

There were inherent difficulties in the AFL. Most strong leaders in the trade-union movement put more emphasis on "trades" than on "union." Many were almost as much opposed to organization of the unskilled as Judge Gary himself. Others were rendered overly cautious by memory of past disastrous failures in the steel mills. Swope thought that Gompers might have overcome these difficulties, but of course he was in no position to appraise them accurately. He could only say, "I do not know to what extent Mr. Green tried to follow up our conversation. But I do know that nothing came of it, at least not then."

That Swope and Young had been trying to get union organizers into their plants was not widely known, but they frightened some of their directors and won for themselves an enduring Bankers Club reputation as dangerous radicals. They were able to laugh over it together because their radicalism, which both regard as the essence of sound conservatism, was paying off. General Electric continued to get its quarter of the nation's electrical business. While the volume was only approaching the peak war total, profits were much greater, not quite in the same proportion as wages but so satisfactory that there was pleasant "extra compensation" for officials at the end of the year and no serious murmur from directors.

There were about twelve hundred men in executive positions in the company by 1927, and Swope thought that an organization was needed to promote year-round exchanges of ideas, to stimulate imagination, which Brandeis said was crushed out of fellows in the bigger corporations. He decided that it would have to be a society "separate and independent of the company . . . where any question may be asked and will bring somebody to his feet to answer it." Textbook procedure for a president with such an idea is to appoint a committee to work it out. But Swope elaborated this one in every detail and kept it to himself until he had a complete plan.

He came to the Camp General of 1928—the summer camp made up of executives from all departments of the company—with a typical speech, a prepared document and a list of names. The speech was an explanation of why he wanted a new organization to add to existing departments, committees, boards and subsidiaries. He thought his listeners needed a special "open forum where critical and radical thoughts may be expressed." The fire that animated him on these occasions was never more in evidence than when he exhorted, "If we could fill this body of executives and leading men with the spirit of adventure to try even unheard-of things, the company would either make progress or go broke, and the older of us would try our best to keep it from going broke."

Swope could rouse this group to a height of enthusiasm, but he knew they couldn't remain on the heights with no nourishment except inspiration. He had brought with him a coldly calculated reason besides adventure for joining his new society. He called it "Elfun," and this fanciful, even pixieish name actually was a contraction of "electrical funds." Elfun was to be an investment trust for its members, who might avoid speculative hazards and concentrate more effectively on their work if they were not distracted by efforts to play the market. When his audience, somewhat carried away by his enthusiasm, agreed that his was a fine idea, he produced his document. He explained that since the plan was new to them, they had had no chance to work out details, so he had prepared a constitution and bylaws which he proceeded to read and they to accept without amendment. He concluded by pointing out that they had had no time to think about suitable officers, but he had a little list, whereupon he placed in nomination eleven members for an administrative committee called for in the new constitution. There were no further nominations, and the minutes-old Elfun Society dazedly elected his selections.

The individual Elfuns did not give up stock market speculation, but they did form a successful investment trust and did create a forum where argument and discussion brought men of all departments together on a professional footing never experienced before. It served Swope admirably. Wherever General Electric had an office or a factory, there was an Elfun chapter. Whenever he visited the place, he had an organized audience, a ready-made channel for his ideas and a carefully cultivated group who could give him a quick summary of what was going on in this particular area.

The members were not always as outspoken in criticism or dissent as he would have liked, or even as he sometimes thought them. They were in general strongly, deeply reluctant to incur the boss's displeasure. This is hardly unusual in business (or elsewhere), but Swope's brisk manner, sharp questions and obvious passion for perfection added more to men's normal fears than he himself suspected.

"I liked it," he said when subordinates stood up for their beliefs against his own. "They were of more use to me."

But this was not the general impression among his subordinates. It was not always clear to them that he ever noted their objections. He would take a press release, for example, and do it over in what he called "the best Swopeian English." This was not a brand which city editors understood, and often the news would be buried far down. But he firmly rejected suggestions for amendment, and releases had to go out as he wrote them.

"Please see page three," the press department was allowed to say in an accompanying letter, but that was as much deference to the rule of giving the best point in the first paragraph as Swope tolerated.

Charlie Wilson remembers another instance of the dread Swope inspired. At the very camp where Elfun had its beginnings, the subject for the set discussions was the most desirable managerial structure—horizontal or vertical. In the horizontal, all authority flows from the central source to each department, and decisions are all made at one place. The vertical system calls for major decisions to be reached and authority to be exercised independently in each main division and passed directly down to the units within that division. Hardly a man on the island that summer did not know that Gerard Swope was one of the most horizontal managers who ever issued an order. But Wilson was as vertical as could be by temperament, and something of a fighter by training.

After nearly thirty years in the company, six of them under Swope, he was prepared to admit that the present incumbent was perfectly capable of being a successful president on the horizontal principle. But he saw no reason for including this admission in his speech. Rather he prepared the most scathing denunciation of the horizontal structure which he could devise.

"It was a flat attack, and I was as sarcastic as I knew how, even about such revered institutions as the Advisory Committee," he recalls with relish.

The session adjourned for lunch when he finished, and as he walked over to the dining hall, some of his confidence oozed away. He wondered if he had been wise to state his convictions so forcefully and impudently. As he passed friends, they murmured sympathetically, "Well, Charlie, it was nice knowing you," or, "Hey, Wilson, let me know when you get located somewhere." He was thoroughly depressed by the time he reached the dining hall, and the feeling deepened when he sat down at a table. One of the island rules was that meals should be taken in the company of strangers or men one knew only slightly, never with close associates. The fellows at the table stopped talking abruptly when Wilson came near, and there was a dead silence for several minutes.

Then he noticed Swope in the doorway, looking around as if to select a place to sit. Wilson turned back to his plate and was staring at it miserably when he felt hands on his shoulders and heard a whisper in his ear—but a whisper in Swope's famous carrying voice was audible half across the big room: "Don't let anyone tell you that wasn't a good speech. I admire your courage."

Wilson felt a little pat on his back, but when he looked up, considerably cheered, Swope was walking rapidly away. Charlie Wilson became a vice-president in charge of the Bridgeport works a year later.

Swope, accustomed to having his decisions accepted and acted upon, thought the recurring charge that his corporation was dominated by bankers very farfetched. Every so often he undertook to refute it, although never to the satisfaction of those who made it.

General Electric often was called "a Morgan company." Brandeis, for example, had included it in one of his more widely quoted denunciations of interlocking directorates when he declared that a railroad of whose directorate a Morgan partner might be a member would use money from a bond issue floated by Morgan to buy rails from United States Steel, on whose board Morgan was represented, which in turn would buy electrical equipment from General Electric for the same reason, and so on ad infinitum. Furthermore, a Board drawn largely from financiers of big business is bound to have that "community of interest" which the elder Morgan had fostered and certainly is tempted to favor insiders even if it resists the urge.

The principal element of fact in this accusation, says Swope, is that General Electric always had one, often two, Morgan partners on its Board, and Morgan financed the merger which created the company in 1892. But it was a fact that the Board also included half a dozen other bankers and underwriters who often were associated with Morgan. Swope pointed out that the chief reason for so many directors from financial houses was that the company would not enlist anyone from a firm with which it did or might do business, so that almost every manufacturing or transportation enterprise in the country was excluded. This was not a policy of other major corporations. General Motors, for example, numbered Young among its directors for years until its increasing competition in electrical appliances led him to resign. Du Pont officials had been his colleagues there in 1917 when that company pulled General Motors out of a financial hole by buying 23 per cent of the stock for $25,000,000. This was only one of the differences between General Electric and General Motors which Swope cites complacently to indicate his own company's superiority. He also says proudly that General Electric developed most of its products while his friend Sloan's corporation simply bought up its principal lines.

In his experience, he adds, sales were so seldom effected by directors that their influence was negligible. The value of these men to his corporation was in setting policy, in bringing to broad industrial problems the point of view and knowledge of able, experienced outsiders. However, this is indirect confirmation of one element in the charges, for the policies which such directors would agree upon are formed in the light of their own interest and belief in big business. In his actual management of General Electric, Swope found this to be true, and he carried out some of his ideas —in labor relations, for example—only by a dictatorial exercise of authority in directions which most of his Board feared or disapproved.

Selling does seem to have been on more substantial grounds than directorial influence. Swope himself soon gained a reputation as his company's best business-getter, and this was enhanced when Henry Ford confided to William Randolph Hearst that he regarded the president of General Electric as a great salesman. Ford said Swope had talked him out of the idea of making an enormous turbine engine in his own plant, and did it in fifteen minutes flat. The mass of figures which Swope quoted in that time convinced the erratic manufacturer of America's biggest-selling car that General Electric could build the 140,000-horsepower monster better than Ford.

Swope had other sets of figures for other customers. He always knew just what General Electric bought from a man or a company to whom he was trying to sell something, and he would mention the total pointedly. It was a practice of which the protagonists of small business complained bitterly; it can very easily give the big corporation many profitable sales of a poorer product or at a higher price.

It was easier to answer critics who complained that the influence and power of large industrial combinations enabled them to suppress inventions in order to protect large investments in inferior products or machines, and to keep up tariff walls to exclude foreign goods which could reduce prices to the American consumer. Swope knew that patents sometimes were acquired solely for the purpose of keeping them off the market. In his own experience, Europe had automatic telephones before the United States simply because competition would provide them if his company did not. Therefore A.T. & T. had acquiesced in the investment required for Europe long before the same facilities were built here. Swope thought such delay was false economy, blocking progress toward his goal of more things for more people at lower prices.

As far as the tariff was concerned, he never defended duties on incandescent lamps and never lobbied for them. He insisted that the real reason the Japanese, for instance, never won a substantial American market was that they could not produce a lamp of GE quality at a price as low as his.

For all its sales techniques, expanding lines, outstanding research, more efficient use of men and machines, his company held no more than its former share of the total electrical business. Swope used to say that this was the most important figure in all the mass of figures which flowed across his desk. He came to regard one fourth of the industry's take as belonging to General Electric almost as of right—at least his remarks at company meetings conveyed that impression. All efforts were directed to the goal of keeping that 25 per cent no matter what else might happen. He and the company did it, too, but they had to run very fast to remain in the same place.

Swope's concentration on this race removed him from much of the zany spirit of the 1920s. It was the era of bootleggers in bullet-proof limousines, of entertainers who achieved wonderful popularity by insulting their audiences, of flappers and sheiks, of tremendous arguments over the coverage of women's bathing costumes and the morality of extramarital sexual relations. It was a golden age of night clubs and spectator sports. Its most respected contemporary chroniclers were savage critics, but it was a complacent society which could enjoy being pilloried by Sinclair Lewis and Henry L. Mencken.

It was not a society in which Swope seemed to fit. He was no frequenter of speak-easies or night clubs. No gaudy scandals pushed him into public notice. His managerial innovations, while bringing him the flattering regard of his peers, and even some imitation, were not so spectacular that the popular press wanted to chronicle them. Even in his own field of business, the intricate corporate manipulations of an Insull attracted more attention.

Despite the hardships of farmers and what then was regarded as an irreducible minimum of unemployment averaging about one tenth of the labor force, the country was so prosperous in relation to any previous period that the goal of a car, a radio, a bathroom, electric light and upholstered furniture for every American family seemed within reach.

The mergers and combinations of the 1920s carried on the trend observable through Swope's entire working life. If they narrowed competition within many industries, they stimulated competition between industries and created new ones. Trucks, for example, now competed with railroads, and airplanes were hailed as threatening both. Movies and radio had become big business; synthetics were on the way.

Wages never had been so high, averaging $25 a week in factories. A theory that the United States had climbed to a plateau of unassailable stability was so widely believed that Australia sent an official mission, in 1928, instructed to learn "the secret of permanent prosperity." The Australians decided to look for the prosperity before going after the secret, and at the end of three months their spokesman said they hadn't found it. High pay for skilled artisans and in some manufacturing lines, they said, hardly compensated for the miserable standard of living they saw in the company towns of mine and mill owners.

They were impressed, though, by the widespread use of electrical equipment in city homes. They thought the rates low, too, although urban dwellers grumbled and the National Electric Light Association spent a great deal of money to block municipal power plants which hopeful citizens thought might bring rates down still more. The private operators had hit upon a device which gave them more substantial profits for less investment. This was the holding company, originally designed to give individual light and power enterprises the benefit of large-scale managerial direction, mass purchasing power and the best engineering skills. But they became in the 1920s a device for pyramiding profits and reached a point where even a professional defender of private power complained that in many areas in the late 1920s rates were three to six cents a kilowatt hour more than they needed to be, or up to double a fair price.

This was negation of the principle of larger business through lower rates, which Swope was preaching. It was a reason why General Electric's sales increased no more than they did, although they had reached a point that established him, at fifty-five, in the words of some newspapers, as an industrial statesman. As his company steadily increased its pay rolls, its profits and its products, there was a growing interest in penetrating Swope's secrets of management. He was in considerable demand as a speaker, and he accepted as many invitations as he could.

Those who wanted to learn how to run a big industrial concern by magic were disappointed. (Swope disliked the growing practice of ghostwriting and prepared his speeches himself; they would have been better organized and more colorful if he had enlisted professional help, but perhaps not so completely his own.) He preached in and out of season his gospel of managerial responsibility. He explained over and over again why the public and the workers should be placed ahead of stockholders in a corporation manager's thinking. He expatiated on the combination of research, organization and engineering which achieved "more things for more people at lower cost."

In interviews for publication he was less expansive but equally clear as to what he thought the head of a great manufacturing enterprise ought to be doing and thinking. He was an unsatisfactory subject for a popular biographical sketch because he had a habit of asking more questions than he answered, and confining his answers to the facts for which an interviewer inquired. He refrained from rambling on discursively about other matters, avoiding the careless talk which can be so revealing.

He was a little more talkative, but not much, at small gatherings of his peers, as at the Bankers Club, for although he was not a conventional clubman and visited those to which he belonged only for business, he often lunched there. His views on management were listened to more respectfully than one might suppose from his reputation as a radical. Myron Taylor of United States Steel and Walter C. Teagle of Standard Oil were congenial spirits for Swope among the industrialists, and Thomas W. Lamont of Morgan's among the bankers. A man at the head of a big business enterprise meets few fellow craftsmen, and Swope seems to have relaxed a little with those few. But more than one among them, as among his interviewers and underlings, came away from a conversation with the profound conviction that this man Swope was a deep fellow indeed, not given to revealing the esoteric secrets of his trade. They apparently were quite unable to grasp a greater simplicity—that Swope never revealed any managerial secrets because he did not have any.

XIII *Boom and Bust*

A workable secret formula for industrial success just then would have been a wonderful possession, although the need was appreciated only later. The year 1929 opened with a chorus of optimism, of which Swope's contribution was a fair sample. He radioed from shipboard a "Business Outlook for '29" which read: "Basic economic conditions sound; inventories not unduly expanded; credits and collections satisfactory; earnings of labor high and employment steady; all presage favorable outlook for '29."

In spite of this public cheeriness, he had gone off on his vacation early in January—he and Mary preferred this to a summer holiday—in a mood of foreboding which Young was at some pains to relieve. On January 12 the chairman sent a long radiogram informing the president that a big transformer order had been landed after difficult negotiations. Young usually ignored such items in his correspondence, but he reported it now in detail, adding, "Will this make your vacation happier? Buck up and have a good time. The world isn't going to the bow wows yet."

Whatever had caused Swope's depression, there was no sign of it left when he returned just in time to see Young off on the most notable of that gentleman's public services. He was to be chairman of an international commission of experts to fix precise limits to German reparations and remove foreign controls. Four months of hard work reconciled French and German viewpoints sufficiently to warrant some more American credits to make this new "Young Plan" work. It was hailed as one of the greatest triumphs of international negotiations in living memory, and businessmen at Harvard's summer session voted Young and Henry Ford the two greatest business leaders of our times.

During all that time, the view from 120 Broadway grew rosier and rosier. Business never had been better and never had so many shared it. Nearly three million firms were dividing a fifth of the whole national income, which explained why ownership was more remunerative than management. Swope, for example, was in the high bracket of salaried executives, but his income was less than 1 per cent of that enjoyed by Andrew Mellon, and the then benevolent tax laws decreed that Swope paid a considerably higher percentage of his to the government than did Mellon.

Although the number of business firms was at a peak, the rate of combinations and mergers in manufacturing, mining, banking, utilities and transportation was accelerating. Since Swope joined the International General Electric Company in 1919, nearly ten thousand manufacturing enterprises had been combined in some twelve hundred mergers. The trend, for the first time, received positive government encouragement, so that in certain industries the majority of the business was concentrated in a few corporations. This was true of Swope's own as well as steel, copper, aluminum, oil, tobacco, automobiles and others. But there was less public opposition to the trend than there had been when Theodore Roosevelt was tilting against the "bad trusts." A.T. & T. long since had completed its telephone monopoly with general approval.

Chain stores and networks of dealers handling the products of single producers such as General Electric or the automobile manufacturers had spread across the land.

The net result was a respect for business and financial leaders rarely accorded to any group of men in this country. Their wisdom was extolled by writer and orator, and they were encouraged by popular acclaim to believe that they were indeed what a more cynical generation called them in jest, "Lords of Creation." In this atmosphere, Swope's letters to Young became positively gossipy, almost the only time in his life he violated his own often repeated injunction not to write anything you wouldn't be willing to see on the front pages of your newspaper.

He took the time to run over to Van Hornesville from Schenectady on a spring day so that he could give a first-hand account of Young's family and how much milk the cows were yielding—he had no trouble writing more than a page. He described his preparations for the annual stockholders meeting—"I will do my best to see that you and incidentally myself and the others are re-elected," a jesting reference to the firm grip they had on the owners of their company. He told of a day at Hyde Park talking over a water-power message which the new Governor, Franklin D. Roosevelt, was preparing—"some suggestions he adopted and others he didn't." He exulted that General Electric's business was running at the unprecedented rate of $465,000,000 a year, at least for eight weeks. He mentioned his decision to have the company sponsor a radio program at last—an hour's musical entertainment once a week by the Damrosch Symphony Orchestra. (Swope kept in close touch with the preparation of these broadcasts as much for the pleasure of talking music with Walter Damrosch as because he liked to have his fingers in every General Electric pie.)

Mixed in with this harmless gossip were a few indiscretions. He wrote, for example, of a Board meeting which "approved lending Mr. Mitchell (of Electric Bond and Share) $50,000,000, and he is highly pleased." At the time such a loan might not have excited much comment, but in a less expansive period would certainly be criticized hotly. Even more open to attack was a sentence reporting on a luncheon he had enjoyed with the new chairman of Westinghouse.

"I think he is going to make an outstanding and able man for the job, and one with whom I hope we can co-operate to constructive ends," Swope wrote.

This had a very suspicious look to investigators years later, although the writer was referring to quite legitimate "constructive ends" in such Association matters as standardization of electrical supplies and fire prevention codes. But it was inevitable that the words standing alone, as they did in his letter, should carry to unfriendly eyes the implication of sinister deals.

One of the items in his company's expanding business which was common knowledge and widely criticized was a series of contracts with Russia. The first, typical of them all, provided a credit of $25,000,000 with which Russia could purchase General Electric machinery over a period of five years. The generators for the most ambitious Soviet electrification project, the Dnieperstroi development, were part of this deal. There was angry comment that Russians couldn't be trusted to pay, and also that help in industrialization was raising up a dangerous enemy to the capitalist system. The first objection was easily answered. Russia paid, even during difficult years, "punctually and punctiliously," said Swope, who, because of the delicate nature of the transaction, was involved personally in the negotiations to a greater extent than usual. On the second point, he declared, "My thought was that it would take at least a generation to transform an agricultural people into an industrial one, and if we kept our leadership in engineering and manufacturing, at the end of that period we would still be in the lead."

As he had in his Western Electric days, he opposed the concept, which in his industry was notably a German one, that other countries should be prevented from developing their own heavy industry. He preferred, he said, to take the risk of competition, confident that continued progress in research and education would preserve American technical and productive leadership better than attempts to maintain a technical or productive monopoly.

Such continued progress, of course, is not automatic. There probably is no way to create the inventive genius of an Edison. But the output of productive research and of engineers or other technicians can be increased.

General Electric has been an outstanding example of industrial research ever since Dr. Whitney had founded its laboratories and Steinmetz given the world some of those products which were meant by "The House of Magic." Swope had pushed this department from the first, but, recognizing his own limitations, he did not try to tell anyone what to look for. He was lucky that Dr. Whitney was a careful spender, but no one in the laboratories ever complained that Swope did not give them a free hand.

"I worried about the money the very first year when we spent about $3,000," says Whitney, "and I worried every year. When we got it up to a million, I was scared to death."

Fortunately, the scared are not always timid. Whitney, a full-faced man of rather stately presence although of no more than medium size, gave an impression of quiet confidence rather than fear. Certainly he did not shrink from any promising scientific inquiry because of the expense, for he adds, "Very often there was doubt in my mind that a certain line of research ever could develop anything commercially, but we always resolved the doubt in favor of going ahead with it anyway."

His successor, Coolidge, does not remember that Swope ever so much as asked for commercial possibilities. In fact, they discussed experiments less than music, a subject which warms the scientist's normally ascetic appearance. The president did insist upon a report of some kind at Advisory Committee meetings, which Whitney, with the confidence of an old teacher, had consistently refused to make. He said no one at the table could understand what he was talking about, and besides, engineers were always rushing off into plans for new products or improvements before the academic studies were completed. But Coolidge did not have resistance. He says he always came prepared to speak at the Advisory Committee after Swope intimated to him that this would be desirable. Asked just what form the intimation took, Coolidge smiles. "He told me bluntly."

Swope knew that the best contribution he could make to research was to keep his hands off except for equipping and staffing the laboratories adequately. But in the education of engineers he played a more active role with the zest he had brought to his teaching at Hull House. As an M.I.T. trustee, he had been nursing opportunities ever since 1914 when he first noted the reluctance of educational institutions to accept new curriculum ideas. The first one he had succeeded in pressing upon Tech was the adoption of "co-operative courses" by the electrical engineering department. This innovation gave selected students fifteen month's work in the shops of a "co-operating" company and turned them out at the end of five years with a Master's degree and more practical experience than had been known hitherto. The shop work was carefully selected—manufacturing practices, testing apparatus, generating power, development and research in communications, etc., rather than routine labor.

Ten years later, Swope came back from England with an even more radical idea. Seeking to learn how English engineers were trained, he had visited Cambridge and one of the eminent professors to whom he talked, the future Lord Rutherford, said, "In America, in your engineering and scientific education, I will admit that the average of your graduates is higher than it is in England, but you can't touch our honors students, the top third of the class. As far as I am concerned, and this is true generally of the professors at Cambridge, it is the honors students only in whom we are interested; the others who go through the University get something from the atmosphere."

In spite of his great pride in M.I.T., Swope realized that there was a lot of truth in Rutherford's boast. It hurt him that there could be a better engineering education anywhere than his alma mater provided. For he always was loyal. When as A.T. & T.'s guest at the first television demonstration in August 1927, held between New York and Washington, he was permitted to ask for someone in the capital to whom he wished to speak, he selected a Tech man. On his travels he was constantly on the outlook for a special lecturer or a new pedagogic idea which he could pass along to Dugald Jackson, head of M.I.T.'s electrical engineering department and soon a close friend.

So now he got busy analyzing curriculum problems to devise a way of establishing the honors system without lowering the high average of students who did not compete. He worked out a plan which M.I.T. adopted in 1925 although it upset some cherished habits and added several instructors to the faculty.

Swope's reward was election to the chairmanship of the Executive Committee. In this post he cut through a good deal of red tape by helping Professor Jackson write letters to the chairman. It was noticed that the recommendations contained in these epistles were adopted by the Committee speedily and without much debate.

Perhaps even more than the curriculum, Swope was interested in the availability of learning and the efficient administration of colleges. He argues that the many youths who qualify for college in everything except tuition are a resource which the country could ill afford to neglect, but he is not convinced that a multiplication of free scholarships is the answer. He thinks people like to pay their way. Therefore, he was both an advocate and a promoter of college loan funds, from which students borrow their tuition, repayable when their earnings make that possible.

His first ventures into this field were personal gifts—as a memorial to his parents, $50,000 to Washington University in St. Louis after his mother died; then to Union College in Schenectady, headquarters of the General Electric Company, and Dartmouth, which one of his sons attended. (Later he established similar funds at Rutgers, in Mary's home town of New Brunswick, and Mary's own alma mater, Bryn Mawr.) But his most ambitious undertaking along these lines was for M.I.T.

Swope wanted to make it part of a broader scheme to insure

financial stability for Tech. Tuition paid only about half the cost of an individual's training, and faculty salaries were low. He proposed broad raises in pay accompanied by a gradual increase in tuition to pay the full costs of a technical education. That full cost would be loaned to students who could not afford it.

In his headstrong way, he would have liked to put the tuition up to the necessary figure at once, but with characteristic caution, recommended an increase of 25 per cent to start. Before he could persuade the Corporation to go higher, several experienced trustees and administrators warned that many otherwise admirable students would hesitate to burden themselves with debt at the outset of their careers, regardless of how easy the terms might be. More convincing was a point of view, best expressed by President Lowell of Harvard, who also was a Tech trustee, that education was not for the sole benefit of the student "but primarily for the public good in supplying the community with a body of men educated for its service."

"Indeed," he added, "it would seem to me unfortunate if a man could say, 'I paid for my education as I did for my automobile. It is mine, and I owe to no one gratitude, nor to the public a duty.' "

So Swope set his goal as payment by the student of what he called "the full operating costs" of education while gifts and endowment would take care of "the capital facilities." But salaries and other costs rose sufficiently to make tuition even on this basis increasingly out of reach of families such as the one Swope had come from himself.

It was not until 1929 that, having covered many slips of paper with columns of neat figures, he was prepared to tackle the problem of raising the loan money. He decided against a wide appeal to the alumni in favor of concentrating on a few men who could give largely, and he got his list down to twenty-one names. His salesmanship was tested by some of them, but he ended a brief campaign with pledges of $4,240,000, the payments to be made in equal installments over a period of ten years. His own was

$250,000 toward what was by far the largest college loan fund in history.

The ease of collecting the pledges varied. Swope got one of $500,000 from Edwin S. Webster, partner in a famous engineering firm, during a walk across Boston Common on the way to a Tech Executive Committee meeting. But Charles Hayden, class of '90 but now a banker and one of the wealthiest alumni, responded, "I won't give you a damn cent; I don't like the way they run financial matters at Tech."

"Charlie," Swope urged, "if you don't like them, come over and help us fix them."

After a bit more talk, Hayden found himself not only subscribing $500,000 to the loan fund but serving as chairman of M.I.T.'s Finance Committee and of the Loan Fund when it began operations in 1930. The others fell into line. Swope's classmate, Alfred Sloan, and George Eastman were half-million-dollar contributors. Four Du Ponts who had attended M.I.T. gave a million jointly, and so on. Actually the donors were tapped for only three installments. With a million and a half in hand and loans running at the rate of $150,000 to $200,000 a year, there was plenty. By the time this was used up, repayments were taking care of the borrowers with ease, even when loans rose to $342,267, as they did in 1956, for in a quarter of a century only 1.12 per cent of the borrowers failed to repay.

About the time he launched this fund, Swope was greatly impressed by an article in which Julius Rosenwald of Chicago expressed his belief that all gifts for educational, health or scientific purposes should be used up, principal and interest, in twenty-five years. Let the next generation, he said, take care of its own problems free from the heavy hand of the dead. Swope, looking back over the unbelievable changes in American life since he was a young manager in St. Louis, agreed to the extent of authorizing the trustees of his loan funds, for example, to use the money at their discretion if they thought the original purpose had been achieved.

At the other end of the educational scale, Swope this same year plunged into the most ambitious of all mass literacy movements—an attempt to teach half a billion Chinese to read and write. The magnitude of the task was attractive. Its originator was more attractive still, James C. Yen, a young Chinese who combined imagination with fervor and the practical ability to use both.

During World War I, Jimmy Yen had been one of eighty Chinese students recruited from American universities by the British to serve as interpreters and letter-writers for some two hundred thousand Chinese laborers brought to France for noncombatant work behind the battle lines. Swope had seen some of them on the ship which brought him home from the East in 1917, "well enough cared for as regards food and shelter, but otherwise treated as animals with a certain labor content," he remembered. Arrived in France, they proved their humanity by giving a great deal of trouble because they were afraid, cut off from their families by the bar of illiteracy and isolated in the midst of the West. The eighty students were scattered among them to write letters home for them, read the replies to them and explain to them the oddities of European life. Jimmy Yen, responsible for about five thousand men in the Bordeaux area, conceived the idea that it would be wonderful if they could write their own letters. Ignoring the ridicule of his fellow students, he selected those of the many thousands of Chinese ideograms which his pupils would find most useful and set out to teach them. To provide practice in reading, he published a crude little newspaper, and when he went back to China he had the basis for a life work. He created a simplified writing—in comparison with the one he had learned—and a new literature to be printed in it. By the time Swope met him in 1929, he had five million Chinese learning to read from one hundred fifty thousand volunteer teachers.

Yen had come to the United States to raise money to spread his efforts, and Swope was so greatly attracted that he accepted the chairmanship of this Chinese Mass Education Movement. It was primarily a fund-raising assignment, and Swope carried it out with the same ease that he had experienced in getting his M.I.T. loan fund. He liked to talk about this new venture, and General

Electric employees on Association Island, for example, heard quite a speech on the life and works of Jimmy Yen.

All this time the nation was rushing gaily toward what hindsight could regard as the inevitable crash. One of the largely ignored signs was that call money in Wall Street—the money that covered the price of stocks which margin did not provide—was commanding an unprecedented 20 per cent, ample evidence that the market was in the hands of speculators. Swope, who had been in the market with a million of borrowed money, now prudently sold all his stock holdings except General Electric shares and invested the proceeds in the call money market.

His next move in the financial world was neither as shrewd nor as conformable to his self-imposed rules. Against all his principles, he yielded to the importunities of Charlie Mitchell and joined the Board of the National City Bank. Mitchell had been repeating this invitation for several years, and Swope had been declining it firmly—as he did many others of a similar nature.

"I have all I can do in my job in the General Electric Company" was his standard response.

Suddenly, in the summer of 1929, he gave in. Perhaps he was infected a little by the ruling hysteria. Perhaps Mitchell raised his usual eloquence a notch or two. But many years later, Swope gave a simpler explanation when he was asked why he accepted the post in obvious violation of what he never ceased to regard as a sound rule for him.

"I was a damn fool," he said.

It was a folly, furthermore, which required some delicate negotiations before it could be consummated. Swope had been asked to serve as director of companies more important to his own than National City. One of them was General Electric's own bank, the Bankers Trust Company, whose officers could be expected to feel unhappy at being passed over for another financial institution, and who had a representative on General Electric's Board. Young thought this was a serious matter, so without telling Swope anything about it, he undertook to win Bankers Trust approval. His rather delicate diplomatic maneuvers were successful, and on July 23, 1929, Swope joined his old friend's Board of Directors.

He could hardly have picked a worse time. Within six weeks, on September 5, came the first premonitory break in stocks. On September 24 there was another, then smaller slides on October 3 and 4, a horrid hour on October 24 when a great many supposedly sound securities could not find a taker at any price, and a final record-breaking day on October 29 when 16,410,000 shares changed hands at prices which averaged 40 points off for the best.

From there the stock market went into its long decline, but in the fall of 1929 the more catastrophic slump in the whole economy was not yet envisaged except by a few Cassandras noting ominous signs in farm distress, overstocked warehouses and the disintegration of world trade. Swope, no more prescient than his colleagues, was occupied chiefly in these months with saving his friends and finding a new president for M.I.T.

The fact that his earlier sale of stocks had left him that rare phenomenon, a rich man with money, enabled him to come to the rescue of a good many whose fortunes were tied up in paper which seemed to be losing all its value. He also organized among General Electric executives a loan fund which extricated some of them from ruinous situations. His freedom from financial embarrassment in these days greatly strengthened his reputation for wisdom, especially among those whom he helped.

The most difficult and time-consuming of these operations stemmed from his National City Bank directorship. He refrained from adding to the spate of brave, foolish phrases with which leaders of finance and industry sought to calm their own fears as well as those of the public. If "prosperity is just around the corner" (Charles Schwab) or "business is fundamentally sound" (Secretary of the Treasury Mellon), that happy state of affairs would prove itself. Meanwhile he kept quiet, but he was not much encouraged by Charlie Mitchell, who turned out to be one of the cheeriest of the optimists with the least reason.

"American markets generally are now in a healthy condition," he cabled for publication between two of the most frightening market breaks. Neither his own nor his bank's condition could be so described, and his new director was not happy about it.

"He'd got into trouble before I came in, but I had to go along with him—or thought I did," Swope says succinctly in recalling those worrisome days when it was apparent that the bank and its securities affiliate, the National City Company, had strayed very far from the path of conservative banking practice.

Mitchell had cushioned the decline of his own fortunes by the then legal device of selling his bank stock to his wife for a paper loss of nearly three million dollars, so he didn't pay any income tax that year. But there was no chance of keeping either him or the bank out of serious trouble, even before the entire country was plunged into much graver difficulties.

While wrestling with the problems which Mitchell's optimism—harsher words were used by others—had brought the bank, Swope was introducing one of his favorite managerial techniques into M.I.T. It was a cardinal principle with him that every executive should have an understudy fully prepared to step into his place. He thought this applicable in educational institutions, so he brought it up at a meeting of his Executive Committee. Although Lowell protested what he called "bringing into the sacred halls of learning some of the methods of business," the Committee authorized Swope to canvass the field for their next president.

One reason he urged a replacement was his desire to end a more direct intrusion of industrial influence at Tech. Because salaries were so low, professors were devoting more and more time to consultant jobs, while with the expansion of industrial technology more and more companies wanted to hire them. As a result they often neglected their classes and their work with each other in the interest of their clients. Swope realized that both the morale and the prestige of the faculty suffered, and thought only a new man could set matters right. So for months, everywhere he went at home and abroad, he inquired about educators who were also scientists and administrators.

He had compiled a rather long list of possibilities when he was invited to the most memorable ceremony in the history of the electrical industry. Henry Ford was giving a dinner for Edison during a world-wide Golden Jubilee of the incandescent lamp. The hero of the occasion, benign and simple at eighty-two, was almost as wonderful as the magnificent technological achievements he had led. It was a time for men to look back over the immense progress of the age with pride and humility, hope and gratitude. The celebration, held just a month after the first serious break in the stock market, dimmed the fears of Ford's guests for a little while. Edison's mere presence seemed to be an assurance that there was magic in man's command of machines.

It was an impressive crowd, but by this time Swope was inured to testimonial dinners and famous people, and he was impressed more by Arthur Compton's brilliant conversation than by the speeches. Compton was the University of Chicago's Nobel-prize-winning physicist, and Swope went over to Chicago to visit him next day. Through him he met an older brother, Karl T. Compton, a professor of physics at Princeton, and decided that his search had ended. He was not impetuous, however. He continued to ask questions, even when he was in England, France and Germany that winter, about who might be the best candidate. It is characteristic that he had confined his talks with Karl Compton to professional discussions of the General Electric Research Laboratory, for which the physicist had been a consultant. Later Compton thought that Swope "may have been really interested in any suggestions I might make but was much more interested in discovering how I might react to the problems which he set before me." The reaction was satisfactory, and then Swope wanted to meet Mrs. Compton, "as the position of the President of the Institute carries with it heavy duties for the wife." After he and Mary had the Comptons to dinner in New York, he asked the professor if he would like to head M.I.T., and the election took place in March 1930. The common industry device of elevating an incumbent to the chairmanship to make way for a new chief executive was adopted, although deplored by Dr. Lowell, and Karl Compton was inaugurated in June.

Swope rode with him to Boston for the occasion and persuaded Owen Young to go along. On the train Compton was treated to a dialogue on the principles of administration—"perhaps for my benefit," he supposed. He was sufficiently impressed by it to remember toward the end of his presidency that the pair agreed on two essentials. The first was "to have someone to take over for a time when he is away." The second was that decisions "must not be postponed because they are unpleasant."

This last point may well have been expressed with more feeling than would have been the case a year earlier. As the stock market crash merged into economic depression during 1930, the president of General Electric was faced with a great many decisions, nearly all of them unpleasant. By far the most distressing were those which threw men out of work.

It was small consolation that General Electric was one of the most solidly based corporations in the country, free from debt and possessed of a handsome surplus which would carry it safely through the worst depression in history only reducing, never passing a dividend. But what about the company's responsibility to its workers? Its assets were impressive as measured against ordinary emergencies. But they could meet the pay roll only for a matter of months even if used entirely for this purpose. There was no getting away from the fact that the orders on which all work depended were drying up, and the figures which crossed Swope's desk were worsening steadily.

As if the remorseless decline in purchases by all customers was not bad enough, some of them tried to set up as competitors. One day, for example, the Chicago manager reported that a Michigan manufacturer of incandescent lamps had been bought out by the Samuel Insull interests and was understood to be infringing on General Electric patents. The manager wanted to sue. This was Young's department, so Swope passed the report along to the chairman, who was on friendly terms with the highly regarded Chicago utilities operator. Young preferred diplomacy to war and sent a copy of the report to Insull inviting comment. The Chicagoan pleaded guilty and agreed to stop, but complained in his turn that Swope wasn't very co-operative. The men had met often, even crossed the Atlantic on the same ship, but had not liked each other. Now Insull objected with a parade of virtue and an arrogant pomposity which came easily to him that General Electric men in Chicago displayed toward his companies a lack of good will, which he blamed on Swope.

The day when Insull's ill will would be an asset was rapidly approaching, but at the time the failure of his companies to buy new equipment was tragic. However, in March 1930, the situation still was so far from desperate in the eyes of well-informed former engineers that when two of them got together at the White House on St. Patrick's Day, they talked of it only in general terms. Hoover invited the Swopes to dinner and to spend the night—they slept in the Lincoln Room—and during the evening asked his guest to a private conversation in his study. The chief point which remained in Swope's mind was a discussion as to whether the President should run for a second term.

"If he had been a perfectly free agent and could have consulted only his own wish and desire, from the way he talked, I do not think he would have been a candidate again," Swope wrote.

He admired Hoover a good deal "as an engineer and especially as Secretary of Commerce . . . the best type of public servant." This admiration did not extend to the engineer as President, however, for Swope never cast a vote for him, and as the depression deepened, he viewed with increasing disfavor the Administration's failure to act.

He himself was busy putting into new form the unemployment insurance plan which General Electric workers had rejected in 1925. A few days before he went to Boston for Compton's inauguration, he submitted it to a vote of the men. The proposal won by a majority in every plant and by four out of five among the entire body of workers. Based on the contributory principle which Swope had defended in all security measures, the plan called for a deduction of 1 per cent from everyone's pay, even that of clerical workers and officials up to Swope and Young themselves—a most unusual provision. The company paid an equal amount, and benefits were fixed at half the unemployed man's average earnings, up to a maximum of $20 a week (the same adopted by the Federal plan some years later) for twelve weeks. This fund eventually paid benefits of $3,828,000, loaned nearly a million more and inspired a report by the Schenectady Mayor's Committee on Unemployment almost a year after the vote that no General Electric employee of a year's standing, which was a qualification for benefits under the plan, had yet applied for relief for himself or his family.

That was a record for any factory which provided so big a proportion of a city's working population, but months before the Mayor's Committee reported, Swope realized that the depression had gone beyond the ability of any single company to handle. So he drafted an ambitious public-works plan by which he hoped the Federal government might provide jobs for hundreds of thousands, perhaps millions, of men and start the wheels of industry rolling. The summer of 1930 offered no signs of economic improvement, and when Swope visited the White House again at the end of September, he outlined his ideas to Hoover.

He wanted the government to display the boldness in a civil emergency which would be routine in war—a line often urged on Presidents but seldom adopted. Specifically, Swope proposed a billion-dollar government bond issue to be sold through a patriotic campaign like the Liberty Loan drives of the war. The money, matched by state and local governments through similar financing, Federally guaranteed if necessary, should be used for variously badly needed improvements. Swope mentioned schools, jails, hospitals, roads and streets, workmen's housing, refuse-disposal plants for big cities, electrification for railroad terminals. He was less concerned about the specific items, however, than that the program be started by winter.

The President gave him some mild encouragement, enough to lead Swope to talk over his plan with Young and Myron Taylor, chairman of U.S. Steel and a friend who shared some of their views on corporate management. Taylor, a big man of mild courtliness whose slow placidity contrasted with Swope's swift impatience to the admiration of both, was keenly interested. But he thought "before reaching a final conclusion additional exploration work should be undertaken." Apparently the President had not indicated any desire that Swope follow up on the idea, for Swope wrote to him:

"Because of our conversation, I did not want to undertake any further work of exploration at this time."

In that letter he enclosed a fairly detailed summary of the plan. He pointed out that a billion dollars of new bonds were less than 10 per cent of the amount by which the war debt had been reduced since 1919. The service charges would add only 3½ per cent to this part of the budget. Furthermore, the various public bodies co-operating would get exceptional value for their money because all prices were so low.

Swope always thought that a prompt program of this kind might have checked the plunge into depression. Two billion dollars flung into works which would give men jobs was an enormous sum by any standards. It bore to the Federal government's then annual expenditures the proportion that forty billions would today. It was a staggering proposal, but it was essential—and on this Taylor and Young agreed—that a start be made by winter.

"If we were faced with war," Swope wrote in his memorandum to Hoover, "the President would immediately call a special session of Congress to declare war and to raise armies and the immense funds necessary to further it. *This unemployment situation in many ways is more serious even than war* . . . the time, effort and money would not be wasted as in war. War, indeed, wastes more than this; it wastes lives, while this will save both money for the communities and will save lives in the most self-respecting manner possible by giving work to men who desire to work, rather than to give them doles or charity."

While Swope did not feel free to undertake the studies which Taylor wanted, he urged Hoover to consult some of his advisers in this field who might have the necessary data on hand. But the only reaction was a three-line note in which the President thanked him for his letter and said he was "making further inquiries in an endeavor to develop some systematic program for the winter."

The inadequacy of that program was painfully apparent as the Swopes started on their regular vacation in January 1931. This time their voyage was through the Panama Canal to California, and then on to Arizona. For some time, men in the General Electric Company had professed some apprehension when their president took what he called a holiday. He was likely to improve his leisure by looking into any General Electric facility or agency available, and he would write or wire some of his disconcerting questions. They were spared this time because he was turning over in his mind all the lessons he ever had learned which might bear upon the national crisis. Gerard Swope was not the only leading industrialist who was thinking about that crisis, but he was the only one whose thoughts crystalized into a definite, nationwide program.

Thinking back over his life—his Hull House experiences, his first groping toward a philosophy of business management in St. Louis, his efforts to organize production and distribution in Western Electric and General Electric, his studies of European social-security systems—he was formulating a set of procedures which might be a solution to the knottiest of national problems: jobs for men who wanted to work. On the backs of Western Union blanks, sheets of hotel stationery, oddly shaped pieces of paper torn from letters or memo pads, he accumulated a background of figures, of questions, of disjointed answers. By the time he got back to New York, he had hammered out roughly a plan about which he was prepared to talk.

XIV The Swope Plan

The first talks were in private, beginning with Young, who as the author of a highly praised plan himself urged Swope to put his in specific form. The next preview was presented to Newton D. Baker, whose administrative talents Swope had admired in the Army. The former Secretary of War, however, had lost the adventurous spirit of his reforming youth, or perhaps the depression frightened him as it did other previously bold innovators. At any rate, he pronounced the proposals "too radical." (Years later, Swope had the satisfaction of hearing Baker say they were "too conservative," so rapidly are the experiments of one day relegated to the commonplaces of another.) Swope preferred Young's advice.

A program of action is important not so much for what it says as for what it accomplishes. In the early months of 1931 Swope had specific goals. The first was to get men back to work. The second was to eliminate for the future the damage which unemployment inflicts on industrial workers and the whole economy. He wanted industry to do both jobs before government stepped in with what he thought would be less efficiency and more danger to the democratic system.

No issue could compare in public interest with this one, and all over the country people of varying degrees of expertness were evolving schemes for remodeling the American economy. Swope had his staff read hundreds of them, to weed out duplications and obvious fantasies. He pored over the remainder, and all through the spring and summer, he worked with his rough notes. At that year's Association Island camps his speeches were tinged with reflections on restoring business and jobs.

He took time out for a trip of several weeks on horseback with his children and a party of their friends through the Vermont countryside. One day the cavalcade rode over to pay a call on Calvin Coolidge, who was in retirement in Plymouth. It was a rainy morning, and the former President, very rustic in high rubber boots and smoking a cigar, graciously took the whole group indoors to see the room where he had taken the oath of office from his father after Harding died. They all refrained from comment on public affairs.

From this trip Swope went on business to the West Coast, and on the train he dictated to Jim Harris the text of a speech which he had agreed to make at a meeting of the National Electrical Manufacturers Association on September 16. He chose for the title of his address "The Stabilization of Industry," and under that heading he set down the principles which had been the chief subject of his thinking for the past six months.

"In the situation that confronts us at the present," he began, "the most disturbing aspect is that men who are able to work, who are competent workers, who above all things desire to work, cannot find work to do. That this condition has ever been present in such periods detracts nothing from its wrongness. That industry must evolve and make effective those measures which will first ameliorate and ultimately eliminate it must be the reaction of everyone who gives thought to what is taking place. I say that industry must do this thing, because it will surely be done."

In his next two paragraphs he set forth his main objectives. His first was to preserve for workers who changed jobs the benefits they earned. Individual company pension and insurance plans helped to create what he called the "forty-year deadline," the reluctance of employers to hire men over that age. So Swope proposed "a system of benefits accruing through the life of the worker and following him where he might go from shop to shop . . . from branch to branch within industry as a whole."

His second point was that "production and consumption must be co-ordinated." Consumption could be restored to a high level, he thought, only if the people felt safe in spending their money. This sense of security could be theirs if they had protection for their old age and against the hazard of unemployment, "protection that they themselves help to provide." Any system for co-ordinating production would have to commend itself to the public, he argued, because an effective one was impossible under existing anti-trust laws.

"It is vain to think of their amendment or repeal," he added, "unless the public is assured of the constructive nature of the steps industry will take, and that the interests of the public will be adequately safeguarded."

He feared that if the separate states undertook to provide the necessary machinery, there would be such a confusion of conflicting and contradictory measures that business would be intolerably handicapped. If the Federal government stepped in, "the power of taxation has no economic restraints." Therefore, he urged, "organized industry should take the lead," but the operation of the plan should be "by the joint participation and joint administration of management and employees" with the public interest protected "through the agency of the Federal government."

"There is nothing new or original in what I am proposing," he said, although this disclaimer would not save him from the charge that the president of General Electric was a dangerous radical propounding wild innovations. "I am merely bringing together well-considered propositions that have found support, including some that have been put into actual practice."

After this careful introduction, he launched into specifics. His plan consisted of eight points. Seven concerned the organization, administration and control of industry, to which he devoted a paragraph each. The eighth, which took up about five times as much of his speech as the other seven put together, dealt with workers' benefits. The eight points were:

1. "All industrial and commercial companies (including subsidiaries) with fifty or more employees, and doing an interstate business, may form a trade association which shall be under the supervision of a Federal body referred to later."

2. These trade associations were to be given extremely broad powers—"outline trade practices, business ethics, methods of standard accounting and cost practice, standard forms of balance sheet and earnings statements, etc., and may collect and distribute information on volume of business transacted, inventories of merchandise on hand, simplification and standardization of products, stabilization of prices, and all matters which may arise from time to time relative to the growth and development of industry and commerce in order to promote stabilization of employment and give the best service to the public." The exchange of information was what trade associations already did.

3. The associations and the companies in them were to be supervised by the Federal Trade Commission or a bureau of the Department of Commerce or a special new Federal agency. This, he said, would protect the public interest.

4. All companies "within the scope of this plan" were to be required to adopt standard accounting and cost systems in a form to be approved for each industry by the Federal supervising agency.

5. All companies with twenty-five or more stockholders were to be required to send them and the supervising agency a quarterly statement of business in a prescribed form and an annual complete

balance sheet and earnings statement so that "the owners will be kept informed on the conditions of business."

6. Standard forms for each industry were to be drawn up, with the co-operation of the Bureau of Internal Revenue to reconcile "methods of reporting assets and income with the basis of values and income calculated for Federal tax purposes."

7. All companies were authorized to adopt these provisions at once but would be required to do so within three years, and new companies would be required to join within three years of their organization.

8. Protection of employees was to be assured by a workmen's compensation act based on the best state laws in existence and a program of life and disability insurance, unemployment insurance and pensions closely modeled on the systems he had inaugurated in General Electric. The additional provision, which made the program a social-security plan for all industrial workers, was that when a man changed his job, his insurance and pension accounts were transferred to the new company. Each company fund would be administered by a board evenly divided between appointees of workers and management. They would be supervised by a general board within each trade association whose members would be appointed one third by member companies, one third by employees of the member companies, one third by the Federal agency. Workers who left industry before the retirement age, which was seventy, could take with them all they had paid into the various funds plus interest. The shares contributed by their employers would be returned to the various companies. But if the worker so elected, he could allow the total amount to his credit to remain in the funds to accumulate until he returned to industrial work or decided to withdraw his share.

It took Swope about half an hour to explain his proposals in his clear, rapid speech. He was greeted not only with applause but with very strong indications that his own association would put the plan into operation as a test without waiting for further action elsewhere. This, of course, had been arranged in conversations which Swope and Young had had with other leaders of the industry before the meeting. At the meeting itself, Young had introduced the main speaker with a strong plea for action, not because the author of the plan thought it perfect, since Swope was well aware that it was open to criticism and could be improved thereby, but because a start somewhere was essential.

No speech made that year of deepening depression attracted quite so much attention. The wonderful dream of a "permanently high plateau" of business which eminent economists had spoken of complacently less than two years before was a bitter jest in September 1931. Newspapers which recorded the reaction to Swope's speech also circulated the grim details of industrial collapse in items such as the one reporting that copper had reached the lowest price in history, seven cents a pound. This, furthermore, was nominal; there were no buyers. Advertisements were an even more somber reflection of the times. Standing rib roasts were thirty cents a pound, but who could afford roast beef? One of New York's newer skyscraper hotels, with an incomparable view of Central Park, called upon the public to note its "rates adjusted to fit present-day pocketbooks." This meant $3 a day, including a continental breakfast served in the room.

Therefore, it was front-page news all over the country that a leading industrialist proposed a program which, one editorial writer noted, "had it been prepared by a Wobbly ten years ago would have landed him in jail." Books and magazine articles were written about it; colleges and universities included it in their curricula. It was damned as pure State Socialism, as a disguised "Capitalist-Socialism," as Fascism, as reckless interference with the sacred operations of free enterprise. There were expressions of surprise that the head of a company employing tens of thousands of workers should be concerned for their security, although Swope had been making speeches on the subject for years. The objectors were answered by exaggerated tributes in which Swope was extolled for having found an ideal solution to all economic ills.

"I don't care to comment on it because I don't believe in it," snapped Samuel M. Vauclain, the elderly, crusty chairman of the Baldwin Locomotive Works.

"An example of constructive leadership" was the pontifical verdict of Nicholas Murray Butler, president of Columbia University, who gave the plan his highest benediction by adding that it fitted in with a line of thought he himself had developed in a speech ten days earlier.

These were mere samples of an extraordinary volume of comment which, without shedding much light on the issues, made the existence of "the Swope Plan" known to millions who were not quite sure just what it was. Much of the discussion, however, was directed to the strong and weak points of the proposals.

It was pointed out that companies with fifty or more workers comprised only about 15 per cent of all business enterprises and employed only about one fourth of the industrial workers, so that much of the productive capacity of the country would be left outside the stabilizing program. The rather vague but extensive powers proposed for the trade associations were too great to be regulated safely, some critics argued. Others said the plan was in patent violation of the anti-trust laws and perhaps of the Constitution itself. The devices for protecting workers offered nothing, it was noted, to the millions currently unemployed, and the number was rising rapidly to the point where from one quarter to one third of the entire labor force would be idle. It was objected that the contributions from workers—1 per cent of wages for pensions, 1 per cent for unemployment insurance, an unspecified amount for life and disability insurance—were too high to be borne.

The proposal to give trade associations power over American industry was greeted by some as the best recovery proposal yet, and by others as a threat to American freedom. Federal supervision was hailed as the answer to all possible objections and denounced as either too little or too much. A businessman thought it undermined legitimate authority; a Socialist saw it as benevolent despotism "to vaccinate the business of this country against the industrial democracy which he sees coming."

There were even incorrigible political dopesters who thought the Swope Plan a clever move to further the nomination of Owen Young for President on the Democratic ticket in 1932. A considerable boom for the "Mr. Outside" of the General Electric Company was developing with no encouragement from him, and the "Mr. Inside" was credited by such popular pundits as Mark Sullivan, who was not very well informed on the lines of authority in General Electric, with an "eager zeal to see his business chief elevated to the White House."

The talk, wide of the mark as much of it was, is a measure of the real achievement of the Swope Plan. As an actual formula for governing industry, it was not put into effect anywhere, not even by the favorably disposed electrical industry. When it came to the point, there was too much doubt of its legality. One school of legal thought held that voluntary agreements of this kind were justifiable in an emergency. The courts had upheld comparable arrangements during the war when the War Industries Board asked each industry to set up a committee to allocate its production and distribution facilities in accordance with the most urgent demands. Electrical manufacturers noted, however, that the initiative then had come from the government. They wanted some assurance that the authorities in Washington regarded the depression in this light, and no such intimation was forthcoming.

Actually, although Hoover as Secretary of Commerce had fostered the formation of trade associations and urged revision of the Sherman Act to enable them to govern industry with more authority, the principal indication of his own Administration's attitude toward the associations had been anti-trust actions against eight of them. The courts had ordered five dissolved, too. While this was not adduced by any contemporary commentator as indicating official sentiment toward the Swope Plan, so far as can be found, memory of these cases could not have faded in association circles. President Hoover declined comment entirely, and only when he wrote his memoirs twenty years later did he reveal that he had sent the Swope Plan to his Attorney General with a covering note in which he said:

"The plan provides for the mobilization of each variety of industry and business into trade associations, to be legalized by the government and authorized to 'stabilize prices and control distribution.' There is no stabilization of prices without price fixing and control of distribution. This feature at once becomes the organization of gigantic trusts such as have never been dreamed of in the history of the world. This is the creation of a series of complete monopolies over the American people. It means the repeal of the entire Sherman and Clayton Acts, and all other restrictions on combinations and monopoly. In fact, if such a thing were ever done, it means the decay of American industry from the day this scheme is born, because one cannot stabilize prices without restricting production and protecting obsolete plants and inferior management. It is the most gigantic proposal of monopoly ever made in this country."

The quotation "stabilize prices and control distribution," upon which most of Hoover's objection is based, did not appear in Swope's speech, although the President obviously implied that it did. The danger of trusts and monopolies was present, of course; that was why the author wanted Federal supervision. Swope, who knew as much about business operations as Hoover, did not agree that his plan would protect inefficient producers or hamper initiative. At the time, however, he had no inkling of Hoover's reaction, and when it was published, he was surprised by the vigor of the belated attack.

The argument that the Swope Plan might lead to the results which Hoover called inevitable could be supported in logic, but the Presidential denunciation went beyond logic. Hoover, as his memoirs made plain, was committed to the thesis that the Government of the United States has very limited powers and should use those sparingly. Swope himself wrote that the Administration "did nothing except follow the usual and ordinary routines." The bitterness of Hoover's attitude toward those who preferred strong action may be explained by the fact that already he was being made the whipping boy on whom all economic sins were expiated.

He includes the Swope Plan in his list of villains because he credits it with a large share in his 1932 defeat.

Hoover relates that he informed Henry I. Harriman, a New England utilities executive then president of the United States Chamber of Commerce, that the plan, which the Chamber had adopted, was sheer Fascism hardly distinguishable from Mussolini's corporate state. He says Harriman replied that Franklin D. Roosevelt had accepted it and that if Hoover did not do so too, the business world would support his opponent with money and influence.

The Swope Plan was not that decisive in Roosevelt's election, but it did give a powerful impetus toward national organized action against the depression, although it was government which took the lead and not industry, as Swope had hoped. The president of General Electric "had shaken the pillars of respectability for the season and thrown a burning brand of thought into the very center of complacency," in the colorful phrasing of Charles and Mary Beard. His plan won the Chamber of Commerce endorsement which Hoover so deeply resented along with that of trade and industry groups. It helped make the idea of economic planning for stability and progress acceptable to many who doubted that academic economists could be practical or politicians trustworthy. Despite a swelling clamor that all the country's troubles stemmed from the folly or greed of the "Lords of the Market Place," great numbers of citizens regarded a successful businessman as a safer guide through the economic maze than any scholar, philosopher or office holder. If the head of one of the largest American corporations which obviously was financially sound amid the wreckage could seriously offer to his colleagues a "revolutionary proposal," for such was the widely used phrase, perhaps there was more respectability to burning brands of thought than the Beards allowed.

A by-product of the Swope Plan was to increase the demand upon its author's time. He was asked to elaborate his ideas before many audiences and finally did accept one invitation, that of the

American Academy of Political Science. His most important addition to the September speech was an answer to those who thought there could be no stabilization without price fixing or agreements to divide the market or combinations at the expense of the public and the workers. He suggested that the Sherman Act be amended to require all agreements under his plan to be filed with the Federal authorities. If trade associations or companies attempted any of the practices which were against the public interest, the government could bring them into court and perhaps with more information to back its case than it had had in the past.

Nothing in Swope's experience caused him to fear that the good will of men, whether they agreed with him or not, was subordinated to their greed. He thought most people in places of public responsibility, among whom he emphatically included business executives, would generally live up to that responsibility. Therefore, he much preferred "to appeal to the understanding of the leaders of industry rather than exercise compulsion through the law."

While he refrained from being drawn into debate about his plan—it was worth acting upon or it was not, but nothing was worth unlimited talk, in his opinion—there were a few invitations he could not refuse. One of them caught up with him at another industry meeting in White Sulphur Springs a week after his speech on the Swope Plan. Governor Roosevelt wanted to see him in a hurry and proposed lunch at his home in New York City the next day.

Across the table, the genial, persuasive squire who had worked out of his own private depression of infantile paralysis to be a leading presidential contender offered his guest a job. Less than three weeks before Swope's speech, Roosevelt had delivered a pretty important one of his own to a special session of the Legislature called to consider the emergency. The Governor was not at all content with Hoover's example of "the usual and ordinary routines." In his speech he said that the state ought to provide for its citizens who were in need. Since then he had set up a Temporary Emergency Relief Administration, which became the first in a long line of "alphabetical agencies," the papers immediately referring to it as TERA. He wanted the author of the Swope Plan to head the organization and accepted a declination with obvious reluctance although "very kindly" at the end, Swope remembered. Jesse Straus, then president of Macy's, who did not have Swope's resistance to what Robert Sherwood called "Roosevelt's incomparable blandishments," took the job, hiring a social worker named Harry Hopkins as his deputy and, within a year, successor. It was his work in TERA that brought Hopkins to Roosevelt's notice, and later Swope liked to speculate on "what might have happened had I accepted the job and succeeded in it." Actually, he had neither the suppleness of mind nor the relish for playing second fiddle to have assumed the Hopkins role as a Roosevelt adviser.

His next inescapable invitations came from the Senate in October 1931. The first was from Senator Wagner of New York, who was coming into prominence as a sponsor of social legislation and served on a select committee studying unemployment insurance. Swope repeated his speech in essentials. In answer to questions, he insisted that industry and workers could handle the job without government contributions but agreed that there should be government supervision. He admitted, too, that General Electric's unemployment program was a failure because it had been started too late in the midst of depression. It was, he said, about to be replaced by a new one.

He already had worked out the details and won their acceptance within the company. By this time the General Electric labor force had been thinned down from a peak of one hundred thousand in the boom to between sixty and seventy thousand. A million dollars had been paid out in unemployment benefits in ten months, and the 1 per cent pay-roll deduction, matched by the company, was not enough. Contributions by both workers and the company were doubled, and the company agreed to meet out of its own resources any costs above that.

At the same time, Swope had asked the Board of Directors to take a bolder step. He proposed to guarantee every employee at least half his average earnings for the next six months, up to a weekly payment of $15. Of course, those who earned more would receive the full amount they earned. By the end of 1931 the family who could be sure of $15 a week was considered fortunate. Swope admitted that his offer might cost the company as much as $5,000,-000. The directors agreed—Swope always thought it one of their most heartening votes of confidence in him—but the next half year was the one period of his presidency that he looks back upon as unpleasant. He came as close as he could to worrying—in another man it would have been worry—and he recorded his thankfulness when the six months ended with General Electric still solvent.

"This was too ambitious a plan for any one company to undertake," he wrote.

On the basis of figures he himself was collecting on company operations, his fears seem exaggerated. The year 1931, which saw heavy cuts in the pay roll, left a profit available for dividends of $41,000,000, eight times as much as Swope feared he might have to spend on his unemployment guarantee and about double the profit in the depression year of 1921 which had led Coffin to call him to the presidency. On the average, therefore, it still was safer to be a General Electric stockholder than a General Electric worker.

A few days after his testimony on unemployment insurance, Swope was back in the Capitol giving a committee headed by Senator La Follette of Wisconsin his views on the advisability of forming a National Economic Council. He thought the various government departments and commissions better prepared to assemble economic facts and figures than a new agency, while he doubted that the proposed Council would be able to take significant action. But he used the occasion to plug the trade association feature of the Swope Plan.

"What led to the formation and development of the so-called Swope Plan?" La Follette asked him.

"I suppose going through these various depressions and seeing the tremendous hardships and tragic facts with regard to unemployment of human beings and in every way trying to ameliorate conditions, not only because of the human aspect, but also because of their effect on industry," Swope replied. "I believe quite basically that contented men without fear in their minds will do a better job than those who are discontented and have fear constantly hanging over them."

But the whole nation was going down into the depths of a fear such as it never had known before, neither in war nor economic or social disaster. In the worst of times in the past, such as the panic of the early 1870s, people literally starved to death and hungry men rioted in the cities. But in 1932, the quiet despair was more frightening than violence and left a more pronounced ineradicable scar. Once crowded streets were as empty as the stores. The air over factory towns cleared as smoke faded from the chimneys. Automobiles were up on blocks because their owners couldn't buy gasoline. Radios and refrigerators and furniture, bought so freely on the installment plan, were carted out of homes on which the rent ran unpaid month after month. The symbol of the age was a pathetic youngish man in a too-large overcoat selling apples on a windswept corner, rather than a ragged, wild-eyed, club-swinging revolutionary bent on loot.

The president of General Electric was making speeches on unemployment insurance all through the first half of 1932, enhancing his reputation for industrial statesmanship but otherwise, as he wrote himself, "not with very much effect." That part of the Swope Plan which called for putting men to work through joint government and industry action would have to wait upon a more imaginative administration than Hoover's. Its social-security objectives would be considered seriously only after a start toward economic recovery had been made.

No signs of recovery were discernible in the reports which came to Swope's desk. The most intensive efforts by even as large a staff as General Electric still employed were quite unable to turn up new sources of business. There were long, searching conferences at every major General Electric office and plant on what might be done to meet the depression, and Swope went up to Schenectady to attend one of them. Chester Lang met him at the elevator to ride down to the auditorium where he would speak. On the next floor, a plump, jovial executive boarded the car.

"Well, we're all going together in this thing, aren't we, Mr. Swope?" he said cheerily.

"Yes," agreed the president coldly. "Down."

Lang remembers that the rest of the trip was made in silence.

XV *The New Deal*

In the summer of 1932 it was clear to observers who retained some impartiality that the Democratic party would be returned to power in the fall. It was not so clear what they would do with that power, for a destined victor does not have to be specific. This one had no special formula anyway, and the electioneering proceeded in a traditional manner of much talk but not very much said, which made it hard for Hoover and the men around him to believe that their political doom was sealed. They ignored Swope's friend, Dwight Morrow, a Republican but not blinded by wishful thinking.

"Those who take credit for the rainfall should not complain when they are blamed for the drought," he had said, recalling that Hoover was elected largely on the basis of what his party called Coolidge prosperity.

Morrow had died in October 1931, the same month as Edison, and Swope was not the only one to miss his wise, good-humored counsel. In his ten years as a General Electric director, he had been a staunch supporter of the Swope-Young team, less uncomfortable than some of his colleagues in the presence of innovations. On one of his last visits to Swope's office, he had brought a little carved wooden bird from Mexico, where, as ambassador, he had won praise for a diplomatic conquest rare in the history of hemispheric relations. He always had smiled a little at Swope's tense but controlled manner, which made Young think of a steel spring.

"Gerard," he said, "what you ought to do is remember the Eleventh Commandment."

Swope expressed surprise and interest in this new version of the Bible, and Morrow explained: "Take thyself not too seriously."

The little bird, which regarded Swope with a mocking expression and which he has kept on his desk ever since, was a valuable reminder in the months after Morrow's death because they were a severe test of his managerial theory and practice. The trick of maintaining an adequate return on a falling business was not easy. He used the method he had outlined in the first speech he ever made as a responsible executive a quarter of a century before. He sought new ways of doing things, shifting work from one plant to another to keep men employed. His and the whole company's best efforts managed to retain for General Electric about one fourth of all the electrical business in the country, but it was one fourth of less and less.

In common with most corporations, General Electric reduced salaries. "Extra compensation" for executives was hardly a memory. But Swope insisted on maintaining one activity at its normal level. In what he thought was the nadir of the depression, July 1932, he informed the stockholders after a preliminary report on how much worse business was this year than last:

"But no worth-while new developments are being unduly curtailed, and engineering and research work which will provide new fields for the company in the future is being continued."

The pessimistic tone of this report was amply justified. The election of Roosevelt, far from creating any upsurge of confidence and recovery, left the country almost without a government for the four months which then elapsed between the voting in November and inauguration in March. The interval was filled with sensational business failures, sensational bank failures, sensational revelations of financial sins committed by the most respectable financial institutions in their frenzied puffing of the speculative balloon. National City was one whose high-pressure selling, syndicate manipulations and extravagant profits for insiders came in for special attention and denunciation—unpleasant reading for a director who was trying to help re-establish the bank on a sound basis.

The entire electrical industry was getting a bad name because pyramids of utilities holding companies were crashing into ruin, dragging down thousands of investors as well as thousands of mere speculators. The Insull network, for example, consisted of two top companies and six layers of subsidiaries under them—a total of two hundred thirty-eight—with the value of the actual operating utilities inflated to give some color of worth to the stock of the higher layers. The "write-ups," always credited publicly to the advantages of reorganization, were very simple; one Insull company increased its paper value by $8,000,000 by mere resolution of the Board of Directors.

But in 1932 the Insull enterprises, which in the past had bought hundreds of millions of dollars' worth of General Electric equipment, not only ordered virtually nothing but in December borrowed $2,000,000 from General Electric on securities which later had to be reduced "to the market value of the collateral," as Young delicately put it. That turned out to be zero.

It was not unusual for General Electric to lend money to a good customer, and in this case the company was rather a victim of Insull financing than a party to his manipulations. The Senate Committee on Banking and Currency, which was looking into these and similar practices, unraveled some of the tangle and heard Young explain that when they made the loan, neither he nor Swope were aware of how much the Insull companies owed to banks.

"Later," he added ruefully, "when I came in contact with the banks, I learned more about it."

At another time the public might have displayed more interest in such testimony. But it was dull reading in comparison with tales of inflated values, stock issued for purely speculative purposes and bonds floated upon mere promises which even a cursory investigation would have shown to be illusory at best and often dishonest. For these were the days when the public learned just how Ivar Kreuger, a Scandinavian adventurer who had pyramided safety matches into an empire, succeeded in getting a quarter of a billion dollars in worthless paper listed on the New York Stock Exchange after even less investigation than American companies underwent. Kreuger, now billed as "the greatest swindler of all time," but only a few years before, the master of governments and a wizard of finance, had committed suicide in March 1932. One of the most bitterly received revelations of this time was the fact that a representative of an American syndicate which launched his stocks here had co-operated in keeping the news secret while insiders unloaded on an unsuspecting public.

By contrast, the General Electric Company and its head emerged from these hearings with high reputations. The thoroughly conservative financing upon which the supposedly radical Swope had insisted was paying off. The company itself, although operating at pitifully low speed so that its sixty thousand employees averaged less than thirty hours' work a week, was riding out the storm. Swope was confident that it could survive anything short of violent revolution.

In January 1933, however, the danger of such an upheaval could not be ignored. This month it had happened in Germany in a particularly virulent form as Hitler took power with the support of leading industrialists who thought him the only alternative to Communism. His policy of exterminating Jews was so abundantly clear that one might almost consider it a blessing that Swope's sister, Golda, had died shortly before.

Some observers thought the American revolution of the twentieth century also had begun on the nation's farms, where angry mobs were preventing sheriffs from executing foreclosures and intimidating judges on the bench. This situation inspired Swope to set down some thoughts on the agricultural problem, a sort of Swope Plan for farmers.

As his program for industry was based on voluntary trade associations, which would become mandatory, so his new scheme was founded on farm co-operatives. Each township or county should have one; they would form a State Co-operative, and these in turn would organize a National Association. The Department of Agriculture would calculate the size of crops needed for domestic use, export and a reasonable reserve, and allocate quotas to the states on the basis of past production. The state in turn would set quotas for local co-operatives which would assign proportions to members. Farmers would sell their crops only to their co-operatives, the receipts to be discountable at Federal Reserve Banks; locals would sell only to states and each state only to the national organization except for the share consumed within its borders. At each level, sales would be limited to the quotas previously set. The National Association would set prices and announce them every day.

Requiring for its success the voluntary co-operation of the nation's most unco-operative citizens, the plan lacked machinery for enforcement or even for inducements, but then it was not intended as a complete blueprint. If it had received the widespread distribution of the Swope Plan, it would have been a target for those who were opposed to any regimenting of farmers and those who demanded price guarantees and subsidies for farmers.

The plan, however, was not known to anyone at the time. It was committed to paper about five weeks before Roosevelt was inaugurated as President of a country whose banks were closing in droves, farmers in near revolt, workers standing in ever longer breadlines. But Swope did not need to wait for the inspiring inaugural address to know that the new administration had very different guiding principles from Hoover's. Like the rest of the country, he was deeply stirred by a warm, confident voice assuring a badly scared people that they had nothing to fear except fear itself. Thanks to his talks with the Governor of New York, Swope was more aware than most men in positions of business leadership that it was no mere oratorical period but a firm declaration of policy when the new President spoke of "broad Executive power to wage a war against the emergency, as great as the power that would be given to me if we were in fact invaded by a foreign foe."

Within two days he ordered all the banks still open, national or state, to remain closed in a "holiday" while Congress enacted emergency legislation to avert runs and preserve what soundness was left in the financial system—more than five thousand banks, or one out of every four in the country, had failed since the market crash. Swope was glad to see bold action, although many industrial managers then began their opposition to a President with such lofty notions of Federal authority over private enterprise.

A month after the inauguration Swope was in Washington and dropped in to see Louis Howe, who was at this time Roosevelt's most devoted adviser and intimate. A former newspaperman who had found in the corridors and committee rooms of Albany a keen interest in social as well as political problems, he had become the Swopes' friend through civic work in which all three were interested. In the White House, he was like a wraith, for he was as small as Swope and much more fragile, but a wraith with power. On this day he was as cordial as usual and spoke of many things without going beyond published facts.

"Don't you want to see the President?" he asked after a time.

"I didn't come here with that idea," Swope assured him. "I have no advice to offer and no favor to ask."

"You are just the man he wants to see then," replied Howe. "There aren't many men who come with such a statement."

"So we went in together," Swope wrote, "and had a very interesting talk about general conditions."

It was then that Swope received some intimation of the sort of legislation which was being prepared to spur recovery, although there were no indications as to how much, if at all, his own plan would be drawn upon. In other quarters, however, the Swope Plan was being discussed as if it were a competitor of a bill sponsored by Senator Hugo Black and passed by the Senate a few days later. This would have limited the work week to thirty hours throughout the country while maintaining the wage level. The House Labor Committee invited Swope's views, and he appeared on April 26, disappointing those who expected an attack on the Black Bill.

At sixty, he had the appearance of a man of affairs, observers thought, because he held himself very straight, had a distinguished amount of gray in his dark hair, used his glasses on a black cord to good effect. The firm set of his jaw and his economy of gesture added to the conviction his words carried. Still as slim as he had been in college, he was a neat but far from gay dresser—"he bought a good suit and wore it for ten years," a friend said.

Speaking rapidly, unemotionally, he approved the Black Bill's objectives but thought it impractical to set a rigid limit on hours across the board on a weekly basis. In General Electric, he pointed out, the average already was less than thirty hours. He suggested a half-yearly limitation, eight hundred thirty-two hours or about thirty-two hours a week, with a maximum of eight in any one day, coupled with authority for the Department of Labor to set minimum wages by localities. This power might be delegated to state industrial commissions if desired. Finally, as one might expect, he advised seeking the co-operation of trade associations and chambers of commerce to administer the program, with final authority always in the Department of Labor. He concluded by warning the Committee that the device it contemplated for spreading available work would raise prices since there would be more supervisory expense to be passed on to the consumer.

The House was not prepared for most of this program, certainly not to the extent of letting the government put a floor under wages, but the proposals before it were soon submerged in a more comprehensive piece of emergency legislation. A National

Industrial Recovery Act was being drafted, and Swope's World War I colleague, General Hugh Johnson, had been selected to head the agency it called for—Roosevelt liked to create a new department rather than expand an old one. Early in May 1933, Johnson asked the author of the Swope Plan to help prepare the final draft.

The NRA of hope and controversy was inspired in part by the Swope Plan. But there were some significant differences, and although Swope had a hand in its operation as well as its preparation, he always disclaimed paternity. The fundamental difference between his original proposal and the one that became law on June 16, 1933, was that the emphasis shifted from voluntary co-operation managed by industry under government supervision to Federal edicts accepted by industry under government compulsion. Trade associations were empowered to establish codes of fair practice, fix the volume of production for each member, standardize wages, hours, working conditions, accounting and reports. Not only were codes to be approved by the President nominally and the Administrator actually, but the President was authorized to impose a code upon any trade or industry which failed to produce its own. In order to speed the process of industrial recovery, the President also was permitted to issue licenses to firms or even individuals who agreed to equitable standards of competition and employment without waiting for codes.

As to labor, the machinery of social-security benefits which made up the bulk of the Swope Plan was not even mentioned. Instead, Congress inserted as an afterthought designed to block the Black Bill a section numbered 7-a which became briefly the Magna Charta of unionism. This gave employees the right to bargain collectively and join unions of their choice free from any employer pressure.

The man who had tried to persuade Green to organize the electrical workers had no objection to this, nor did he oppose the other provisions of the bill. In fact, he accepted NRA with the enthusiasm which was general in the country, even so keen and critical a student of government intervention in industry as Thayer applauding.

"I have always believed," he wrote from retirement in his beloved Maine to his former protégé a week after the bill's passage, "that trade combination was one of the valuable agencies which our legislators find it easier to prohibit than to regulate, and I therefore was very glad when the President's Industrial Recovery Bill was passed. It seemed to me to be almost worth the price of the depression."

He added that Swope's share in it made his satisfaction complete—"Go to it, young man."

The young man of sixty already had settled down with right good will to helping make NRA work. This meant spending most of a hard, hot summer in a Washington which as yet was sparsely equipped with air conditioning, and commuting to New York several times a week since he did not seek leave from his General Electric duties.

Washington made up in interest and excitement for its climate. Swope, who had been an innovator to such an extent that he often was called radical by his peers, was now in the midst of innovations on a scale which dwarfed anything seen in the United States before. The entire pattern of "the American way" was being redrawn with a rush which brooked no check for two years although some of the hasty improvisation would need adjustment later. If NRA was a revolution in commerce and industry, there were equally revolutionary experiments in agriculture, finance, labor, housing, regional development, even the medium of exchange.

The doctrine of *laissez faire* in which Swope had been reared but about which he had harbored doubts ever since his Hull House days was in even greater disrepute than Socialism. The doctrine of planning had taken its place. While there was very little of the orderliness of Swope's "analyze, organize, deputize, supervise" in the mélange of extraordinary Federal activity to which, almost at once, the world gave the title "New Deal," there was a new spirit.

The men closest to the President were such an unusual group in government that reporters took to calling them a brain trust. Actually they were not so much more intelligent than previous public servants as they were free from the dead hand of political tradition. They made the mistakes of their inexperience but they brought a new point of view and a zest for experiment with them which compensated for the errors. A remarkably high percentage of these lawyers, professors and farmers never had held office, elective or appointive. Swope, with the advantage of his World War I background and his understanding that the ways of government are not the ways of business, got along with them so well that he was the only industrial leader numbered among the brain trusters by so keen an observer as George Creel.

His admiration for Roosevelt remained high. As a man who had been making decisions for a good many years, and knowing that the mere making of them was as important as their rightness, Swope appreciated to the full the tremendous burden of responsibility upon this one man as the New Deal spread its ramifications into every phase of American life. The President seemed to thrive on it; the cartoonists were right to portray his cigarette holder always at a jaunty angle. Swope, who was closeted with him occasionally on NRA matters, noted: "I was impressed with the absence of strain in his manner. He was unhurried in talk or gesture and often quite genuinely merry. He was blessed with a real freedom from worry."

He himself had worked hard to achieve that freedom, and he expressed his amazement.

"I marvel, Mr. President, at your calm and poise in the way you carry the load in these fearfully hectic days," he said.

"I'll tell you, Gerard," Roosevelt replied, "at night when I lay my head on my pillow, and it is often pretty late, and I think of the things that have come before me during the day and the decisions that I have made, I say to myself, 'Well, I have done the best I can'—and I turn over and go to sleep."

Swope's own duties multiplied. Immediately after the enabling act was signed in June 1933, NRA was set up with two highly important advisory boards, one industrial and one labor. Swope was a member of the first and took part in a famous joint meeting of the two which, sitting from nine o'clock one morning until nearly two o'clock the next, hammered out an agreement which he was not alone in thinking a miracle. It provided that throughout American commerce, manufacturing and mining, pending adoption of separate industry codes, the maximum work week should be thirty-five hours and minimum pay forty cents an hour.

Also this June, Swope was asked to form a Business Advisory Council for the Department of Commerce and be its first chairman. In July, Roosevelt appointed him chairman of a Coal Arbitration Board, especially set up to avert what began to look like civil war in the coal fields. The miners were demanding their rights under Section 7-a with undisguised belligerence; the owners resisted arrogantly and General Johnson blustered loudly but ineffectively. It was a situation which could disrupt the slow trend toward industrial recovery unless apparently irreconcilable forces could be brought to see reason.

At the head of the miners was one of the strong men of the labor movement, John L. Lewis. Swope's first impression of him was of physical power, his second of vocal power, his third of suppleness of mind. The man's size and strength were obvious at first glance; his eloquence poured forth on the slightest provocation, but the keen thinking was not quite so immediately apparent. A miner at the age of twelve, Lewis had educated himself with the help of his wife, a schoolteacher, and although he had become best known to the public for handy use of his fists and voice, he had a scholar's knowledge of the American economy. Introduced into the higher circles of labor by Gompers, he had crushed opposition within the union ruthlessly, and in 1933 had been its president for fourteen years. Now he was out to organize the "captive" coal mines, which presented one of the most thoroughly tangled features of an economically difficult and distressed industry. Most of these mines belonged to steel companies which were no more willing to admit union organizers there than in the mills.

In preliminary discussions, Swope found that his talk with Green in 1926 was known to some of the labor leaders. Lewis had heard the story and was willing to believe the hero of it would not be unfriendly to miners. The union chief, a congenitally suspicious and cantankerous man, therefore looked to the chairman with more confidence than he had in the labor member of the board, George L. Berry, president of the pressman, a tight craft group, or the employer member, Louis E. Kirstein, a vice-president of Filene's store in Boston, of whom he knew nothing.

Meanwhile, under Swope's leadership, the advisory boards of the NRA had gone into action on the labor front. Coal mines were not the only scene of conflict as employers and unions disputed the meaning of Section 7-a. Strikes and lockouts could destroy the beneficial effects of industry codes and of a President's Re-employment Agreement under which work and production were slowly rising. In midsummer 1933, Swope proposed at a joint meeting of the Industrial and Labor Advisory Boards that a National Labor Board be created to safeguard the interests of both sides in labor disputes, avoid aggressive action by either and avert causes of irritation for both. On August 4, the labor and industry members unanimously approved and signed a statement he drafted, the key paragraph of which read:

"This board will consider, adjust and settle differences and controversies that may arise through differing interpretations of the President's Re-employment Agreement and will act with all possible dispatch in making known their findings. In return, the employers and employees are asked to take no disturbing action pending hearings and final decision. This board will promptly proceed to establish such central and local organizations as it may require to settle on the ground such differences as may arise in various parts of the country."

This first National Labor Board went into operation under the chairmanship of Senator Wagner, who was coming to be regarded by labor as its champion but whose stolid common sense still made him acceptable to employers. The union representatives were Green, Lewis and Dr. Leo Wolman, a facile, astute economist with an academic reputation more impressive than his years. Management served in the persons of Swope, Kirstein and Walter C. Teagle, president of the Standard Oil Company of New Jersey, who had received considerable acclaim for enlightened thinking when he organized a "share the work" movement.

More significant than the membership were the signatures to the document creating machinery to settle disputes in ways which involved no stoppage of work. Labor signatories besides those suggested for the board were Sidney Hillman, president of the Amalgamated Clothing Workers; Rose Schneidermann, president of the Women's Trade-Union League; Father Francis J. Haas, a Catholic priest who supported Labor with great intelligence and influence for many years; John P. Frey, secretary-treasurer of the Metal Trades Department of the AFL; J. R. Franklin and Berry. The list of employers was longer and better known. It included the members proposed for the board and Alfred P. Sloan, Jr., president of General Motors; H. I. Harriman, chairman of the New England Power Association who had been president of the Chamber of Commerce; Edward N. Hurley of the Hurley Machine Company and War Shipping Board chairman under Woodrow Wilson; David R. Coker and T. Austin Finch, leading manufacturers in the South, and Pierre Du Pont.

In six months this board and its regional branches handled one thousand, eight hundred and eighteen disputes and settled more than two thirds of them on the spot. Cases involving collective bargaining were three times as numerous as those in which wages were a major factor. At the national level its panels established some precedents which had permanent effects upon labor relations generally, and Swope was responsible for at least two of them.

In one of the first cases before the Board, he brought into disputes between unions and employers the use of the secret ballot, which had worked well in General Electric's Plans of Representation. The occasion was a controversy between a Pennsylvania hosiery mill owner and his workers which was especially bitter, Swope thought, because all concerned were Germans. Their quarrel arose from the employer's refusal to recognize a committee of his employees for purposes of collective bargaining. He said that he didn't know they truly represented the men. Swope suggested a vote by secret ballot to decide this point, the result to be binding on both sides, and the rest of the panel agreed. The manufacturer, however, objected. He didn't see why the men should have any say in the matter at all; whose factory was it, after all?

"This is the American way," Swope told him firmly.

He was a bit premature, although the vote was taken over the mill owner's protests. But the Wagner Act's "consent election" clause soon did make it the American way.

Another panel on which Swope served dealt with the Denver Tramways case, a dispute arising over the contention of the workers that the bargaining agent selected by a majority vote should represent all the employees. Management argued that even a majority could commit only themselves; the minority could choose their agent, too. The panel ruled that majority vote was binding as to all the employees, not the least compelling reason in Swope's mind being that any other results must lead to confusion intolerable for men and management alike. This, too, became an accepted principle in labor relations.

In 1933, however, the situation in the captive coal mines was thought to be the key to labor peace, and General Johnson twice had failed to bring the owners and the union together. In the last few years, Lewis had watched helplessly while his United Mine Workers dropped to a third of their past peak membership. Now he saw an opportunity to rebuild to even loftier heights upon the foundation of the captive mines. He came to the first formal session of the Coal Arbitration Board on a hot summer day full of fire and determination, but Swope wasted no time in preliminaries.

"The first question to determine," he announced, "is whether the men at the mines want the United Mine Workers or some other organization to represent them in collective bargaining."

"There isn't any question about that," Lewis asserted promptly in his forthright manner. "The United Mine Workers of America are the dominating factor."

"That may be true," Swope conceded. "You may know it, but I don't, and I would have to be shown."

He swiftly suggested that the men indicate their choice in an election. Lewis willingly assented, for he knew he would win any honest vote by secret ballot, and Swope asked him where the first election should be held. In the same definite way, the mine leader answered, "There isn't any question about that; the election should be held at union headquarters."

"Mr. Lewis," Swope told him, "you know this situation much better than I do and maybe all the men in the mines are members of your organization, but let us assume for a moment that there are a few who are not; what do you think would happen to them if they were to go to union headquarters?"

A broad smile came over Lewis's face, giving him a far more attractive appearance than the scowl with which cartoonists usually ornamented his features, and he replied simply, "Well, I guess they would have their heads bashed in."

This, in the state of warfare which had marked the coal industry for generations, was a tragic matter of fact. It was not the sort of introduction to a new era in labor-management relations which commended itself to a former Hull House resident. He insisted that the first election, to select the bargaining agent, be held at the mine pit.

Elections do not guarantee industrial peace, and before long the differences between labor and management in a score of industries were being fought by strikes and lockouts—often violently. But Swope made a point of recording that after the vote at the mines, most of which were won by the union, Lewis was quick to act in any work stoppage.

"He had agreed that there should be no interruption," Swope wrote, "so that whenever the men went out on unauthorized strikes or we had any other difficulties, all I had to do was to call him.

He would get the men back to work promptly. Many of the other strikes were more troublesome and involved hand-to-hand battles."

It was no accident that the General Electric Company, whose president had informed himself about labor problems from the viewpoint of the worker as well as of the employer, should have experienced less strife than any other of its size.

"I have noticed in studying labor relations abroad that, as in England for example, where strikes are carried through without physical violence, the settlement leaves no scars, and negotiations to reach it are more easily concluded," Swope wrote. "Industrial democracy does not need to be founded upon industrial warfare; in fact, warfare is incompatible with democracy in this as in any other phase of life."

This philosophy was confirmed by Swope's handling of General Electric labor relations. Throughout the depression and into the first months of the New Deal, the company's Plans of Representation had seemed to him to be working well. But while he was serving on the National Labor Board, he heard that an independent union had been formed in the Lynn plant. It was asking to be recognized as bargaining agent, the first request from within the company to change the system.

"I certainly had no desire to stand in the way of a form of representation the men wanted," Swope declares. "The managers of the Lynn plant were convinced that the request was being made on behalf of a minority. Much to their surprise, when the vote was taken under the auspices of the Boston branch of the National Labor Board, the union won. In the next few years, the Lynn example was followed at the other works of the company."

The NRA codes, in which minimum wage scales and maximum hours of work were embodied, proceeded with infinite difficulty in some industries, notably steel, and relative ease in others, such as Swope's own. He was pleased that the electrical code was the second one to be completed and—he himself serving as government's adviser—set the pattern for many. There were no restrictions on production, but the maximum work week was put at thirty-six hours.

Executives were exempt so that the activities of the president of General Electric were not curtailed. Besides rushing back and forth between Washington and New York, he managed his usual trips to General Electric offices and factories. This year a typical day in Chicago gave him morning conferences with the company manager and a General Electric director who lived in this city, lunch with the heads of Sears, Roebuck and Montgomery Ward to discuss their purchase of appliances, a tour of the World's Fair as guest of its management, a reception at the Fair, a forty-five-minute question-and-answer session with the Chicago Elfuns, a dinner meeting with his local managers and delivery of the principal address at a National Electrical Manufacturers Association affair, which was his main reason for being in Chicago. On the midnight train to the East he did his NRA homework, arriving fresh and prepared for his day in Washington.

He was aware that the electrical code stimulated production only slightly, which was true in all heavy industry. The New Deal's major contribution to immediate improvements in business was its expanded relief program—in February 1934, more than one out of every seven American households was on relief, a total of four million, seven hundred thousand families. They were not starving—that was a great accomplishment—and the effects were felt first in consumer goods industries, reaching to such producers as General Electric only slowly. In fact, the trickle of new orders was so small that Swope found in an analysis of six typical apparatus departments in five cities that there was little advance from a year before. The hours worked ranged from 22.7 a week to 30.6, and five of the plants were running at less than one-third capacity, one at only 18 per cent. The sixth, the Lynn turbine works, was operating at what was then a robust 54.4 per cent of capacity.

Under the circumstances, he could work up little enthusiasm for the continued proposals to impose a thirty-hour work week generally. They "would not in any case increase work and would not in most instances increase employment," he told the House Labor Committee which had a thirty-hour bill before it and once more invited his opinion. He had not receded from his position that industry was a better administrator of these matters than government. He kept urging self-governing bodies for industry even beyond those set up in the codes, a speech on the subject before the Business Advisory Council attracting almost as much attention as the Swope Plan.

"There was much discussion but little action," he wrote.

With the nation's economy just beginning to stir off dead center, Swope turned once more to questions of social security which the New Deal in its first hectic year had not touched. The New Deal, although its enemies would accuse it of having delayed recovery, had put into effect programs which were restoring confidence more rapidly than they achieved prosperity. Blue eagles, the symbol of compliance with NRA, bloomed in shopwindows and on factory walls. Farmers were subsidized to limit production while orators talked about an economy of abundance, and at one time during January 1934, more than four million, two hundred thousand men were employed on direct Federal public-works projects, from road-building and school improvements to leaf-raking in parks. The Tennessee Valley Authority was actively in business, home-building and slum clearance were supported. Measures to protect investors in stocks and depositors in banks had been taken, and Swope thought it high time to extend similar security to workers.

He had been preaching the gospel for years without seeming to have accomplished anything outside his own company except to enhance his reputation as an enlightened industrialist with some and as a dangerous radical with others. But four years of the Great Depression had revolutionized the attitude of most Americans toward protecting themselves from the consequences of economic accidents. They were prepared to accept a strong lead, and Roosevelt, with his instinct for a popular trend, was prepared to give it to them. While the subject was not new to him—he had been pressed to consider it even before his inauguration and had advocated it in general terms in a number of speeches—he had given no indication to any of his close advisers that he was contemplating specific action until he asked Swope to come to the White House for a private discussion of it over luncheon on March 8, 1934.

Swope was in Washington that day for a meeting of the Business Advisory Council, which was considering plans for a permanent organization to succeed NRA. Its session was big news, although nothing came of it. The two men lunching in the White House that Thursday were a better story if only a reporter had been there. Swope had made no special preparation of his case; he had been stating it so often that all the necessary facts and figures were at his fingertips. He was there, rather than another, because Roosevelt was not only genuinely fond of him but had a high regard for Swopian energy and ability to marshal facts in support of opinion. Once when Herbert, out of admiration for his older brother, signed a telegram "Swope the Lesser," F.D.R. replied, "As a matter of fact, you and Gerard between you should rate not as twins but as quintuplets! And, strictly between ourselves, you amount to a whole lot more than the Dionnes."

At luncheon Roosevelt wasted little time in preliminary chatter. He spoke of several bills on the subject of old-age pensions, unemployment insurance and disability benefits. But he was not putting his seal of administration approval upon any of them and wanted his visitor's opinion as to what a sound system should include.

Swope needed no more encouragement, because this was an opportunity to get the social-security objectives of the Swope Plan adopted not only for industry but on an even wider scale. He started by saying that a Federal system ought to include these items: life insurance, old-age pensions, payments during periods of disability or invalidism, widespread unemployment benefits.

"But," he added in recalling the interview, "I wanted it set up in such a way that every American's personal, individual account in this security system should start when he was born and continue until he died. As I outlined this concept, I could see that the President's enthusiasm was mounting. He caught the fire of the idea."

Swope spoke then of the General Electric Company's experience with its life insurance and pension plans. He described how the unemployment fund had been rejected by the workers in 1925 and adopted eagerly in 1930, with the men and the company contributing equally. He mentioned the pension plan he had originated at Western Electric.

The talk shifted to systems used in Great Britain, Germany, Scandinavia. Swope pointed out that in these, the most advanced in the world, the individual contributed to the whole package; of all the countries which had social-security plans, only Russia did not require payment by workers. He thought Russia a very unhappy precedent for Americans.

"Gerard," Roosevelt broke in, "I agree with you that fifty-fifty is the thing we ought to have."

"I think it might be satisfactory to have the employer pay two thirds and the employee one third," Swope replied. "The main thing is to keep the employee's interest through his feeling that it is his plan and he has paid for it."

"No," the President insisted, "I think fifty-fifty is about right."

"I suppose you know that the Federation of Labor doesn't agree with you," the visitor pointed out.

Roosevelt made no comment on this but went on to ask about other phases of Swope's experience in these matters. The problems of administration were canvassed lightly, and Swope urged that in spite of any difficulties every worker should be included, industrial, commercial, agricultural, domestic. As he was leaving, Roosevelt asked him to summarize all these ideas in a memorandum. Two weeks later it was completed, a fairly detailed document bristling with statistics and a covering letter outlining the proper method of protecting a citizen from birth to death so that he would grow up with a sense of his own personal share in a great system of social insurance.

"When a child is born," Swope wrote, "the parents take out life insurance from the Federal government, with a minimum payment of two cents per week—in stamps—which will be secured at the post office and put in a book supplied for that purpose. This book is to be retained by the parents of the child and payments thereon maintained until he is twenty years of age, or gainfully employed, when the book is to be handed to the child."

At this point the individual was to pay sixty-five cents a week as long as he was employed at half or more of the normal hours for his industry, while the employer paid seventy cents, all by stamps from the post office pasted in the book. A worker kept his book all his life so "as he goes from employment to employment, his protection goes with him."

The package which these payments paid for was life insurance, graded upward to a top of $2,000; an old-age pension of thirty dollars a month, which once had been a subsistence income; unemployment benefits of six dollars a week minimum ranging up to half the individual's full-time pay. Benefits would be paid out through the employer but the administration would be in the hands of "a committee of the employees of such employer, to secure the best administration and to lessen malingering and improper claims." Swope was sure that only the workers themselves could keep the system from being abused and then only if they were protecting some of their own money. He liked to tell of a General Electric worker who applied for unemployment benefits when he had a milk route which provided a good living. His fellow workers on the fund's administration rejected his claim indignantly; management would have been put on the spot if it had been their sole responsibility.

That Roosevelt's enthusiasm had not cooled was soon evident. After he received this letter he began to push for an administration social-security measure. His Secretary of Labor, Frances Perkins, has written:

"At Cabinet meetings and when he talked privately with a group of us, he would say, 'You want to make it simple—very simple. So simple that everyone will understand it. And what's more, there is no reason why everybody in the United States should not be covered. I see no reason why every child, from the day he is born, shouldn't be a member of the social-security system. When he begins to grow up, he should know he will have old-age benefits direct from the system to which he will belong all his life. If he is out of work he gets a benefit. If he is sick or crippled he gets a benefit."

He had absorbed the Swope proposal so completely that the Secretary also quotes him as saying, "The system ought to be operated through the post offices. Just simple and natural—nothing elaborate or alarming about it."

He argued repeatedly that benefits should be extended to all workers and their families.

"I don't see why not," he would say. "Cradle to the grave—from the cradle to the grave they ought to be in a social-insurance system."

So firmly had he accepted this idea, she relates, that when Sir William Beveridge's British plan was announced in December 1942 as a "cradle to the grave" program, Roosevelt protested, "It is my idea. It is not the Beveridge Plan. It is the Roosevelt Plan."

A lot of people think it was the Swope Plan, although Swope himself is the first to say that it comes from a great variety of sources and is the composite of the thinking of many men and women. The important thing in 1934 was that Roosevelt, the one man in the country who could get a bill passed, consented to adjournment of Congress that summer only on condition that social security be "must" legislation at the next session. He appointed an Advisory Council on Economic Security, of which he asked Swope to be a member, and in the fall, the extent and manner of coverage was being hotly debated by spokesmen for labor, industry and just plain people.

The Council was not the last word on social security, but the debates among its members were an accurate reflection of the final decisions. Apparently no one except Swope and Roosevelt had been fired by the cradle-to-the-grave ideal. The system covered only adults, and employed ones at that. The simplicity of a book with stamps bought from the post office was eliminated in favor of a new Federal agency and a complicated system of payroll deductions and levies on employers.

Swope and a few others argued for features which lost out in the final votes. Old-age pensions were put on the fifty-fifty basis. But when it came to unemployment insurance, the opposition was determined and powerful. Swope never forgot the words of Green in objecting to any worker payments.

"We grant," he said, "that old age may be an incident in the life of each man, and therefore provision for it should be participated in by the employee as well as the employers. But unemployment is an incident in industry for which management is responsible, and therefore management must accept the entire burden."

Swope disputed this thesis. In the climate of opinion then prevailing, it was useless to say that management was neither so omnipotent nor so omniscient as to merit full responsibility for unemployment. But it was worth while to point out that management was sufficiently alert not to bear the full cost anyway, since it would be added to the normal expenses of business and eventually paid by the consumer. Therefore, it was on the ground that it would make for a better administration and a keener interest on the part of workers that he argued for employee contributions. He pointed out that in the better European systems workers paid a share, and so did the government. He also urged that a feature of a Wisconsin statute on workmen's compensation be adapted. This would permit companies with a record of low unemployment to pay less than firms with high unemployment histories. He thought it would stimulate management to smooth out the peaks and valleys of employment in seasonal industries.

He lost this round, as he did a proposal to widen the coverage beyond commercial and industrial workers. He wanted to include farm laborers, domestic help, employees of nonprofit educational, religious and health organizations.

"Curiously enough," he wrote, "this proposal was opposed by the representatives of the educational and philanthropic institutions themselves."

Swope joined several other business leaders and one member of the President's brain trust, Raymond Moley, in presenting a minority report on these points to the Secretary of Labor. But none of them was included in the bill which finally was signed on August 14, 1935, after a stormy passage through Congress. On the whole, though, it was a triumph for the advocates of social security. The major objectives were achieved, above all recognition that the Federal government should organize protection for its citizens against the hazards of the economic system. This was not exactly the principle upon which Swope had reared his earliest programs in the field; he had thought that industry itself should do the job. But he had been converted to the need for Federal legislation, certainly to extend the protection to others than industrial workers.

During this debate, Swope had his finger in a few other New Deal pies. He talked with the President and Louis Howe about better housing programs, testified before the new Securities and Exchange Commission and annoyed a few industrial diehards by urging not only rules requiring full and regular statements on the business of the company but by agreeing to publication of certain corporation salaries. He wanted that last limited, though, to the two highest officers. In General Electric that meant himself and Young. He was willing to lump the salaries of the next group as a whole, but he feared that publication of the earnings of individual vice-presidents, for example, would lead to unnecessary jealousies.

Since he couldn't get the Federal government to include domestic workers in its Social Security Act, he put into effect a system of his own for his household staff in the country. Then he won the consent of the General Electric directors to some improvements in the company's profit-sharing program. For a long time executives had shared, but now, although 1934 was hardly a good year, he put through an arrangement whereby workers shared too, and as business picked up, they split about one dollar for every eight paid as dividends to stockholders. It was the first example in a major company of profit-sharing by everyone from porter to president.

All in all, his service in Washington had been interesting and rewarding. As he passed his sixty-second birthday, as alert and brisk in movement as ever, but with a lot of white in his hair, he was looking forward to new opportunities, opportunities for growth which the depression had interrupted but not destroyed. He was coming back to a new office in New York, perched on the forty-fifth floor of a building at Fifty-first Street and Lexington Avenue. He could look out over the East River one way or to the Hudson the other and see in between the green strip of Central Park. He is not a great one for looking out of windows at any time to dream, but he used to contemplate the view occasionally while he listened to reports, and say to himself with satisfaction, "This city isn't going to hell."

XVI *Recovery*

The forty-fifth floor of General Electric's new building had become the company's holy of holies. Vice-presidents measured their importance by the proximity of their offices to that of the great chief, a common business standard, so that a move nearer often was as gratifying as a raise in salary. Their president, credited with bringing the company safe and sound through the Great Depression, was looked upon by many younger men as infallible now. He wasn't, of course, but the reputation gave his decisions the force of gospel, and few were bold enough to object. This was strange, because it was apparent to any impartial observer that Swope liked and promoted these few.

"He seemed to love an argument," says one retired vice-president. "Looking back, I seem to have had quite a few with him. The battle was always good while it lasted. I cannot recall at this moment ever having won any such argument, although I must admit I still think I was right on many of them."

There were no counteracting legends of men fired for disagreeing. Yet there always was the feeling, apparently, that lightning might strike. For example, Swope attended a meeting of the board of the General Electric Supply Company, which distributed appliances and, like all subsidiaries, had directors drawn exclusively from the company officials. A statement was presented comparing the year's business with that of the Graybar Company, whose profits were large despite a slightly smaller volume and notably fewer but more highly paid employees. Swope asked the gathering what such a situation might mean. His then favorite vice-president, Quinn, broke an uncomfortable silence with "One clear meaning is that we don't pay our people enough."

He recalls that there was almost a gasp of horror around the table at such impertinence, for Swope was supposed to have a strong aversion even to talking about high salaries. But to the surprise of the audience, he said approvingly, "That's absolutely right."

At the same time, he was inclined to regard a post with General Electric as carrying with it advantages in prestige and security which compensated for smaller salaries than might have been earned elsewhere. His own experience in Western Electric, where he had carved out a notable career at small pay but big opportunity, influenced his attitude, and he made no secret of the fact that the only time he ever had asked for a raise himself was his adventure with Barton in the nineties. Quinn has written that during the depression he had an offer of another job at $50,000 a year, and consulted Swope, who said it wasn't good enough for him.

"But," Quinn adds, "he did not offer to raise my salary to the $50,000 figure."

Quinn remained anyway, for there was a strong suspicion, which Swope since has confirmed, that he had destined the outgoing, likable and alert redhead for the presidency. Not the least of the reasons was that he asserted himself. So did a different but equally forceful executive upon whom Swope had his eye, Charlie Wilson. So did one of the few men in the company who could bandy figures about as easily as Swope, Jesse W. Lewis, promoted from an accountant to treasurer. But they were emulated only by young men with a strong belief in their own views and enough iron in their souls to express them against opposition. This combination is rare; Swope encountered it seldom and cherished it when he did.

Quinn, a maverick who came to think that the large, diversified corporation is dangerously inefficient, crushing smaller competitors by sheer weight of capital advantage, also reached the conclusion that Swope was only a hard-working, machinelike, ambitious person with no great talents. But he recalled that one day he was summoned to the president's office, where he found the leading officials of the National Lamp works.

"Would you mind repeating what you have just said?" Swope asked them.

The spokesman obligingly recited a suggestion that all incandescent lamps made by any General Electric factory be called GE lamps. When he finished, no mention was made of the day years ago when a younger Quinn had met the new head of the company. Swope wasted no time explaining to the others or inviting Quinn's comments, but he had taken the trouble to show a man that his ideas bore fruit.

By this time, Quinn argues, General Electric had what he calls effective monopoly control of the lamp business. Swope, who would reply that even a large majority of the business is not necessarily monopoly, is more interested in the fact that lamps have become progressively better and cheaper. Behind the by now traditional policy of the whole industry to get the price as low as possible was a reason which Swope seldom stressed but of which he was fully aware. The chief makers of lamps always had been the makers of generating and transmitting apparatus, too. The more widespread the use of electricity in home and office, the greater the demand for the expensive equipment.

Swope cited lamps as the supreme example of his "more things for more people at less cost." Thanks first to its research—notably by Coolidge and the laboratory's Nobel Prize winner, Irving Langmuir—and then to its manufacturing skills, he declares, General Electric made the best bulbs although licensing competitors to use its patents. The research, he maintains, is something which no one much smaller than General Electric could undertake. It was one of his favorite themes in talks to officials on the advantages of their company. Because General Electric could afford even Langmuir's pure research, the electrical industry and the public were enriched, and the company got its fair share of the benefits. Similar research, perhaps, could be conducted under the auspices of government and universities. Swope was not one to minimize the value of their studies. But they do not take the place of industrial research, and there is no certainty that they would if the corporations gave it up.

He lost out on the fruits of research elsewhere, though. A new Dutch flash bulb for photographers was offered to General Electric and was refused, eventually being bought by a small independent, the Wabash Company, which in a few years had three fourths of the country's flash bulb business. At about the same time, General Electric (and every other American company) turned down fluorescent lighting on the ground that incandescent lamps were better, leaving the new field to a French subsidiary.

It may be that these slips were due to Swope's concentration in 1935 and the next couple of years upon new home appliances. Throughout the depression, one of the very few commodities which showed no decline was the use of household electricity. Its cost had come down, partly because abuses revealed by the depression investigations were corrected but mostly because the load made reduced rates possible. Public projects—big dams and rural electrification—were spreading lines into remote corners.

Swope liked to tell how he had electrified his own home in the country because rates came down. Current in Westchester had been ten to fourteen cents a kilowatt hour, so he could not afford such luxuries as electric ranges or heaters. In fact, he had countered an objection to the high prices of GE stoves by telling the utility people they couldn't even give such things away unless they reduced rates.

Now, in 1935, he put Charlie Wilson in charge of a new appliance division which was to expand GE products into virtually everything that the American household could use. The company's plants still were working at less than half capacity. But there were ample reserves to finance growth, and General Electric had won in the depression a large following of investors to replace the speculators who had bid the stock up in 1929. Swope never had any illusions about the loyalty of shareholders; they would have been naïve to seek anything more than the best return they could get on their money, but he was proud of the fact that General Electric was one of the few corporations which had increased the number of its stockholders through the depression although the price of a share had gone from a high of 100¾ after a four-for-one split in 1930 to a low of 8½ in 1933. The company remained fourth largest in the country, passed by General Motors but passing United States Steel—A.T. & T. and Du Pont were the two others. Swope thought his company had come through the depression strong enough to go after the 25,000,000 customers who had been his objective ever since 1922.

To do it, he was prepared to modify his managerial principles, adapting them to growth. He established the appliance division on almost vertical lines. As Wilson describes this partial conversation, he doodles with a pencil and says, "Mr. Swope told me, 'We won't have a vertical organization [the pencil draws a short up-and-down line] nor yet a horizontal one [quick stroke across the page]. We will use something between the two [careful diagonal line] and lean on one another.' "

All he asked of Wilson was perfection and a clear set of figures. He talked a good deal about "GE quality" and one way he expected to get it was to have a top executive try out a new appliance until he was satisfied with it. Wilson set himself on fire twice before Swope would let the GE blanket go on the market, brushing aside pleas that someone else might get there first. Once he was convinced he had the best product, his supposed aversion to spending money disappeared. In his new radio department, for example, Wilson calculated the business for its first four months in time to be prepared when Swope called him in for questions. He recalls that the dialogue went like this:

SWOPE: How much business will you do in these four months?
WILSON: Eight million. ("We did eight million, eight hundred thousand," he explains, "but you always were supposed to go at least 10 per cent over the estimate.")
SWOPE: How much will you lose?
WILSON: That depends.
SWOPE: I didn't ask you that. How much will you lose as you've set it up?
WILSON: A million dollars. ("That was a lot of money in those days.")
SWOPE: Not enough.
WILSON: I know—you think I haven't figured enough for advertising and promotion, but more wouldn't do any good in four months.
SWOPE: (*closing the conversation*) It's your job.

By the time the year was out, the boy from Hell's Kitchen was the new heir apparent, for Quinn had resigned in November to embark upon a career in advertising and merchandising which eventually converted him into one of the most persistent, vocal critics of what he calls "giant business."

At this time Swope was hearing that side of the argument from one of its most notable advocates. During his sojourns in Washington, he visited his old teacher, Brandeis, and on at least one occasion the talk turned to the merits of size. Swope mentioned that a savings bank life insurance plan which Brandeis had fathered in Massachusetts was pitifully small because people hadn't been educated—or sold—on its advantages. In the whole state, the total of life insurance under this program was less than General Electric had for its employees. Brandeis preferred it that way.

He didn't want even insurance to get big. For he was still of the opinion he had expressed in 1933: "Able, discerning scholars . . . show that size alone gives to giant corporations a social significance not attached ordinarily to smaller units of private enterprise . . . sometimes to dominate the state."

He and Swope did not convert each other. Swope saw that the power of industry was great, but that the big corporations were no more danger to the state than powerful, organized concentrations of other forces—of veterans or consumers or minorities—if they were sufficiently ruthless and insufficiently regulated.

He had watched Brandeis's philosophy prevail in one instance, however, and because of it he had a new office. General Electric, along with the other sponsoring companies, had accepted a decree divorcing them from the Radio Corporation of America. The government had invited them to organize RCA in the first place, and some industry officials thought it was a double cross when the Department of Justice complained that the relationship was a violation of the anti-trust laws. Neither Swope nor Young, who had always been much more concerned with radio, took this position. Wireless had become a very different business since RCA was formed to rival the cable companies. Broadcasting into the home, which even so sanguine an electrical pioneer as Rice had thought never would be more than a toy—he had advised the company to keep out of it—had become a major industry. Young for one could see a justification for separating the major manufacturers from ownership of the major broadcaster. General Electric distributed its share of RCA stock to its own shareholders. However, there was a substantial sum of money owing from RCA, and it did not have the cash. Swope went against the advice of most of his colleagues to take in part payment the fine new building on Lexington Avenue, valued at $7,000,000, for this transaction, which RCA could not use since it had moved into John D. Rockefeller's new Radio City. Few General Electric officials thought it wise for a solid concern like theirs to move so far from the financial district. But Swope preferred to decide on the basis of a study of employee and customer convenience trends of business rentals in various districts and prospects for profitable leases since his own company then could use at most one third of the building. Once again he had displayed that fondness for figures which explained why one of his favorite limericks was:

A snake-charmer came from Bombay.
"I just love my adder," she'd say.
She had a position
With some statistician—
Which adder she meant, I can't say.

He was arithmetically meticulous; his expense accounts were models of precision, detailing each penny down to small tips and taxi fares. Of course, Jim Harris kept the details and prepared the sheets, but Swope always saw them. He never gave them more than a glance, but that was as much as he needed. Once, after putting down the many items which added up to a $400 or $500 trip to Washington, Harris was surprised and annoyed to have Swope give the product a swift look and say, "This can't be right."

"How, not right?" demanded the secretary, who long ago had ceased to be intimidated by his chief's positive manner.

"Oh, all the items are here," Swope conceded, "but it doesn't check."

He had spotted at once the error of $10 in addition which it took Harris some minutes to locate. This ability, whether operating on an expense account or a complicated profit-and-loss statement, was the talent which enabled him to keep abreast of the company's steadily expanding activities. His mind would translate graphs and figures into an elaborate story of a year's operations, showing him more precisely than words just where the weaknesses might be. For he was mightily concerned about weaknesses.

"I very seldom report to my directors about the profitable lines," he once confided. "I only report on those which are losing money. If we look after our weaknesses, we don't need to worry much about our strength."

Perhaps this is why he seemed to distribute more criticism than praise, although there are men who think he was generous with both. He himself was perfectly willing to take criticism as long as he thought it was sincere and open. His close association with the New Deal, for example, led to a great many rather barbed requests "for information" at employee meetings, especially as administration of the NRA codes bogged down and dissatisfaction with them grew among workers and consumers as well as businessmen. This was the reason that, when the Supreme Court struck NRA down on May 17, 1935, there were few to mourn, and that summer some provocative questions were asked about it at Island camps. Swope would reply with stories of sweated labor which NRA exposed and corrected in its early days, of a mill owner who was paying eighteen cents an hour but got the weekly wages just over $15 by working his employees eighty-four hours, and then defended it by saying, "Our people like it."

"I realize that my activities in the last year or so must have embarrassed your salesmen," Swope confessed at one of the camps, and went on to explain his work with associates from highly respected companies. "Of course, they are not all radicals like I am."

When someone asked him whether business improvement was not being accomplished in spite of the New Deal rather than because of it, he replied disarmingly, "I don't know," but went on to add that he personally thought it was due "to a large extent to NRA. . . . I do know that there have been some tremendous results from NRA."

He cited as just one the abolition of child labor in textile mills and an agreement by Southern mill owners to pay $12 a week, "ever so much higher than the wage that had been paid." Repeatedly he replied to expressed fears that the government was going to take over complete control of industry by saying he expected more regulation, which he thought all business ought to welcome, but not regimentation. Even when a bill abolishing utility holding companies was passed, the fruit of the abuses which the depression had revealed, he refused to echo the chorus of doom which many of his fellows joined. He didn't like the bill; he testified in Washington that regulation was better than abolition because holding companies could serve a useful purpose. In this he spoke not only for a manufacturing company which wanted solvent utilities as customers but for the biggest single holders of utility shares, the various General Electric employee funds.

For a time this stand cost him some of his popularity. He got letters from stockholders accusing him of "acting as catspaw to pull the Electric Power Clique out of the fire," of being "stupid and shortsighted," of putting out "shallow propaganda . . . false deductions, twisted facts and lies." On the other hand, he got letters from people who told him they were selling their stock because the president of the company was fostering regulation of business, social experiments and employee welfare over owner dividends.

"We get it every way we go, but that is part of the job," he said philosophically, and went on to add that business is mistaken to oppose regulatory legislation or worker benefits. "All these advances have always been opposed by manufacturers. I suppose they always will, but finally I think industry and manufacturers get a worse bill than if they had taken a little more liberal stand in the first place."

That General Electric's business suffered from Swope's identification with the New Deal, or at least that salesmen thought so, was plain in the summer of 1935. One of the most recalcitrant, outspoken industrial foes of the New Deal was Weir of Weirton Steel, and one day Swope, answering a long-distance call, heard the voice of an agitated salesman.

"Ernie Weir thinks you are the devil and won't give us any business," he said, and proposed that he fly up to New York at once to accompany Swope on a mission to pacify the steel man.

"You don't need to fly to New York," Swope replied. "I will see him."

He liked to tell this story to fearful associates, because it pointed a moral.

"I found, as is so often the case, that our gentleman was entirely wrong in his assumpton," he would say. "I called up Weir and went to see him—we had a very lovely hour together. I have great respect for him—and he gave us the business."

One of the few political issues on which he would have agreed with Weir, however, was municipal ownership of power plants. He thought government never could give service as cheaply or as well or with development of the latest discoveries as could properly regulated private utilities. But he gave public projects their due, if a little reluctantly.

"Someone might say, 'Hasn't the government been instrumental in lowering rates?' and I am sorry to say they have," he admitted in pointing out that under private ownership, the United States had developed the highest per-capita use of electricity in the world.

Those lower rates were the key to the progress of General Electric, both in apparatus and appliances. They were a big reason why Swope was able to say in 1936 that the company had come out of the depression stronger than ever before. The plants all were working at better than half their capacity; nearly ten thousand more men were employed, and the average work week was up to thirty-seven hours. By the end of the year the minimum starting pay in the shops was seventy cents an hour, and he enjoyed contrasting it in his speeches with his own twelve and one half cents because, he said, the difference was due entirely to more production at lower costs.

The upward trend was noticeable also in the close questioning about salaries to which he was subjected at almost every meeting of officials. During the depression men had been glad to be on a pay roll. With returning confidence, they wanted to know why more of the profits didn't go to them. So they asked fairly blunt questions and got equally blunt answers. In 1935, Swope had instituted an adjustment in pay for everyone earning less than $4,000 a year, tied to the Department of Labor's cost of living index, 1 per cent increase in salary for every point up in the cost of living, and vice versa. (He overruled people who said workers would accept the increase but not the cut, and he proved that he was right when, after going up 7 per cent, wages came down again

5.) When someone asked when executives would have their salaries similarly adjusted, he replied, "Never."

Men at or near the subsistence level, he explained, were too surely endangered by small rises in the cost of living, but "you people are above that" and were paid on the basis of contribution and responsibility. He liked to cite the shift in Russia, where, he said, the old line "to each according to his need" had been changed to the capitalistic concept of "to each according to his contribution."

In these years, too, he used his own case as an illustration to defend payments of extra compensation only to officials whose departments earned more than 8 per cent on the money invested in them, a small list for a long time.

"Neither the chairman nor the president has received any extra compensation in the last five years," he told one group in 1936, "simply because we didn't earn it."

That was a year, too, when questions about his political views were sharp, and often a little smug before November. During the campaign he never went any further than to admit he was a Democrat and to reject a few of the more outrageous charges being made against Roosevelt as a dictator, Fascist or Communist. He had no desire to influence votes by his position in the company, and he was careful to speak well of Landon, the Republican nominee. But when Roosevelt won his smashing electoral victory, 523 to 8, Swope allowed himself a bit more freedom of speech. He addressed the Elfuns of Schenectady the day after the election, and when someone asked how he liked the result, he replied that certain people in the audience "have equipped me for almost a year of simple living in backing their opinion against mine." He admitted that "the discrimination the American citizen exercises . . . excites my great admiration." Then this apostle of efficiency in industry startled some of his listeners with a remark which showed why he got along so well in Washington.

"Happily when you come to a democracy, well-being is much more important than efficiency," he said. "Maybe that is a curious thing for me, as head of an organization that must be efficient to maintain itself, to say. But efficiency isn't the ideal of life. The ideal of the American family, of your family and mine, is to secure the greatest happiness from life, and it is not always the most efficient government that is going to give that."

He had his own notions as to the extent to which government could promote happiness. It was not much on the positive side; rather he saw government as supplying basic protections, keeping open the channels of opportunity so that the individual could achieve his own happiness. Perhaps because he had done it well himself, he was an optimist, and because he was acutely aware that others were not so fortunate, he tried to help.

Because he did not think government the proper agency for all relief, he accepted in both 1935 and 1936 the chairmanship of the National Mobilization for Human Needs which sought to promote the success of community chest campaigns throughout the country. Newton D. Baker had headed the organization for its first two years and asked Swope to take over for the next. The chests were facing special difficulties because many donors thought that government social-security acts eliminated the need for private philanthropy.

Swope, fresh from the social-security battlefield, knew how mistaken this was, and set his executive talents to organizing an educational program to combat the mistaken point of view. He also made another trip to Washington at which he won the support of Roosevelt and the Secretary of the Treasury for legislation to permit corporations to write off on their tax returns donations up to 5 per cent of their profits. The measure opened up a new source of funds for health and educational institutions. But, of course, Swope had to convince some of his fellow industrialists that they should participate. Henry Ford, for example, replied to his first suggestion of assistance: "Swope, you know I don't agree with this thing you are doing."

"Well, Mr. Ford, how would you do it?" Swope asked.

"That's the worst of it. I don't know," the master of mass production confessed.

Ford was a more reasonable being than many gave him credit for, and when Swope urged that he ought to go along on an existing plan until he could work out a better, he agreed to attend a Detroit luncheon to open the big drive. But he was so shy that on the day appointed, he waited outside the hotel, trying to nerve himself for his appearance, and the organizers of the luncheon grew frantic. This diffidence was one of his unsuspected charms. Most of his public ventures unconnected with industry had been unfortunate—a libel suit, a campaign of anti-Semitism, a peace ship in the midst of war—and had brought ridicule and even hate where he had hoped for good will. It had become a real sacrifice for him to take part in public ceremonies, although now that he was in his seventies, his years and his success had mellowed the popular attitude toward him. On this occasion, Swope went out after him, and when they came back for the inevitable picture-taking, one observer commented, "It looked like Public Enemy Number One being led from the courtroom by the chief of detectives."

Swope, however, was fond of him—"Mr. Ford was simply and genuinely my friend," he says—and presented the millionth GE refrigerator, gold-plated for the occasion, to Ford's museum in Dearborn. Eccentric at times, the father of the tin lizzie had a keen mind when it came to things that interested him and an endearing fuzziness about those that were of small importance. One had to feel a little protective and therefore affectionate toward a man who didn't even know where he lived when he was in New York. Swope once assumed that he was at the Waldorf-Astoria, and mentioned it during a conversation in his office.

"Oh, no," said Ford. "I am staying at a little German hotel near Broadway and Forty-second Street, and I always talk to the waiters in German, which they don't like."

He couldn't think of the name of the hotel, which Swope was unable to identify from his description, so he stepped out to the anteroom to ask his secretary.

"Where am I staying here in New York?"

"Why, Mr. Ford, you are staying at the Ritz Carlton," said the secretary, naming one of the city's proudest hostelries, and definitely on the other side of town from Times Square.

On the other hand, Swope's affection did not lead him to blind admiration. He recognized a master of mass production when he saw one, but he recognized, too, the great mechanic's blindness in human relations. Commenting on Ford's phobia against middlemen, he explained, "He sells direct to his distributors and dealers, and he does it drastically; he doesn't consider them as human beings but simply as cogs in the wheel in bringing his product into the hands of the consuming public. His cost of distribution isn't much better than the others, like General Motors, who sell through dealers."

These were the days when automobile manufacturers were resisting the stimulus which NRA and later the Wagner Act gave to collective bargaining. Ford was only the most outspoken, stubborn, unrelenting foe of labor organization in an industry which was so anti-union that Detroit had passed Pittsburgh and Los Angeles as the citadel of the open shop. In the fall of 1936, when Swope visited Detroit for his second Mobilization of Human Needs campaign, the United Automobile Workers were just beginning the drive which would carry them from a membership of thirty thousand to four hundred thousand in a year of bitter industrial battles featured by wildcat and sit-down strikes, brutal beatings of union organizers and assorted violence in word and deed.

In this situation—paralleled in other previously unorganized mass-production industries—many industrial managers were unable to resist the temptation to brand all union leaders as dangerous demagogues or Communists and condemn all their works out of hand. A fair number of questions hurled at Swope during open meetings challenged him to say what he thought of unions now. Temperately he replied that he did not defend sit-down strikes or breaches of contract, but he reminded his audiences that the unions they were referring to had sprung from bitterness and violence. In spite of all the trouble, he thought his classmate, Sloan, was better off for having signed union agreements than if he had refused. Now, Swope pointed out, the public attributed work stoppages to the automobile workers, whereas in the absence of a contract, General Motors would have been blamed. But there was a more important point.

"Whether you like it or not," he said, "you have got to open your minds to the fact that labor must have more protection than it has had before. . . . Maybe unionization is a justification of the manager's job; it makes that job much more difficult and therefore he has to do better if he is to continue to hold it. . . . I don't say I like it, because every man would like to do what he thinks best for the other fellow, but I feel that if you have the confidence and respect of your people, you won't have nearly as much difficulty as you thought you would. . . . It takes time, it takes patience, because many of these people have had no background and experience; they are young and want to accomplish things without due process of time. . . . I am sure that few of you, if any, would sympathize with some of the methods that have been followed by some of the employers to prevent organization amongst their people."

He was not talking for publication or public acclaim in these extemporaneous answers to what at the time was the burning question for American industry. In fact, he was speaking off the record, often making a point that he not be quoted.

"If I am going to tell Gene Grace or Tom Girdler what I think of them," he said, referring to two of the most anti-union employers then in the news, "I am going to tell them myself, but I don't want you fellows to do it."

All this time he knew very well that he would be called upon to practice what he preached. The organizational work he had proposed to Green ten years before was taking place in the electrical industry with a rush, but not exactly to his prescription. Here and there elections to select bargaining representatives were demanded in General Electric plants, and Swope, remembering the surprise union victory in Lynn, picked up some easy money betting factory managers and Charlie Wilson that the men, although without major grievances, would pick the new CIO Electrical Workers.

A rash of strikes in other industries during December 1936 was followed in January by the biggest sit-down of all at General Motors. It began and ended in company concessions, while Swope was on his vacation, in Mexico this time. It left a bitter aftermath, with workers reinforced in the opinion that they could win their rights only by proving their power, and employers convinced that unions had proved their untrustworthiness and would never live up to a contract.

Swope, coming back into this atmosphere in mid-February 1937, found that the president of the new Electrical Workers, James B. Carey, had asked him for a meeting. The advice of plant managers and other top executives was that Swope decline—"it would give them too much prestige." Besides, such discussions were not a normal part of the company president's duties, and a pattern of plant-by-plant negotiations had been established. Swope acquiesced at first, but ten days later he changed his mind.

"I remember very well, just as though it was today," he said some six months later, "that evening, February 24, which was a Wednesday. I went home in the subway and read in the paper that Chrysler had agreed to meet Lewis and the other people, and I said, 'Swope, it isn't time for you, a little king, to say you won't meet with anybody.' So I called our managers together the next morning and I said, 'I think you are all wrong; I have never objected to meeting anyone, even refrigerator specialty dealers [this small dig was delivered to an audience of merchandising executives; he eliminated it in telling the story to others], and I can't begin now.'

"So while they sat there, I called up Jim Carey, the president of the union, and said, 'Mr. Carey, I have got your letter; you have been very patient in regard to a reply. I don't know you and you don't know me; maybe it would be well to have a meeting and just see what kind of people we are. Won't you come up and see me?' He said he would be glad to, but would like to bring his secretary along. Well, I had visions of some platinum blonde, and that might cramp my style, so I said, 'Oh, no, come alone and let us meet man to man, all off the record."

Only much later did he learn that the union secretary was a man (at this time Julius Emspak, a former worker in the Schenectady plant who had used Swope's Union College loan fund to finance his education, and already had paid it back), an important figure in the organization. Also that the Electrical Workers had a rule requiring at least two officials to be present at any negotiation. Apparently Carey knew when to waive a rule. He came alone, a good-looking twenty-five-year-old, slim, with a lot of dark hair and the appearance of an intense college senior. The two had what Swope called "a fine intimate talk," mostly about Carey, his background, his hopes, his beliefs.

"You seem to know all about me from the age of six," the young man commented.

"No," replied Swope, smiling, "from the age of two."

Their talk finally turned to various phases of the electrical industry, and it paid off for the union and the company. Carey came away convinced that Swope could be trusted, that he understood labor relations and that nothing to which he agreed would be overruled by anyone. As a result of their conversation, Swope arranged a meeting—at which no objections to the presence of the secretary were raised—between union and General Electric officials. That ended Swope's personal contacts with the union leaders on bargaining, although he saw them occasionally on broader industry matters. He delegated chief responsibility for union negotiations to Burrows, the vice-president in charge of manufacturing, with this brief admonition: "If you can't get along with these fellows and settle matters, there's something wrong with you."

Thus forewarned, Burrows always did settle matters without coming to the president for help, and without any work stoppages, a record which no other major corporation could boast through all that era. Swope was glad enough to be spared entanglement in labor problems, although even after Carey was ousted and a reputedly pro-Communist element gained control, Swope called the union "well led, the discipline good." But most of all he was pleased that the experience vindicated his view of employee relations, which he has summarized:

"Under the American principle of free and responsible private institutions for both industry and workers, the best results are obtained through voluntary co-operation with a minimum of legal compulsion. I had been arguing for a long time that management's duty was first to the public it served and then to the workers, even before the stockholders or the industry itself. By the middle of the 1930s, these views were well known. Probably they had some influence upon the manner in which the union representatives approached us and negotiated with us in good faith.

"Such an attitude on the part of labor is essential to industrial peace because, of course, management cannot do it alone. The union must share many of the same objectives, although I am not suggesting that its leaders go so far as to put the interest of stockholders above that of the men. Part of this mutual philosophy should be a willingness to share relevant facts as to costs, earnings, production and so on with each other and with the public. Under these circumstances, the most difficult situations can be resolved peaceably. This has been proved not only in the General Electric Company but in the experience of the railroads, the garment trades and others.

"Nor is it only in the negotiation of wages and hours that the rule of co-operation applies. In fact, even in our first negotiations with the Electrical Workers, neither of these points was raised seriously by the union. But often the good effects of high pay and short hours are lost because of other grievances or hardships under which work is done. One of management's tasks is to devise ways of overcoming these hardships or other legitimate grievances. So small a thing as a ventilator to draw off unpleasant odors can work wonders in labor-management relations.

"In the long run, the people who should be management's chief concern are those who give their lives to the business, the workers, and not primarily those who buy in and out because a company pays good dividends."

In the midst of industrial strife which saw the CIO's rise to power in the mass-production industries, this seemed more the view of a cloistered scholar, even if not couched in scholarly terms, than of a major participant. It had stemmed from Swope's experiences and observations in more than forty years, but it was flavored by his incorrigible belief that on the whole people are pretty nice folks. It might enrage his liberal friends that he could see the good points of Henry Ford and Ernie Weir. But Weir and Ford were no less outraged when he insisted that Jim Carey and John L. Lewis were reasonable men. But Swope was not disturbed. He picked up a little story that summer of 1937 to prove his point that the more you treat people like decent, respectable human beings, the more they will behave that way.

He and Mary went to Italy in June, and as usual he dropped in on General Electric plants wherever they went. One of them, a big one, was in Milan, and Swope's visit lasted beyond closing time. Coming out of the office, he saw the workers moving off down a path in single file. He joined the line to see what happened, a new Fascist ceremony perhaps. No; at the gate every woman and about one man in ten were "frisked" to see if they were stealing material.

"I asked the manager about it, and he said that was a customary practice in factories in Italy," says Swope, who characteristically refrains from expressing moral indignation, but simply adds, "I asked him to make a trial of giving up the practice and appeal to the workers' honesty."

Nearly three years later he learned that the experiment had succeeded. No one was being searched at the gate, and losses from pilfering had declined.

Besides visiting factories, listening to Toscanini's last concerts at the Salzburg Festival before the Nazi *Anschluss* the next year, sight-seeing with Mary and calling on old friends, Swope spent a good deal of the summer at his favorite indoor sport of amassing and arranging figures. He had been wondering just how it might be possible to get a statistical harness on standards of living so that one could measure their difference in various countries. He thought he had hit upon an appropriate unit by calculating the length of time an average worker had to labor in order to buy certain basic commodities. One hitch was that the commodities which the people of one country considered basic were not much of an item in the living standards of another. But he decided upon a few for his comparison.

The most significant ones were rent, five foods—bread, butter, beef, eggs and milk—and a kilowatt hour of energy. On the basis of this selection, he gathered a great mass of data on wages in various localities and prices of his selected commodities in those localities. The results, when compared with similar United States figures, were explained in an article published in the *Atlantic Monthly* in March 1938, his first venture at popular writing. The piece attracted a good deal of attention as a novel method of measuring standards of living. The amount of time spent in earning the family's shelter varied little from country to country. But for one unit of the basic foods Europeans worked from two and a half to four times as long as an American. Of course, they seldom had that unit of food because of the cost, and Swope's article indicated why the American market for comforts, labor-saving devices and even luxuries was out of all proportion to the population.

Writing for the magazines usually is a pastime for retired executives, and by the time his article was published, Swope was well on the way to retirement. After his return from Europe, he and Young talked it over in some detail. They had agreed long before that there should be advance preparation for the succession and that they should leave as they had come, together. A couple of years earlier, Swope had listened to Professor Dugald Jackson apologize for appearing tired with: "I'll be seventy years old soon, and then I'm going to retire."

"I'd hate to think that I'd not retire before I'm seventy," Swope had replied.

In accordance with his axiom that a Number Two man should be in line always for the Number One spot, he long ago had made his selection, first Quinn and then Wilson. The Board of Directors, men "not intimately and closely associated with the everyday affairs of a large corporation," were not qualified to choose, he thought. Management, he held, ought to be self-perpetuating—far from being a feature to be criticized, it was a positive advantage. He said he had seen the tragic consequences of leaving the decision to directors in other corporations. So he and Young recommended to the Board that Wilson be appointed executive vice-president in preparation for the presidency, and Philip D. Reed, a younger lawyer who also had an engineering degree, assistant to the president as a steppingstone to the chairmanship. Reed, affable, handsome and polished, an obliging piano player and almost as tactful as Young himself, was especially familiar with the legal aspects of the business. The directors having duly ratified this arrangement, Swope decided to make the first announcement of it to the Elfuns of Schenectady.

He called them together two weeks after his sixty-fifth birthday in December 1937. With a sense of drama which he seldom indulged, he delayed his important news. He spoke first of his dream that one day the men and women who worked in General Electric would own so much of the common stock that they could control the company. If each of the eighty-seven thousand workers would put 10 per cent of their pay into General Electric shares, he explained with enthusiasm, they could do it in twenty or thirty years and have a fine protection for their old age as well. He saw this as an alternative to eventual state ownership of major industry, although he conceded that in this country it might be five hundred years before the state took over.

"It is the men who are giving their lives to the business, their minds and their thoughts, who should have a greater voice in the management," he said.

He went on to scoff at people who thought the great days of

technological progress and of General Electric expansion were past, that the pace of the last twenty years could not be maintained. He insisted that the pace of the future would be even faster and that opportunity was unlimited.

Then at last he got around to his announcement. He explained that there was no question of health involved. He had undergone a thorough medical examination that morning, and the doctor could find nothing wrong. But in line with his well-known principles, often expounded to this audience, he was selecting two men "to help me carry the burden." The first, he said, was Wilson and this was no stunning surprise to his hearers.

"One very interesting thing," the speaker interpolated, "and I glory in it, to you highbrow people particularly, is the fact that he is not a college man."

While his audience waited in some suspense to learn who the other man was, he digressed for a moment to enlarge on his favorite theme that cheap electricity made for the greater glory of General Electric. Finally he told them about Reed, and wound up his little speech by adding another precept to his familiar "analyze, organize, deputize, supervise."

"That is to advise," he said. "That is going to be my job. I am going to watch these men carry the load; I am going to advise."

But in case anyone should think he really meant it, he added hastily, "I am going to act still as president."

XVII *Elder Statesman*

At sixty-five, Gerard Swope was about to learn whether his principles of management were at once tough enough and flexible enough to survive radical changes in the problems and opportunities of the corporation. The basic mechanical techniques of mass production, of which Henry Ford was the outstanding pioneer, had proved themselves valid in spite of new processes and inventions. The basic human-relations techniques, of which Swope was the outstanding pioneer in his generation, had to face the test of changes which the depression imposed and which recovery and war would modify still further.

One legend which the crash demolished was that men who amassed great wealth performed a useful social function in so doing and by the same golden token proved themselves possessed of social wisdom. The public still wanted to know what Mellons,

Fords, Rockefellers, Du Ponts and Vanderbilts were doing, how they spent their money. But neither they nor the newer "grand acquisitors" were accepted as safe guides through the mazes of an increasingly complex economy. Reliance on government had come to stay. The influence of men who had studied economics was greater than that of men who had garnered vast fortunes and would have been greater still if the scholars could have agreed upon desirable policies. Since they did not, there was an opportunity for a new kind of businessman to assert leadership, the corporation manager.

At this time a confidential rating of "the best brains" in industry gave the first five places to Gerard Swope of General Electric, Alfred P. Sloan, Jr., of General Motors, Walter C. Teagle of Standard Oil, Myron Taylor of United States Steel and Walter S. Gifford of A.T. & T. None of them could have been included in any compilation of great American fortunes. When they began their careers, however, a similarly compiled list of "the best brains" certainly would have numbered Carnegie, Rockefeller and Vanderbilt. That Swope was in first place in this 1937 chart can be attributed chiefly to his influence upon managerial thinking.

The principles which he had given to the science or art of corporate management were in essence these:

1. The chief executives must subordinate their concern for those who hire them to the interests of those they hire and the public their industry supplies.

2. They must use the advantages of their corporation's large resources and many minds to overcome the natural disadvantages of size and develop the advantages for greater efficiency rather than use the power of these resources to crush or eliminate competition.

3. Their goal must be "more things for more people at less cost," for that is the justification for their existence.

4. They must keep the channels of opportunity constantly open to talent, not allowing the growth of routines which will choke off the emergence of promising young men.

5. They must inform the stockholders, the workers and, therefore, the public about the progress of the corporation—a policy

of "full disclosure" up to the point of the rights of these groups to know—a point upon the exact location of which not everyone will agree.

None of these is affected by the differences between horizontal and vertical theories of management, the greater or lesser responsibility of committees and boards, the centralization or dispersion of authority, the location of the decision-making and policy-making functions of management. In many of these matters, Swope was well aware that his own methods of operating General Electric could not be copied successfully by anyone else, perhaps could not be continued indefinitely by himself. As the company grew still more, one-man rule would create bottlenecks which it was his theory that management existed to avoid. This theory was largely responsible for his choice of Wilson as a successor. The man who had had the courage to speak out for vertical management in 1928 would not shrink from authority in 1938, and Swope was not surprised that the first thing his new executive vice-president outlined to him was a plan for partial decentralization. Furthermore, he insisted on it when Swope argued that it was not yet time, and the president, admitting that he had delegated power, agreed to abide by the younger man's decision.

Wilson, although he reached decisions, *Fortune* magazine reported, "as a ferryboat gets to its slip, banging both sides on the way in," could use committees in ways which Swope would have found uncomfortable if not impossible. There were plenty of them in the company, of course, but they had not been responsible for decisions up to now. When someone once suggested a general planning board directly under the president, composed of three men without administrative functions of any kind, Swope replied, "Personally I don't believe in more committees. I think that is the trouble with a big organization like General Electric, the feeling that the moment a problem comes up we say, 'Let us have a new committee'—and we have got to fight it constantly."

The pace of industrial organization outmoded his thinking on this point, and by 1938 he would not have been so positive. He saw the changes coming, but he saw too that they did not repeal his basic principles. He had taught industry how to treat its people. When the supremacy of the machine was in danger of becoming an industrial fetish, he had established the truth that men are more important than the tools they use.

This lesson, of course, was not conned in all its implications by every manager. Swope would not assert that he himself always had observed every one of his principles in actual practice, because men do make mistakes. But the philosophy is accepted by manufacturers and distributors. If it were not, one may doubt that the American people would have consented to leave in the hands of men who manage a few dozen corporations the power to guide the destinies of American industry. If Brandeis's pupil had not established principles which management honors, although sometimes in the breach, Brandeis's own views on breaking up the largest concentrations of capital into their component parts might have made greater headway. For this Swope must bear the criticism of those who think that the large corporations have been a drag on the economy and remain a threat to initiative. But he must receive the credit from those who argue that these same corporations have proved themselves the bulwark of our prosperity, and of our national defense.

Either way one looks at him, he was fitting gracefully into his role as an elder statesman of industry. It placed a great many new demands upon his time. Most of the calls were for speeches, which he was able to avoid except when the theme and the audience appealed to him. But his views also were demanded by state and Federal legislative committees on industrial matters, labor relations, social security. He served on several governmental advisory committees and spent a good many hours bringing together the private utilities and the Tennessee Valley Authority to establish a working agreement both could accept.

On one side was Wendell Willkie, president of the Commonwealth and Southern Corporation, who had taken the lead in opposing the entrance of the Federal government into the production of electric power. On the other were David Lilienthal, TVA director, and Donald Richberg, a lawyer whom Swope had known in the NRA days. Both Willkie and Lilienthal appealed to Swope The utilities executive, outspoken and outgoing, conveyed in these talks, as he did to a national audience a couple of years later, the deep sincerity which animated him. He was disarmingly willing to change his mind on good evidence, and the TVA director, a milder and more scholarly type but quietly forceful in discussion, was equally reasonable.

With TVA's legality established in the courts, Willkie was trying to get as good a price as possible for the private utilities in the area, arguing that the government should pay the value of the business and not just of the physical plant. He won this point in the end, and also Swope's high regard. When the settlement finally went through, the Willkies and the Richbergs spent a week end with the Swopes to celebrate.

A more widely publicized recognition of his leadership came in the summer of 1938 when a commission which Roosevelt appointed to study industrial relations in Great Britain and Sweden unanimously elected Swope chairman. He had not wanted to be even a member. He knew a good deal about the progress of these countries in workers' welfare and thought them well ahead of the United States in several important practices. He doubted that his views would be regarded anywhere as impartial.

"Mr. President, you and I know that I am not a radical," he explained, "but other people, and especially people in industry, the employers, think I am radical."

He suggested, therefore, that industry be represented by the president of the National Association of Manufacturers or Sloan's successor in the presidency of General Motors, William Knudsen. Roosevelt promptly named both, as well as Henry I. Harriman, former chairman of the United States Chamber of Commerce. But when Knudsen said he was unable to make the trip, Swope took his place with pleasure. Besides Harriman and Charles R. Hook, the president of NAM, the other members were William H. Davis, a patent lawyer who was later chairman of the National War Labor Board; Lloyd Garrison, Dean of the University of

Wisconsin Law School; Anna Rosenberg, a labor-relations expert; Marion Dickerman, principal of a girls' school and an intimate co-worker of Mrs. Roosevelt's for many years, representing the public; Robert J. Watt, the AFL's leading international authority, and W. Ellison Chalmers of the Department of Labor.

Their mission, which was to find useful procedures which could be adapted to the American economy, was likely to be interesting but unproductive, Swope thought. Later he gave his reason to the President, pointing out that in England, for example, the practice would have been to appoint a commission before legislation was taken up in Parliament.

"In the United States," he went on, "we first pass legislation such as the Wagner Act and establish such an agency of government as the National Labor Relations Board, which are entirely new and almost unheard of in our industrial practice. Then we appoint a committee to study what Great Britain and Sweden have done."

His conviction that nothing much would come of the study did not prevent him from working hard and enjoyably. The commission turned out to be a congenial group, perhaps because of the variety of their backgrounds, and all readily acquiescent in Swope's ideas of orderly procedure. They spent several weeks in meetings with employers, officials of trade associations, workers and union leaders. Their reports, one on each country, were miraculously unanimous—"due to you more than anyone else," Garrison wrote to the chairman, whose driving leadership he credited with achieving harmony "without dodging a single issue."

The reports, published as public documents, were of more influence than Swope's disclaimer would indicate. They were widely studied, commented upon, argued about, and they contributed in profound although perhaps unmeasurable ways to the attention which was paid in these years to what was called "the middle way" of the Scandinavians. The findings showed how both Britain and Sweden had achieved successful collective bargaining on a completely voluntary basis. In England, for example, the time lost in strikes was only about one third of that per man in the

United States, and violence had been unknown for years. Yet the bargaining was just as keen, the issues as great. Neither the employer nor the union leader thought he was sacrificing his interests by reaching agreement before a work stoppage instead of after one. Swope, of course, was especially attracted by the large role which employer associations played, since unions seldom negotiated with a single company but with an entire industry. The net effect of the reports was to confirm the views of those who thought that strikes and lockouts need not be part of the manufacturing process.

Swope, who had been of this opinion all his adult life, made a few speeches on the subject, but before they were delivered, he enjoyed a surprise which he owed in part, at least, to this European mission. In September, only a couple of weeks after his return, he was awakened late one night by a long-distance telephone call. A voice, speaking from the Democratic State Convention in Rochester, wanted to know if he would accept the nomination for Governor.

"Ridiculous!" Swope exclaimed.

"It isn't ridiculous," said the voice. "It is a suggestion made by Jim Farley and Ed Flynn [the national and state chairmen of the party] and has the sanction of the President."

This assurance did not sway Swope's opinion. He replied that he never had been in politics and was as busy as he wanted to be. Firmly he quoted General Sherman: "If nominated, I would not run; if elected, I would not serve." He was pleased to hear that Herbert Lehman, his friend who had served two terms with distinction already, was then prevailed upon to run again. Swope thought little of the incident until some time later, in conversation with several labor men, one of them mentioned the offer and explained that labor had been consulted.

"I suppose labor said 'thumbs down,'" Swope commented.

"No," was the reply. "The American Labor Party and the CIO said they would back your candidacy."

The idea of such support for the chief executive of one of

America's largest corporations was piquant, but, as Swope wrote, "they weren't put to the test."

Within a year, however, he and Young were put to a test of their own sincerity. In 1937, they had agreed that if all worked out well with Wilson and Reed, they would bow out in two years. Young would be sixty-five on October 27, 1939, and they had set that as an appropriate retirement age, although Swope would be nearly two years past it. But in September, the world erupted into war, and while the American people were dividing angrily on the best way to keep out of it, there was from the first all too much danger that the United States would be drawn in. It was an emergency in which two elder statesmen might have been forgiven a reconsideration of their plans to quit. Neither Young nor Swope remembers such an idea crossing his mind. They had developed the habit of sticking to a decision, and on November 17, 1939, they presented a joint letter of resignation to the Board of Directors, to be effective at the end of the year.

"We took up these offices together, and we wish to lay them down together," they wrote.

According to plan, the directors thereupon elected Wilson and Reed, and the end of a dynasty was announced. Apparently it struck no one as significant that in the offices and shops of the General Electric Company there wasn't a single quiver of apprehension, so far as can be found. The calm was a wonderful contrast to the situation which had prevailed in many of these same places eighteen years before. Swope could walk away from the forty-fifth floor of the General Electric Building with the comfortable feeling that he had done what Coffin put him there to do—and more.

He also walked away with the even more comfortable feeling that there were a lot of other things to do in the world. It was a revealing glimpse of the extent to which his reserve and concentration had hidden him from all but his closest associates that many officials were quite sure he would either be miserable in his retirement or would never give Wilson real control. Because he worked so hard and so single-mindedly, they assumed he had no strong interests outside of business. They had heard him—some of them had heard him more than once—quote Justice Holmes: "The longing for repose and certainty is in every human mind; certainty generally is illusion and repose is not the destiny of man."

They had not noticed that he had been troubled by illusions in statements of policy, but they were sure he was not destined for repose. There were expressions of commiseration for poor Charlie Wilson, who would find himself, these worriers thought, in a position of responsibility but not of power.

The object of these speculations, however, was quite satisfied with his prospects as he walked rapidly on that snappy fall evening over to Park Avenue and up to his apartment. He and Mary would have more time for travel now. He would be able to promote a few of the causes in which he believed, such as expansion of social security to groups not covered in the Federal system, international understanding, education. He would be able to read some of the books for which the presidency of General Electric allowed no time, listen to music more often, ride and swim. Of one thing he was sure: he would not be one of those tiresome retired men of affairs who bore their busy friends with idle chatter. He had been the victim of a few in recent years, but not often because it had been his practice to give their names to Miss Marratt with the admonition. "Don't put him through. He talks too much because he has nothing to do."

His golfing experience was hardly a memory now, and one word which did not enter into his thinking as he stepped briskly along to the Valhalla of all good business executives was: "Relax."

XVIII *Curtain Call*

The Swope-Young resignation hit the morning papers of the following Saturday. War or no war, it was front-page news, often accompanied by editorial comment—in itself a good indication of the recognized importance of General Electric to the average man—in marked contrast to the relatively brief notices of their appointment which had appeared on business pages eighteen years before. The very first telephone call to Swope's country place was from Mayor Fiorello La Guardia of New York—Swope always wondered how he got the unlisted number.

"What do you mean by retiring?" the Little Flower demanded in his shrill, urgent voice. "You are entirely too young. What are you going to do?"

"First we are going to South America, but after that I have no definite plans," Swope informed him.

"I want you to accept the chairmanship of the New York City Housing Authority."

"You are very kind, but I am not a citizen of the City of New York."

"Oh, that doesn't make any difference in your case."

Swope was not tempted but did not like to decline without giving the Mayor a chance to explain further. At this conference, La Guardia persuaded him to take a quick tour of some developments in Harlem and Williamsburg. They went first to a new Negro housing project in what had been a miserable slum very much like those around Hull House in the 1890s, and Swope was recruited on the spot.

"I tell you, I got a thrill from seeing these people, in clean surroundings, fine upstanding people, some seventeen or eighteen hundred of them, all so proud of their housing development," he explained some months later. "I was tremendously impressed."

La Guardia was as quick to capitalize on an opportunity as Swope himself. Three weeks before his General Electric resignation was effective, the new housing executive was called down to the Mayor's office to be sworn in as a member of the Authority, and to be elected at once as chairman by the other members, one of whom was his companion of the mission to Great Britain and Sweden, William H. Davis. There were picture-taking and handshaking and much smiling. Swope had insisted on his trip—after all, he had taken his winter vacation no matter what was going on when he worked for a living and saw no reason to change his habits now that his employment was unpaid. He had served notice that he would start real work on his return.

Meanwhile letters and telegrams and telephone calls inspired by his retirement poured in, a flood almost as great as those which had greeted his rising star in 1922. There were almost wistful letters from some of his peers who wondered how he dared quit, such as this from Sloan of General Motors, who had resigned the presidency only to become chairman:

"An action of this kind is more important to the individual than it can be to anyone else, yet it is very important to other individuals who, sooner or later, and perhaps sooner than they realize, are confronted with a similar problem.

"I want to congratulate you on your courage in taking the step that you have taken. To my mind, it takes a great deal of courage because of the fact that anyone who has been intensively occupied, as you have been down through the years, has a real problem when he divests himself of the daily urge of accomplishment and takes time to look around and to see what is going on, in a broad way. The question whether one who has lived such an intensive life can be happy under such circumstances and is willing to face the problem causes me to say that it took a great deal of courage to act as you have done."

The president of General Motors went on to say that "many of us" ought to retire earlier, but his next words explained why he himself waited until he was in his eighties:

"I think also that there ought to be more opportunity in our scheme of things for capitalizing on the broad experience and contacts . . . that men like yourself have had . . . in the interests of the community as a whole, particularly in correcting the many mistakes that exist, economically and otherwise, but unfortunately we have no such opportunity."

Swope thought that there was no dearth of opportunity for men who could learn the difference between administration in government and in private business. So he did not feel as brave as Sloan thought him, and he turned without qualms from such rather sad letters to the expressions of real regard from men who differed from him but had found him reasonable even in the differences. Such a one was Thurman Arnold, Assistant Attorney General, who was at this moment working up an anti-trust suit against General Electric but wrote:

"It is difficult for me to believe that there is anyone who can adequately replace you from the point of view of relationship between government and business. The only bright side of the picture so far as I am concerned is the thought that your counsel must inevitably continue to have the greatest weight with the company."

There were the more public expressions of esteem, represented by *Fortune*'s tribute to him as one "whom many call the finest corporate executive officer that ever struck a balance sheet, precise, exacting, a man of almost frightening purposefulness."

Finally there were the cordial, the admiring, the respectful and the affectionate notes from old friends in business, government, social work, from artists and scholars, scientists and engineers, businessmen and workers. Then, as the effective date drew near for what *Fortune* called "the voluntary breakup of the most illustrious team United States industry has ever known," there was a series of farewell ceremonies—luncheons, speeches, presentations of scrolls—all very heartwarming to a man who was not given to displaying his emotions but now tried his hand at translating Goethe, with this result:

Would you constantly seek afar,
See that happiness lies near;
Learn happiness to understand,
For that is ever close at hand.

The torrent of words came to an end at last, although for once Gerard Swope had not been wearied by even the most long-winded, and he and Mary were off for their first long trip of his retirement. It was a thorough one, lasting three months, via Cuba to the Panama Canal, down the west coast of South America to Chile, across the Andes to Buenos Aires and then by boat, plane, train and car up the east coast. Swope asked questions and collected figures as enthusiastically as if he had been preparing to start a new General Electric appliance division, or as he had done in Japan nearly thirty years before. He came back with two ideas.

One of them was another *Atlantic Monthly* article on standards of living. He had applied his measure of the time needed to earn certain commodities and arrived at a sound reason for much of what observers called Latin-American backwardness. Mindful of the job waiting for him in New York, he paid special attention to housing.

His second thought was that the United States should purchase all British, French and Dutch possessions in the Western Hemisphere, removing the threat that they might fall into the hands of the Axis and giving the owners funds for needed war supplies. He was not alone in this idea, but he dodged the implication of United States imperialism by proposing that the various territories be turned over to the Latin-American republics nearest to them at cost, with provisions for extremely liberal payment terms, and for the admission of European refugees.

As the so-called "phony war" came to an end in a series of bewildering Nazi conquests in Europe that spring, he expounded his ideas to Roosevelt and Secretary of State Cordell Hull. After he got home, he wrote a long memorandum with details. He thought England, France and Holland would be quite willing to sell although even in their extremity these countries had given no indication of their readiness to accept an offer which certainly would be interpreted as taking advantage of their necessities.

Swope received pleasant acknowledgments of his proposal, but no indication of enthusiasm. Within a few weeks, both France and the Netherlands had fallen, and in June he received a friendly note from Roosevelt calling his attention to a statement handed to the German and Italian governments that the United States would not recognize the transfer of any Western Hemisphere territory from one non-American power to another.

After this essay into foreign affairs, Swope settled down to his housing job. As industry moved into its war-boom stage, the United States' preparations for defense competed for heavy production with Allied needs. Civilian shortages developed and the actual building program in New York was hampered, but in two years Swope's program completed four times as many rooms for people as the Authority had finished in its first five years—a not very fair comparison perhaps since the earlier period had emphasized employment rather than construction. Nevertheless, in Swope's administration the number of rooms in Housing Authority projects rose from 8,022 to 36,821 and the rental per room was reduced from an average of $104.92 a year to $84.45.

His colleagues—La Guardia had given him an able engineer

as Director of Public Housing—say that he improved the management of both projects under construction and those already occupied. But his principal contribution in their eyes was an entire refinancing of Housing Authority bonds, which saved $6,000,000 in subsidies and another $6,000,000 in interest charges. Under his direction, too, sites were acquired and demolition work begun for housing which could be erected after the war. In these plans, Swope insisted, crowded districts ought to have a better design than the customary six-story maximum for lowest-rent apartments. Loftier buildings accordingly were put into the blueprint stage against the day when it would be possible to build them. Swope also thought that private business ought to be enlisted in the drive to house the American people adequately. Insurance companies seemed to him to be the most likely developers, and for New York he proposed that they see what they could do with some of the blighted areas along the East River. He and the chairman of the Metropolitan Life Insurance Company had frequent conferences, from which stemmed postwar projects in both low- and high-rent categories.

Outside of his housing work, Swope was enjoying his role as adviser, the fifth wheel of administration which he had claimed for himself when he first announced his retirement. But he learned that advice is not always heeded. At the White House luncheon the day he gave Roosevelt his views on the Western Hemisphere, talk also turned to the Democratic Convention, which was only a little more than a month distant.

"Dear Mr. President," Swope said earnestly, "you have accomplished so much of the great constructive program in your two terms that you will have a great place in history. I think it will be further enhanced if you maintain the tradition set by George Washington for not more than two terms."

"He seemed interested, and we discussed other possible candidates," Swope wrote, but of course his and Roosevelt's opinions of the emergency which the country faced as France fell and England faced the Axis alone were not identical.

The nomination of an admired friend on the Republican ticket made Swope's political decision that year easier.

"Because I felt so strongly about the two-term tradition, I voted for Wendell Willkie in 1940," he has explained, "but in 1944, feeling even more strongly about the foreign situation, I again voted for Mr. Roosevelt."

In the General Electric Company his advice was thought to be more valuable, but he gave it less spontaneously. He was careful not to offer unsolicited suggestions here. Those who had expected him to be leaning over Charlie Wilson's shoulder were surprised. But Swope, although he always insisted that Coffin never interfered with or bothered him, was meticulous in avoiding his own predecessor's habit of dropping in on the new president with comments or questions. When he was asked, he answered. For the rest, he was confident that Wilson knew what to do. So he and Young waited for their successors to come to them.

"Charlie and I hesitate to muscle in on the standing luncheon date that you and Mr. Swope have on board meeting days" was the typical preliminary to such a request, made by Reed to Young in suggesting that this time the elder join the younger team for a discussion of matters to be put before the directors.

The elders were pleased with this procedure and with the progress of their protégés, so that Swope agreed heartily when Young one day quoted to him a remark attributed to John Finley: "Nothing succeeds like successors."

Actually the miracle of industrial production which amazed the world and even some of the men who took part in it was beginning then, as the United States adopted its first peacetime conscription and Roosevelt called for what seemed an impossible flotilla of fifty thousand war planes. In January 1941, Swope heard of what he thought was a monkey wrench to be thrown into the electrical machinery of this program. He was attending a public dinner at which he met Thurman Arnold, who remarked, "I am sorry, Mr. Swope, that the government will have to sue the General Electric Company in the conduct of its incandescent lamp business."

"Why, we are operating under the unanimous decision of the Supreme Court in 1926," Swope objected.

"I know that," said Arnold, "and because of it the suit will be civil and not criminal. I think that decision is a bad law."

"If it is bad law, why don't you have a good law passed by Congress?" Swope inquired.

"Oh, hell," Arnold replied, "that takes too long, and besides I think I can get the interpretation of the law I want from this Supreme Court."

Some months later, the suit was filed in Federal Court in Trenton, New Jersey, but the deepening emergency led to what seems to have been a misunderstanding. General Electric officials understood that the government would postpone action until the emergency was over so as not to take key men away from defense work. Arnold understood that his department had agreed only not to seek the dissolution of the company. Therefore, Swope and the active officers of General Electric paid little attention to the matter, which in any case would have been pushed out of their minds when the Japanese struck at Pearl Harbor.

December 7, 1941, was a day of personal as well as national tragedy. The Swopes were entertaining friends at The Croft and Gerard's sister, Dolly, was coming out from New York to spend the day. Possessing much of the curiosity of her brothers combined with the gentleness of their father, Dolly had become very close to the family since her return at the outbreak of the war after many years' residence abroad. On this Sunday morning a telephone call announced that she had collapsed and died instantly in Grand Central Station just before her train left. Hurrying into the city, her older brother heard the first news from Honolulu, and the sorrowful arrangements for a funeral were made against the background of disaster.

Mobilization of men and industry brought a wonderful array of the nation's talents to Washington in the next few weeks, and Swope was among them. He had been serving most of the year on a National Defense Mediation Board set up to avoid work stoppages in essential industries, and he had not endeared himself to fellow industrialists. They were displeased to hear that Swope had found hourly rates in General Motors fair enough but annual earnings "irregular and low." They complained of his radicalism when he said that Bethlehem Shipbuilding ought to accept a union agreement since thirty-eight other Pacific Coast shipbuilders had done so.

"In general," he wrote, "it was my impression that the labor leaders who appeared before the Board were sincere, honest, upstanding men and compared favorably with the representatives of the employers. But labor organizations and collective bargaining in this country are young, and the membership of the unions are undisciplined and are impatient with the legal technicalities often brought forth by the representatives of the employers."

He resigned from this board, as well as from the Housing Authority, the National City Bank directorate and assorted civic posts to be an assistant to the Secretary of the Treasury and supervise the Treasury's procurement program. Lend-lease and war orders generally were expanding this section into what some emergency planners thought might be the principal procurement office for the whole government. Swope, assigned to a somewhat more imposing room than ever he had occupied at General Electric, was asked to prepare for just that, and also to supervise the activities of the Mint and the Bureau of Printing and Engraving. He was just getting into the swing of it, visiting warehouses, seeing money printed, talking with foreign and domestic suppliers, when he resigned abruptly. On March 2, less than two months after he came to Washington, he wrote to the Secretary:

"I have just been informed that a civil suit instituted some months ago by the United States Department of Justice against the General Electric Company is to go to trial this month, and that the counsel estimates that the trial will last several months. As the suit involves matters on which the Supreme Court of the United States rendered an unanimous decision in favor of the General Electric Company in 1926 when I was its president, I am advised that it will be necessary for me to appear as a witness and that I must be available at the call of counsel and the Court."

Before his resignation became effective five days later, his brother, Herbert, who was consultant to the War Department—and followed Gerard's World War I example of refusing a brigadier general's commission—was invited to lunch at the White House.

"Tell your little brother to come and see me," said Roosevelt, who enjoyed the disparity in size between the brothers.

"If you say so," Herbert replied, "but it won't do any good."

"Why not?"

"The first thing he'll say is, 'If the President wants to see me, let him tell me so himself.'"

Roosevelt, says Gerard, decided not to press the point, and for the next few months the energies which Herbert believed had been intended by the President to direct industry for the war effort were devoted to helping lawyers and accountants work up the answer to Arnold's charges. Swope's own statement was relatively simple. Patent control, to the extent General Electric practiced it, was what the patent laws intended, he said. The system of fixed prices and exclusive territories for agencies had given Americans the best lamps in the world at the lowest prices. The foreign contracts, many of which Swope had negotiated himself, did forbid sales of lamps by foreign companies in the United States and by General Electric in industrial nations abroad. But since no foreigner could make good lamps at General Electric's price, and since quotas and tariffs effectively barred American products from these industrial markets, the clauses were irrelevant.

Before the case came to trial, the War and Navy departments asked that it be postponed until after the war because a hearing would interfere with war production. The court decision, when it finally came in 1949, vindicated both Arnold and Swope. The law was reinterpreted to rule out the clauses in foreign agreements to which Arnold objected and General Electric's contracts limiting the number of lamps which could be manufactured by a licensee using the company's patents. On the other hand, as Swope contended, his company held its share of the business through the legitimate advantages of research, design and manufacturing efficiency, and foreigners still could not meet the low American prices.

Swope's preoccupation with the anti-trust case was ended in the late summer of 1942 when Roosevelt asked Charlie Wilson to take the vice-chairmanship of the War Production Board, key agency on the industrial front. Reed already was in government service as chief of the United States Economic Mission in London after a try at organizing the nation's rubber program. Swope had gone to Nantucket for a little sun and swimming when Young telephoned him to say that General Electric's directors wanted the old team back for the duration. The War Production Board had offered to appoint Wilson "without compensation," the phrase used in this war instead of "dollar-a-year," so that he could keep his General Electric title and salary. But he, Swope and Young agreed that he ought to resign from the company and take the pay of his new post so that no charge of conflict of interest could stick. These details settled, Swope came back to New York the day before the September board meeting and for the second time heard himself and Young elected president and chairman of the General Electric Company.

"Gerard immediately got under the load in his characteristic fashion," Young wrote to Reed, "and spent the first two weeks visiting Schenectady, Fort Wayne and Lynn, and intends to make the rounds of the other places very soon."

Once more "the most illustrious team" was in harness, and both men were touched by the reception they got from old friends. To Young the welcome "had been so warm on this resurrection that I looked with less apprehension on the next one." Swope, who recalled that some people thought he had retired prematurely, added, "Well, I think this merely proves they were right."

So he celebrated his seventieth birthday as the president of General Electric after all, and the corner office on the forty-fifth floor echoed once more with staccato dictation, sharp questions, rapid-fire instructions. "That stunning performance" of managerial virtuosity which *Fortune* attributed to the extraordinary intelligence of a very special man was about to be repeated, but with a difference in accent. Gerard Swope was as brisk, as slender, as erect as ever. People who caught a glimpse of his back as he strode rapidly down the street, careless of traffic or traffic signals, thought they were watching a rather limber boy. Those who saw him coming, strong-jawed, firm-lipped, sharp-eyed, supposed him to be in vigorous middle age despite his white hair. But his manner had altered subtly, the change being a reflection of the different concept he brought to his job in his "reincarnation."

"I was a caretaker," he explains. "It was not for me to initiate new methods or change policies but just keep things running smoothly. This was especially easy because the government was our main customer; no problem of selling there."

Swope, who never had had an easy job before, is not much impressed with his performance in this one. He was rather pleased when, taking the regular physical examination required of all new employees, he passed with flying colors. He was a bit disconcerted when a waitress in the executive dining room told him severely that there was a rule limiting lunchers to one cup of coffee each. He was slightly amused when Roosevelt, asking for an extension of Wilson's War Production Board service, added "on condition, of course, that you and Owen do not try to overtax your strength."

He recognized at once that the principal duty of the company was to deliver war orders on time and up to specifications. The engineering and manufacturing organization he had built up over eighteen years was superlatively well able to handle these matters. Swope thinks he has told the story of his leadership of General Electric through the two most critical years of the war in two paragraphs. He wrote:

"On assuming the office of president again, I called a meeting of the Advisory Committee of the Company, which consisted of all the vice-presidents who had charge of operations. They were all responsible men who had been long in their jobs, and I had confidence in them. I told them I expected them to keep me advised promptly of any impending trouble either of delivery or quality, and I expected to hear of these troubles from them before I heard of them from the government.

"In the two years of this second presidency, no instance arose where I did not know of trouble before the War and Navy departments called me up. My work was largely one of general supervision of production, and this job I found much easier and lighter to carry than the work of president in times of peace when sales had to be made, competition had to be encountered, and costs of production were involved. Now it was only a question of production in quantity and quality. This was very important, but the well-trained and seasoned engineering and manufacturing organization carried on the work very well indeed."

Swope knew all this because, while he gave the impression of having mellowed considerably, he was on top of the production figures, and on top of the production, too, as he maintained the pace of his old travels. If he deprecates his own share, he does not minimize his company's contribution to the victory. One of the notable differences between the previous war and this one, as someone has said, was that the first was mechanical and the second electrical. General Electric, its own historian says with some justification, "produced a greater variety of complex war equipment and was called upon to solve a greater variety of difficult technical problems than any other manufacturer."

Swope had so much leisure that he accepted an assignment from the National Community Chests and Councils early in 1943 to preside over a Budget Committee for War Appeals. In a congenial atmosphere of figures relating to every American relief organization, whether working on behalf of United States forces, the Allies or the people of occupied areas, he reviewed the budgets so that they could be recommended (or not) to local community chests, and finally merged into a single National War Fund.

Wilson served in Washington for two years, and on his resignation from the War Production Board, Swope promptly tendered his own as president of General Electric. The company was doing its part in the miracle of production, and some of his associates were giving Swope more credit than he took himself. The confidence he inspired merely by being there, making decisions and infecting people with his passion for perfection was a considerable factor in the company's smooth operations, they thought.

Swope, glad to give back the forty-fifth floor to Wilson, was sure that this time his retirement was for good. Young, who resigned with him, of course, went off to Florida, and they exchanged notes on a new joint statement which would take them out of official positions in the General Electric Company completely. This was their resignation as directors now that the new administration had established itself. Swope delivered it for both of them on his seventy-second birthday, and wrote happily to Young:

"I sang our swan song this morning, which, with proper reluctance and great regret, was accepted."

XIX *Happy Ending*

On a July day in 1944, Swope was reading *Yankee from Olympus* and it reminded him that Owen Young would have a birthday in just three months. He saw no reason to wait until then to send a gift because, he wrote, "we have endeavored to look ahead and do things before the necessity for doing them was upon us." He wanted Young to have a biography of Justice Holmes, whom they both admired, "as a token of everything we have tried to do together for so many years, and in appreciation of the joy of our association and the affectionate remembrances of the things we have lived through together."

Young's reply was a pleasant memento to carry into retirement and a summing up, too, of the relations between the members of "this most illustrious team." He wrote:

DEAR GERARD,

I quote the final words from *Yankee from Olympus*:

"Whether a man accepts from Fortune her spade and will look downward and dig, or from Aspiration her ax and cord, and will scale the ice, the one and only success which it is his to command is to bring to his work a mighty heart."

This applies to you.

I know it by the experience of unnumbered years. I can prove it by your letter accompanying this delightful volume as an antedated birthday present. The book I could have gotten for myself, but only you could create the letter. I will paste it in the volume so that they may live together.

Do you remember that on our way back from the Orient, you said, "I will do all the work—I like it." No promise has ever been more completely fulfilled.

Well, it was good to recall those days, but at seventy-two Gerard Swope was far from any desire to withdraw from the world for a life of contemplation. He remained one of the least reminiscent of men. His swan song at the end of 1944 came at a time when victory in the war seemed sure—reassuring to a man with three sons in the services and another son and daughter hard at secret war work, although few were predicting the end for 1945—and Swope began his own postwar planning. He still was active in the Community Chests as chairman of the Budget Committee, and still dissatisfied with the failure of the Federal social-security system to cover employees of nonprofit organizations. If the government wouldn't, the organizations and the employees themselves might. So he launched and for years headed the National Retirement, Health and Welfare Association, which carried out a pension and insurance program along his favorite lines.

At the suggestion of Mayor La Guardia, he joined the Board of the Health Insurance Plan of Greater New York in 1945, scornful of those who argued that it was a step toward socialized medicine. He desired insurance against all possible hazards much more than he feared Socialism, and has been an active director of HIP ever since. Just as he wanted industry to make itself responsible for social security before government took it over, so he argues that voluntary, comprehensive group health insurance will work better, if widely adopted, than compulsory state coverage, which he regards as the inevitable alternative.

There was some unfinished business in housing, too. For all the ambitious postwar developments, public and private, there was a glaring omission which a good many people were deploring, but which very few did anything to repair. This was the absence of housing for middle-income families, those with from $5,000 to $7,000 a year. They couldn't get into the low-cost public projects and couldn't afford the rents of new privately built apartments. Swope organized a company, of which he was very much the working chairman, to build co-operatives for people in this bracket. He provided the benefits of his managerial talents and negotiating skills to set up terms, deal with banks and obtain tax exemption under slum-clearance laws, and in at least one instance some personal underwriting.

The first project, built in Queens, became something of a show place. According to plan, the residents gradually elected their own members to replace Swope's original directors until only he was left. For both sentimental and practical reasons, they then insisted that he himself remain as their chairman. Another project in Queens and one in Brooklyn eventually provided homes for 1,388 families. Swope, who almost always found that people were as fine as he expected them to be, was delighted with the families who moved into these buildings. He thought they proved his contention, held for half a century, at least, that human beings grow up quickly to opportunities.

He was so sure of it that, when $200,000 had to be found in two days in order to obtain a site for one of the projects, he offered to guarantee the sum himself. His colleagues were worried. Each applicant had been told that he would have to make a down payment of from $1,000 to $1,500 depending upon the size of the apartment desired. Suppose, Swope was told, they backed out when it came time to pay the money. Swope merely laughed. He realized that plenty of worthy folk cannot put their hands on a thousand dollars in two or three days. But, he said, the sort of people who signed the co-operative applications were good for the money or they wouldn't have signed, and they needed the apartments badly. He was right, of course, and he never had to make good his guarantee. He spent a lot of time with architects, builders and suppliers, surprising one young manager with the efficient results he got from a few decisive words at the right moment.

The Far East, which had fascinated him ever since his first trip in 1917, continued to attract him, and he was now able to gratify his interest with more reading and, in 1949, travel to the Orient. He had long been a friend of Edward C. Carter, who was the chief organizer in 1926 of the Institute of Pacific Relations and its guiding spirit for more than twenty years. The two men had been associated in raising money for Jimmy Yen's mass education movement, and Carter's ideas for a clearing house of information and opinion on the Far East appealed to Swope's predilection for facts. As early as 1938, he had authorized the International General Electric Company to contribute to the work. By 1949 he was sufficiently familiar with it and keen enough about it to accept the chairmanship of the American Institute of Pacific Relations, one of the ten national groups which formed the international body. He succeeded Ray Lyman Wilbur, who had been Hoover's Secretary of the Interior, and Newton D. Baker, too, had held the office. His chairmanship, beginning in the year that the Chinese Communists completed their conquest of the mainland, was promptly enlivened by an attack launched against the Institute by a Senate Judiciary Subcommittee on Internal Security. The chairman of this investigation was Pat McCarran of Nevada, who did his best to give his name to an inquisitorial technique which became known as McCarthyism. No one in these years did more to discredit Congressional investigations than this shrewd, often genial, unscrupulous Senator who was proud of a successful career at the bar and on the bench. He now sought to show that Communist triumphs in the East had been aided, abetted and perhaps made possible by the hidden machinations of their agents and dupes in the Institute of Pacific Relations.

He could succeed only by torturing the facts out of all reasonable shape. For its "documentation" the Subcommittee had to rely upon false witnesses, adroit insinuations which linked the Institute to suspected or actual Communists who never had any share in its work, and the attribution to the Institute of views expressed by writers in its publications who were neither employees nor officials—a technique by which it is easy to brand the Congressional Record as an instrument of subversion. The credibility of the Subcommittee's reports and public hearings, therefore, depended upon an atmosphere of almost hysterical suspicion. Once that had been created, the most fantastic stories would be believed.

One thing the investigators did not want was to have the chairman of the American Institute as a witness. Not even in the climate of opinion in which it was possible to create the impression that some of the country's most persistent foes of communism were Soviet stooges was there much hope that the American people could be led to believe that the former president of the General Electric Company was a Russian tool. Nor, if he appeared in person, would it be easy to paint him as the dupe of craftier men. So the Senator from Nevada carefully refrained from putting Swope to the question.

He was equally careful to keep out of his Subcommittee's record any analysis of the Institute's real work, embodied in some two hundred research volumes, "which," Swope said, "represent the Institute's principal contribution to American knowledge of Asia and the true measure of its influence on American thinking." As a forum for ideas and information on the Far East, the Institute had published articles by men of all shades of opinion, from extreme left to extreme right. So had every American magazine with any pretensions to reliability and impartiality. The Subcommittee, therefore, fell back upon allegations and insinuations which Swope, a notably temperate person in his speech, called "flimsy" and "outrageous." Two examples of the "smear" technique which especially roused his resentment were typical of the Subcommittee's methods.

Louis Budenz, an ex-Communist who for many years seemed to have an inexhaustible reservoir of new charges against people accused of subversion, was a star witness. Although he never had mentioned it in many previous interrogations about Communist plots and plotters, he now swore that he knew John Carter Vincent had been a member of the Communist party and on a mission to China in 1944 with Vice-President Henry Wallace had influenced Wallace in the direction desired by the Communists. Vincent, a State Department official, had been a trustee of the American Institute of Pacific Relations from 1944 to 1946. McCarran refused to allow the record to show the facts of the mission. Swope summed them up in a public statement, saying, "Mr. Wallace in 1944, with Vincent's concurrence, actually recommended measures, including the replacement of General Stilwell by General Wedemeyer, which were the exact opposite of what the Communists wanted at the time."

The second example was even more flagrant. With a great fanfare of publicity, Subcommittee investigators "raided" Ned Carter's home in Lee, Massachusetts, and seized the Institute's old files, which were stored in a barn there. The strong implication was that incriminating documents, hidden for sinister reasons, had been unearthed. The truth, which came out later but, of course, not in such sensational form and therefore without so much impact upon public opinion, was that the FBI already had examined these files thoroughly. They had been sent to the barn to save New York storage costs.

Unable to persuade McCarran to permit the Institute's side of the story to be presented before the Subcommittee, Swope decided in October 1951 to issue a statement and hold a press conference. Some of the Institute staff suggested that, much as this would help correct false impressions, it might be an ordeal which he would regret. His conference would be attended by some reporters and commentators who were upholding the McCarran investigation, and they could be expected to ask insinuating, even loaded questions.

"What harm can they do to me?" Swope asked.

Of course, they were unable to do any, but it was not for lack of trying. Swope explained exactly what the investigation had done and failed to do, outlined the Institute's work, detailed facts which controverted McCarran's pledge of "a truly objective approach" and concluded: "I am naturally concerned to defend the good name of the American Institute of Pacific Relations, a useful organization with which I am glad to be associated, and that of the loyal men and women who have served it. But I am even more concerned to defend a basic principle of American democracy, the principle of free inquiry and free discussion. If the day ever comes when it will not be possible for a private nonpartisan society like the American Institute of Pacific Relations to seek and publish facts without fear of political reprisal, and to present to the public differing opinions on controversial issues, something essential to the American way of life will have been lost."

Five years later it could be seen that the stand of men and women like Swope against the ruthless drive for conformity by smear and intimidation, which at this time reached an intensity known only once or twice before in our history, preserved that "something essential." Meanwhile, its chairman kept the American Institute in funds almost singlehanded. The organization had relied largely upon the substantial contributions of large corporations with interests or connections in the Far East. The attack of so powerful a Senator as McCarran and the resulting publicity at a time when the epithet *Communist* was more to be feared than *leper* normally would have dried up this source of revenue at once. Almost any vice-president in charge of public relations would have argued that a business cannot afford to be mixed up in this sort of political controversy. But Swope did not ask the vice-presidents. He went straight to the presidents, informed them that General Electric was continuing its financial support of the Institute, and in at least one case added, "I won't take less from you."

It is one of the facts of big-business life that the men at the very top of large corporations are likely to be more adventurous and less timid than those who are only hoping to get there or are simply concerned with keeping their jobs. And by the early 1950s Swope's own principles of the responsibilities of management had been widely accepted. So where a vice-president must shrink from exposing his company to attack, a president can take the attitude that he will not be intimidated. He is not in the habit of abdicating his judgment, and certainly almost the last thing he is afraid of is being called a Communist. So Swope came away from their offices with enough checks to meet the Institute's modest budget.

There was criticism, to be sure, but he was used to that—hadn't he been a radical in industry almost all his life?—and it did not check a steady flow of honors. He was used to that, too, the honorary degrees, medals and citations from professional and civic organizations, foreign decorations. They had been among the rewards of his work in industry, education and social service ever since President Wilson had conferred a DSM upon him for his contribution to victory in World War I. Of them all, the one which brought him most into the public eye was one he would not accept.

In May 1947, he was notified that the ninth ranking of the thirteen British orders of chivalry had been awarded to him, and he would be entitled to sign himself Honorary Commander of the Most Excellent Order of the British Empire. The honor was to be conferred in Washington on June 15, 1948. The delay was later explained as due to the time consumed in manufacturing the badges of silver gilt, pearl gray and crimson, and the priority given to military members.

The year's interval saw the climax of Israel's fight for independence, actually proclaimed after much British opposition and confusion on May 14, 1948, as the result of a United Nations decision. Swope never had been much of a Zionist. In fact, he had been so little a practicing Jew that a great many of his closest associates had assumed that he was a Gentile. His own faith was in people and in practical works, never in professions or in the ceremonies or formalities of revealed religion.

"I don't suppose that Mr. Barton or Mr. Coffin ever knew that I was a Jew," he once said in recalling how little part Judaism had played in his life.

But he was aroused by British policy in what had been the mandated territory of Palestine, and on June 8, three weeks after the proclamation of the new state, he wrote to Sir Oliver Franks, the British Ambassador to the United States:

"Naturally I was gratified at the recognition accorded me by the British government. My many trips to England and other parts of the British Empire; my many friends over there; and my high esteem for your great wartime leader, Winston Churchill, all filled me with admiration of what your country had done in the development and defense of democratic government.

"In this last year, however, in spite of the repeated recommendations of several commissions of your own government, of an American-British Commission, and then finally of the action of the United Nations on a separate state in Palestine, the vacillating, reprehensible and nonconstructive attitude of your government has left me without respect for its position.

"Because of my feelings, it seems more fitting for me to decline the decoration your government has tendered me."

The letter got into the papers, creating comment and attracting a lot of mail, mostly from strangers. The majority were enthusiastic supporters of the new state of Israel, by no means all Jews, but some were sorrowful or indignant Englishmen and a few echoed the sentiments of the angry Arabs. At his office Swope saw reporters and disclaimed any fervent Zionism. Nor was he protesting as a Jew. He objected chiefly, he explained, to Great Britain's failure to support the United Nations.

Other honors were more pleasing. General Electric established a Gerard Swope Foundation for scholarships similar to the one Swope had created for Coffin. Degrees came from a variety of institutions of learning. The one from Dartmouth was typical: "In recognition of the unflagging quality of your exemplary citizenship." For he had, Dartmouth said, "built one of the most broadly used and respected careers of our times."

The busy years continued that career into a singularly green and vigorous age. His health remained the envy of younger men—Stuart Crocker, one of Young's brilliant young assistants who had become chairman of the Columbia Gas System, saw him in the subway a few days before his eightieth birthday but walking so fast, as usual, that Crocker, a man of fifty but bulky, couldn't catch up. Swope still counted that day slightly lost if he didn't ride; he slept on a porch so open that in winter he sometimes awoke covered with snow; he still was so eager to be the first into the lake that early one April he wrote to Young:

"Sunday was such a lovely warm day that I was tempted to go in swimming, but I was restrained by more conservative people."

He was not an easy man to restrain, though, and he retained undiminished a dangerous contempt for red traffic lights. He gave up riding shortly before he was eighty-three, not because of any frailty but because it wasn't much fun riding alone and everybody was too busy (or too lazy) to get up early for a brisk canter. He and Mary celebrated their Golden Wedding Anniversary in 1951, surrounded by children and grandchildren, Herbert and his family, Mary's sister, old business associates, friends from the Hull House days and the Institute of Pacific Relations and all the years and projects in between. There is something both inspiring and touching about a half-century of close companionship between two people, and at the Swopes that day a writer said as much to an editor. Fifty years of a really happy marriage is something to write home about, he said.

"But not to write to the magazines about," the editor warned. "A successful family life is the most wonderful thing in the world to live and the dullest to read."

By this standard, Gerard and Mary Swope's had been very dull indeed. He kept telling people, "I have been very fortunate"—fortunate in his health and energy, in the three men who had most influenced him, Barton, Thayer and Coffin, and in the two women who had been of equal or even greater influence—no, he would say three—his mother, his wife and Jane Addams. He had worked hard, of course, but he had enjoyed it and he still agreed with Holmes that repose is an illusion.

Through his eighties, Swope has continued the busy life which led Robert Moses, New York's energetic czar of parks, to say to him, "Eighty indeed! It's a matter of spirit." To the remonstrances of physicians and family that a few concessions to the climate if not to his age might be in order, if only a hat when it is raining, he replies, "I'm going to go on living my life the way I always have, and when it's over, that's that."

Of course, the tremendous driving energy, once the distinctive characteristic of General Electric's president, no longer is so much in evidence. The steel spring has relaxed a little bit. The expression on his face is softer, his voice a trifle milder. But he has resisted the greatest temptation of age, if indeed it has tempted him at all, to live in the past. When a man can remember seeing most of the houses on Olive Street lighted by gas and has not only witnessed but shared largely in the making of the Electric Age, it might be expected that he would enjoy reliving those days in a spate of anecdote and reminiscence. But even after Mary died in 1955, leaving a void in the lives of husband and children and friends which could neither be filled nor described, Gerard was not given to babbling about "the good old days."

Two or three days each week he walks from his apartment on Seventy-ninth Street to the office on Fifty-first, where General Electric maintains a Mount Olympus on its forty-sixth floor, symbolically just above the president, for retired presidents and chairmen. That means for Swope, Young and Wilson now. The company has grown enormously, with business topping four billions, and into new fields of electronics and nuclear energy in ramifications which Swope admires from a distance but does not attempt to follow in detail.

It is a powerful demonstration of the permanent effectiveness of Swope's managerial principles. These are proving flexible, adaptable to changing conditions and procedures, and therefore more important to the industrial scene than the most brilliant expedients of a moment. Swope's basic innovations in industrial human relations and in the philosophy of managerial responsibility are so thoroughly accepted that younger men in corporations all over the country, not just General Electric, are likely to think that they have prevailed always. This is what has survived of a regime which was so brilliant in its own time, according to *Fortune* magazine, that we are not likely to see its match again.

General Electric men, those who worked under him anyway, are inclined to talk more about that legendary exploit, about his amazing grasp of figures or his tireless energy or his reputation for omniscience in business or even his coldness and impersonal hardness than about his philosophy. But they act, as do their successors who knew Swope only by hearsay, in the more important tradition which he established.

One day recently Wilson was explaining that the great significance of his predecessor in American life was that he "introduced the new concepts of management into industry which made it click." Someone remarked that after all General Electric had its most spectacular expansion in Wilson's own presidency. The big man nodded.

"But it was on Gerard Swope's foundation," he said. "Wilson couldn't have done it."

Sources

For writing the biography of a living man, the written record discloses far less than the subject himself and those who know him can tell if they will. In the preparation of this book, therefore, talking has been more rewarding than reading.

First of all were my interviews with Gerard Swope himself. For a period of nearly two years we met about once a week for sessions to which I came armed with questions. He answered all of them frankly but, as the reader will have gathered, his replies were concise, strictly to the point and without any of the revealing "that-reminds-me" which elaborates an incident or a policy. Extra detail was obtained only by asking extra questions and persistent discussion.

Only a little less valuable were my interviews with Owen D. Young, Gerard's friend and colleague; Charles E. Wilson, his admirer and successor; James Harris, his clear-sighted secretary throughout his GE presidency; Theodore K. Quinn, his critic and one-time heir-apparent; Herbert Bayard Swope, whom I am not alone in regarding as the best reporter the American press ever had; Dr. Alice Hamilton, an intimate friend since his Hull House days; Dr. Willis R. Whitney, his old teacher at M.I.T. and colleague at GE; Chester H. Lang, former GE vice-president who collected Swope anecdotes as some men collect stamps.

I also owe much to interviews, some of them years ago, with many others who knew Gerard in varying degrees of intimacy, including his sister-in-law, Margaret Swope; his son, Gerard Swope, Jr., Charles E. Mitchell, Myron Taylor, James Carey, Ralph Cordiner, Karl T. Compton, Dr. William Coolidge, W. W. Trench, Dugald Jackson, Clark Minor, Gordon Campbell, William L. Holland, Stuart M. Crocker, Kenneth Patrick and Jesse W. Lewis.

The spirit of the book derives largely from the sum of all these interviews. The substance comes quite as much from documentary sources. The unpublished ones have been primarily Gerard's own letters and papers; the vastly more complete collection of Owen Young, who has preserved and arranged a biographer's treasure trove; and a mass of formal data from the files of the General Electric Company. Newspaper and magazine files and books, including a variety of industrial histories and memoirs, rounded out the story.

There also is some personal reminiscence which stems from my own lifelong acquaintance with Gerard. Our families were neighbors and friends in St. Louis; as a boy I often listened respectfully to Ida Swope when she talked about her sons to my grandmother, whose brother was the David Goldsmith for whom both Gerard and my father named their sons. Later I was privileged to know Mary Swope, first as my mother's friend and then as mine. I must leave it to the reader to decide whether this personal factor has affected the work for good or ill.

Finally, I would like to acknowledge gratefully the suggestions for elaboration and condensation, especially in presenting the business and industrial background, which were made with a wonderful blend of kindness and frankness by my editor at Simon and Schuster, Joseph Barnes, and Frank Ernest Hill, whose literary-historical talents helped me greatly.

David Loth

Piermont, N.Y.
September 19, 1957

Index

Index

ABOUT THE AUTHOR

Shortly after he received his degree in journalism from the University of Missouri in 1920, David Loth joined the staff of Herbert Bayard Swope's New York World. *He remained with* The World *until its demise in 1931, and by that time he had been reporter, rewrite man, cable editor and editor of two of the Sunday sections. Since then he has traveled extensively, published his own newspaper in Spain, been a member of the staff of* The New York Times, *served as information director of the Columbia University Bicentennial, and contributed articles to* Reader's Digest, Look, Esquire *and other magazines. He has been appointed an associate Nieman Fellow in Journalism at Harvard for the academic year 1957-1958.*

He wrote his first book—a biography of the Brownings—in 1929 and has followed it with a varied list ranging from biographies of Lorenzo the Magnificent and Woodrow Wilson to studies of American Communism, the Kinsey report, and the Seven Seas.

The Swope and Loth families were friends and neighbors in St. Louis, and Mr. Loth has known the subject of the present biography all his life.